Policing for Profit

D1556755

Sage Contemporary Criminology

Series editors

John Lea ● Roger Matthews ● Geoffrey Pearson ● Jock Young
Centre for Criminology, Middlesex Polytechnic

Sage Contemporary Criminology draws on the best of current work in criminology and socio-legal studies, both in Britain and internationally, to provide lecturers, students and policy-makers with the latest research on the functioning of the criminal justice and legal systems. Individual titles will cover a wide span of issues such as new developments in informal justice; changing forms of policing and crime prevention; the impact of crime in the inner city; and the role of the legal system in relation to social divisions by gender and race. Throughout, the series will relate theoretical problems in the social analysis of deviancy and social control to the practical and policy-related issues in criminology and law.

Already published

Jeanne Gregory, *Sex, Race and the Law: Legislating for Equality*
John Pitts, *The Politics of Juvenile Crime*
Roger Matthews, *Informal Justice?*

Policing for Profit

The Private Security Sector

Nigel South

SAGE Publications
London • Newbury Park • Beverly Hills • New Delhi

© Nigel South, 1988

First published 1988

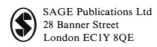

SAGE Publications Ltd
28 Banner Street
London EC1Y 8QE

SAGE Publications Inc
2111 West Hillcrest Street
Newbury Park, California 91320

SAGE Publications Inc
275 South Beverly Drive
Beverly Hills, California 90212

SAGE Publications India Pvt Ltd
32, M–Block Market
Greater Kailash – I
New Delhi 110 048

British Library Cataloguing in Publication Data
South, Nigel
    Policing for profit: the private security
    sector. —— (Sage contemporary criminology; 1)
    1. Private security services
    I. Title
    363.2'89

    ISBN 0-8039-8174-0
    ISBN 0-8039-8175-9 Pbk

Library of Congress catalog card number 88-062327

Typeset by AKM Associates (UK) Ltd
Ajmal House, Hayes Road, Southall, London
Printed in Great Britain by
Billing and Sons Ltd, Worcester

Contents

For my mother and father
and their headlines from Morecambe
(I hope I got it right this time)

Acknowledgements

As is customary, I will admit that any deficiencies in this book are my
fault alone. However, the research interest on which the book is based
goes back over ten years now and there are many people who have, in
various ways and at different times, helped me see this book and
related articles through to completion. They deserve more adequate
thanks than a mere mention here – but that's life.

The research on which the book is based started life as a PhD
project, funded by the Social Science Research Council (now ESRC),
at the (then) Centre for Occupational and Community Research at
Middlesex Polytechnic. Despite the fact that I pursued a somewhat
different line of research to the one originally envisaged, it is to the
great credit of Gerry Mars that he remained that best kind of
supervisor and friend – one who asks sensible questions, picks up on
problems and makes constructive suggestions. My thanks to him and
Val and to the members of the seminar group at Hampstead. James
Cornford and the Outer Circle Policy Unit brought together a
Working Group on the subject of private security from which I
benefited out of all proportion to my own input into the group. My
thanks to the members of the group. I owe a long-term debt to Stan
Cohen both as a committed teacher, who sharpened my interest in
criminology at the University of Essex, and as a supervisor in the early
stages of the research before his departure to Israel. I owe a similar
debt to Jock Young, as a supervisor who contributed much to the
research and the book that has resulted, and, as a friend, for much else
besides.

I offer my grateful thanks to all those who talked to me about issues
mundane and sensitive during the course of the research, whether for
the record or not. Special mention must be made of Bruce George, MP,
whose help has been extensive, and also of Emma MacLennan and the
Low Pay Unit and Tom Wilson and the Managerial, Administrative,
Technical and Supervisory Association research staff. Middlesex
Polytechnic, despite perennially stretched resources, provided a
supportive environment for the project in its early stages. My thanks to
Daphne Clench and Shirley Webb, to Audrey Hardwick and others in
Administration at Enfield, to various members of the Social Science
faculty, especially those associated with the MA in Deviance and

Social Policy. In particular, thanks to Roger Matthews, Geoff Pearson, John Crutchley and John Lea. The Library staff at Enfield helped enormously and were it not for their professionalism and efficiency in helping to trace obscure references, I would not have had the dubious pleasure of typing out such a long bibliography.

Ken Plummer, who is simply the best teacher I ever had, first awakened my interest in the issue of who are the subjects of surveillance and stigmatisation in society – and hence in the mechanics of social control generally. My thanks to him and Ev for subsequent years of friendship. Over many years as friends as well as colleagues, Nick Dorn has been supportive about and interested in my work on private security, despite the frequency with which we seem to be working to impending deadlines for joint work at the Institute for the Study of Drug Dependence. For his forbearance and example of professionalism in research, I am grateful. Both of us still miss the conversations that we had with the late John Auld about research – and sundry other matters of even more importance. Other colleagues at ISDD, Christine James and Lorraine Lucas, should also be thanked for their interest and for helping to make a frequently demanding project schedule survivable.

As I acknowledge throughout this book, the pioneering work of Clifford Shearing, Philip Stenning and their colleagues, on private security in Canada, has been invaluable to me. They have my deepest thanks for generously sharing material, ideas and for keeping up a mutual correspondence over nearly a decade. It should also be acknowledged that the title of this book is, at the very least, third hand, being used by Steven Spitzer and Andrew Scull in an early article and then, in a broader sense, by Shearing and Stenning in later work.

The research of Jason Ditton and Stuart Henry was influential in initially spurring my interest in the hidden economy and its control, and I am grateful that despite my early criticisms born out of that youthful certainty that everyone else is wrong and you are right, they remain good friends. Phil Scraton, with whom I co-authored those early critiques, remains an inspiration in his commitment to civil liberties issues and I thank him (and the Flying Scratonis) for things shared over the years. Since the late 1970s, the exchange of papers and ideas between Bob Weiss and myself has grown into another good friendship and has been invaluable in keeping me in touch with developments relating to private security in the USA. Robert Reiner examined the thesis on which this book draws and I do not think that I could have had a more scrupulous and helpful reader. My thanks to him for his comments and also to Mike Brogden for also looking at the thesis. The research overall benefited, albeit indirectly, from the time I spent in the Department of Sociology, Hofstra University, New York, in 1980. Special thanks to Donna DeCesare, Jeff and Sue Rosenfeld and Steve Rayner for their help, friendship and hospitality, then and since. Thanks also to Gordon West for exchange of work and for discussions in Toronto and London.

In more recent months, various friends have been supportive, subscribing to the reasonable belief that spending all one's time reading private security journals and texts is 'just a phase that will pass'. Perhaps invidiously, special mention must be made of the following: Ian Johns for a friendship that goes back a long way; Roger Smith and Celia Angel (the Terry and June of Charlton) for many good times and late nights; Sue Harris for friendship, help, advice and for always being Sue; and Ann Singleton for her support, help and political good sense. During the last nine months over which this book has been written, Bev Holmes has put up with a lot of rambling about 'the damm book' – as we have so affectionately referred to it. My thanks and my love to her. Finally, despite the fact that my father still thinks that being an electrician would have been a wiser career move than being a criminologist, this book is dedicated to my parents with love and thanks.

Nigel South
London

The Author and Publishers would like to thank Securicor for permission to use the photographs on the front cover, and Frances Pinter Publishers for permission to use extracts from an article originally published in Michael Clarke (ed.) (1983) *Corruption: Causes, Consequences and Control*, London: Frances Pinter. Thanks also to Michael Clarke for permission and for his encouragement in the preparation of that article.

1 The Criminological Context

One need only pause for a minute to see that although in areas like mental illness the private sector might genuinely displace the state, this would be an impossible outcome in crime control. For the state to give up here would be to undercut its very claim to legitimacy. (Cohen, 1983: 117)

The research on which this book is based began as a straightforward observational study of private security 'at work'. It ended up as a somewhat more ambitious examination of the range of activities within what I came to call the 'private security sector', an exploration of issues of accountability and an attempt to develop a new and more comprehensive account of the phenomenal growth of private security.[1]

I came to this study with a criminological interest in what is broadly termed 'social control' (Cohen, 1985). From an original interest in industrial sociology, I had moved through undergraduate and graduate work on the 'underside' of industrial relations, looking at the 'underworkings of the work-place' (Scraton and South, 1981), to a recognition that there was another little-noted side to this area apart from workers' involvement in what came to be termed the 'hidden economy' (Ditton, 1977; Henry, 1978; Mars, 1974, 1982; South, 1982), industrial sabotage (Taylor and Walton, 1971), workplace resistance and so on: this was the dimension of *control*.

Initially, the literature on the area of social control in the workplace seemed not merely underdeveloped but virtually barren. However, at the same time as my interest developed, some of the original 'hidden economy' writers began to indicate the significance of areas of commercial justice (Ditton, 1977) and of private security (Henry, 1978). In a co-authored critique of some of this early work (Scraton and South, 1981), I began to explore one arena of what we referred to as 'private justice'. By this time I had already embarked on what had been conceived of as an ethnographic study of private security workers. What follows reflects the questions that it began to raise for me about broader features of the private security enterprise. (For the results of my observational research, see South, 1985: ch. 2).

As a system of social control with strong superficial similarities to the police, private security nonetheless remains unique by virtue of its private status and many other characteristics. For example, despite the heterogeneity of functions across the private security sector, there is a strong homogeneity in terms of occupational values shared from low-grade operational staff to the most senior members of the board. These values are reinforced by a variety of factors. Perhaps most striking from the fieldwork was that this is a business with confidence and optimism. Uniquely, when other enterprises are sorely beset, even in the service sector to which the present Conservative government pins such hopes, the private security business has been expanding rapidly and significantly (see Chapter 2). Sociologically, this has a strong significance. Workers' attachment to the values of their occupations and the goals of their organisations may be undermined where they see their industry in decline or stagnating. In private security, workers can (but, of course, do not always) not only feel that they are doing a 'good and useful' job, supporting the police and the status quo, but also that the evident demand for their services and success of the industry indicates public approval and demand. Such ideological 'good value' is also attractive to investors, sponsors, company directors and so on.

At the same time, these reinforced occupational values and sense of worth, common from guardroom to boardroom, bolster the idea of a strong boundary between the occupation and the rest of society that private security services. This affirmation of boundary, contributed to by a host of features of private security such as the uniform, the secrecy of undercover work, the accountability to clients and so on, was made clear throughout the fieldwork (South, 1985). This theme is taken up in Chapters 3, 6 and 8 in considering the relationship between private security and the public police and the changing division of policing labour in society (Chapter 9; South, 1988). Similarly, the recognition that certain features identified in fieldwork were occupationally specific – for example, long hours, low pay, little training, lack of impact of unionisation – suggested, among other things, that these would also be found in private security in other countries and that legislative responses in other jurisdictions would have to deal with parallel problems. These matters are discussed in Chapter 8. Hence, although a survey of private security in practice in other countries could not be attempted, fieldwork conclusions strongly suggest that there are enough features of private security that are occupationally specific to make reference to other models of licensing and regulation abroad a sound exercise. In other words, examining models of licensing in other countries would be of relatively little value if we could not take it that they shared at least some strong common ground.

When I began this research, in the late 1970s, the significance of the expansion of private security had been evident to various representatives of the police service and the Police Federation for some years, and periodically various media reports had focused on either 'heroic' or 'sinister' aspects of private security in operation. In other countries, policy debates had flourished for a number of years, resulting in various schemes for the licensing and regulation of certain aspects of the private security sector. Meanwhile, the fruits of pioneering work by Shearing, Stenning and others in Canada and Spitzer, Scull and Weiss in the United Sates were just beginning to receive attention (Freedman and Stenning, 1977; Shearing et al., 1980; Shearing and Stenning, 1981; Spitzer and Scull, 1977a, b; Stenning and Cornish, 1975; Weiss, 1978, 1981).

My own fieldwork had begun to generate questions about the legitimacy of private security, 'hidden services such as undercover work and an interest in the origins of private security – what was its history and antecedents? Such queries were stimulated further by this burst of new work on the subject, and the parameters of my own research expanded dramatically. However, the present volume attempts to provide a rather more condensed picture of the private security sector today than would be possible if I had tried to pursue all these different directions here.[2]

Some general debates and reference points

At one level, an adequate definition of private security might perhaps be simply a good description of it, covering how and where it operates, how big it is as an industry and so on. But a rather more sophisticated enquiry might ask about its relationship to other social institutions, for example, the police, government and so on. Exploring these avenues might raise questions about underlying features of the phenomenon – its legitimacy, its *Weltanschauung*, its deeper mechanisms and functions (in the senses developed by Foucault, 1977) and even, beyond the face value of the terms, what can be said about the *privatisation* of that security which all members of the commonweal quite naturally desire for themselves, their families, friends and communities. In the following chapters I shall attempt to explore such diverse questions. Here I can only offer some initial reference points.

The first consideration concerns terminology. Although some writers have opted for the term 'private police', this would seem generally inappropriate, suggesting an unhelpful contrast with the public police. Private security is a very broad enterprise and the concept of 'security' itself is complex (Spitzer, 1987). Here and elsewhere (South, 1984), I argue that 'private security' is a more useful term than private policing because the services and activities engaged in are broader than, and not confined to, those associated with 'policing'. Use of the term 'private police' may have been favoured by some commentators in cases where, as for example in the United States, 'private police' have often had the status and legitimacy of legal deputisation for the civil/public police; however, this is generally exceptional and some may also find a more dubious polemical attraction in referring to 'private police' (Klare, 1975; Spitzer and Scull, 1977b).

Shearing et al. (1980: 16) move towards a definition of security in suggesting that we identify the common theme which characterises security services. This theme, they argue, 'is *protection*, and in particular, the protection of information, persons and property. Thus, security may be defined as those activities which serve to protect these valued goods.' In one sense, however, this attempt at clarification is actually misleading, for 'protection' is also a part of public policing responsibilities and activities. But the similarity of such functions does not mean that both kinds of service should therefore be called 'police'. The critical point is that, although similar activities may be undertaken, there is a crucial difference with regard to legal status, control and accountability.

Importantly, these authors make the point that the very term 'police' has come to be associated with members of a 'government con-stabulary' (Parks, 1970): 'that is, persons with a special legal status employed by governments to preserve the peace . . . To talk of "private police" rather than "private security", given the connotations we associate with the term "police" thus tends to be misleading' (Shearing et al., 1980: 16). The term 'police', and our sense of who the police *are*, carry strong 'connotations of government control and governmental authority' (Shearing et al., 1980: 17). This point obviously raises the question of the relationship between private security and government (South, 1984).

As their resolution of this problem of terminology, Shearing et al. (1980: 17) opt for the use of the term 'private security' as more accurate than 'private police', but employ the broader concept of 'policing' as appropriate to the description of the activities of private security. In this book I shall be suggesting that, in many ways, private security is a *broader* enterprise than public policing, with a *wider* range of functions. I have therefore adopted the term 'private security sector' to embrace the provision not only of services which seem recognisable as 'policing' but also activities outside the scope of conventional, common-sense ideas of policing.

Taking the exercise of defining private security further, we might start by asking how the 'industry' defines itself. One of the most articulate, vocal – and relatively liberal – representatives of the private security guard, alarm and transport industries, is J. Philip-Sorenson of Group 4 Security. Speaking at a Cambridge University, Institute of Criminology, Cropwood Conference in 1971, Philip-Sorenson defined private security services as operating:

almost always in private industrial and commercial premises, behind the traditional and legal boundary of the factory fence, which the police cannot lawfully cross unless by invitation or in other special circumstances. Our principal task is to prevent loss and minimise risk to people and property in private places and we have no function in the preservation of law and order in the public sector. (Philip-Sorenson, 1972: 44–5)

Building upon Philip-Sorenson's statement, Garner (1978: 72) offers a 'workable definition of the private security industry' as: 'firms offering services or products designed as protection against fire and/or theft primarily in the private sector of property where the police have limited access.' Having offered her compromise definition, Garner then goes on to note several very pertinent problems with it. First, the commercial term 'firms' may exclude 'in-house' security which constitutes a separate department within larger organisations and provides the organisation with private security services but does not offer them for hire to others. A focus on private security firms or the 'industry' is, then, too narrow. Secondly, Garner suggests, the range of 'products' to be included poses a problem. The example of curved-mirror manufacturers is offered as what may seem a mundane example, but which in fact represents a highly profitable industry in itself. Is this *part* of the private security industry because the product is often used for security purposes? Similarly, Garner asks, although lock and key manufacturers are obvious inclusions in any definition, where does one place the services of the 'heel bar' key-cutting counters which have proliferated? Thirdly, even the term 'services' must come under scrutiny for its vagueness. This poses a problem for Garner in the distinction between protecting property and guarding people. Percep-tively, she hints at one solution to this dilemma when she observes that: 'the guarding of illegal immigrants at airports, undertaken by Securicor, does equate people with property and treats them as commodities not persons' (Garner, 1978: 72).

A fourth confusion arises over determining where public and private territorial limits are drawn. For example, in the Prevention of Crime Act 1953, a public place is defined as: 'any place to which, at the material time, the public have or are permitted access, whether on payment or otherwise.' Thus, private security guards working in shopping precincts find themselves working in a privately owned space but in a public place (Garner, 1978: 73), an anomaly which is a source of some legal confusion and which has implications for the role of private security in those functions which Philip-Sorenson refers to regarding 'the preservation of law and order in the public sector' (Philip-Sorenson, 1972: 44–5). (Shearing and Stenning, 1981, 1983, 1987; Stenning and Shearing, 1980b).

If the task of *defining* what private security does and where it operates is difficult, open to debate and in need of clarification, then the related question of how big 'it' is – logically – becomes even more of an obdurate problem. Bowden (1978), for example, concedes that it is extremely difficult to estimate the size of the private security 'industry' (let alone the make-up of what I refer to as the rather broader private security sector, see Chapters 2–5). However, one can at least, he suggests, be 'a good deal more precise about the logistical capability of the larger commercialised companies' (Bowden, 1978: 255). Where such precision is actually to be found remains unclear unfortunately, for Bowden then resorts to the estimates of capability provided by Bunyan (1976), which were certainly open to some question as accurate for the mid-1970s. This is not to be critical of Bowden or Bunyan; rather to take the first opportunity (which I shall repeat!) to emphasise the dearth of information available in this area.

In 1978, a report, *The Private Security Industry*, was prepared by a working group of the Outer Circle Policy Unit and submitted to the Home Office as it considered a Green Paper on the subject. The report discussed a wide variety of issues related to private security but observed that 'the problems are created not by the existence of the industry', since it is no affront to any formal constitutional understanding, and indeed obligations remain on the public to help to 'maintain the peace'. Rather, problems stem from:

> its size and pervasiveness, and the gradual assumption of quasi-public duties and the claim to authority implicit in the wearing of uniforms. The security industry has become in effect an auxiliary of the police in crime prevention and an important exception to the general trend of regarding the police as exclusively responsible for the prevention of crime. (Outer Circle Policy Unit, 1978: 9)

I shall take up several of these issues later (particularly in Chapter 6) but here, considering the latter points, perhaps private security could be construed as an affront to certain *informal* 'constitutional understandings'. Could then the nature of 'general' expectations about policing, provision of security and crime prevention provide clarificatory and conceptual leverage?

In an essay on private policing in the USA as a suitable case for research, Becker (1974) asked if we could use the idea of 'sponsorship' as a basis for distinguishing between private and public forms of policing. This proposal excludes vigilantes and voluntary deputies who are unpaid, although the distinction between the two is still clearly between private and public spheres. But convergence and overlap render 'such a simple distinction not possible' Becker finds. Examining the nature of services performed, Becker concludes that:

at best private and public functions seemed to be turned around from traditional images. Thus we find private police performing the more aggressive crime control and apprehension functions, while public police perform more prevention, order and maintenance and community service functions . . . The area in which private police seem to be taking over is that of theft prevention, protection of private premises and the types of more minor crimes that used to be curtailed by the presence of policemen on the beat. (1974: 443)

Thus, shifting bases of role and responsibility, whilst analytically very useful in addressing the changing division of policing labour, does not really provide a clear definition of the two policing/security forms or one which helps us better to understand their development and practice.

To move beyond the narrowly didactic approach to discussions of private security (for example, private security can be defined in *this* way because it differs from the police in *that* way; it performs these services for these interests; it is such and such a size with so many employees and so many armoured vehicles), I must briefly refer to some broader sources of theoretical influence and relevance.

A new criminology with an old focus?

The mythical, but often assumed, unilinear march of theory in criminology and the sociology of deviance (Young, 1981: 250) has only relatively recently moved on from the situation where, as Spitzer (1975: 638) writes, 'prior to the 1960s, the subject matter of deviancy theory was taken for granted and few were disturbed by its preoccupation with "dramatic" and "predatory" forms of social behaviour.' After the labelling and conflict theorists of the 1960s and early 1970s had reappropriated the rationality and humanity of the deviant, occasionally to the point of panegyric, the materialist romanticism of many writing in the wake of the 'new criminologists' (Taylor et al., 1973, 1975) reawakened interest in the control agencies engaged in what Spitzer refers to as 'deviancy production'.

In his subsequent discussion of the 'production' and control of 'problem populations', Spitzer (1975: 640–1) places emphasis upon locating systems of control and their discernible features *under specific conditions*. This is one prescription for broadening the criminological enterprise. Yet still, as Edwards and Scullion (1982: 322) have noted, 'systematic attention to the controllers of deviance has been rare.' Plummer (1979: 110) has persuasively argued that it is not the province of the sociologist of deviance to be overly concerned with the agents of control, for the subject of the deviancy tradition is properly the study of the devalued groups who are controlled. More surprising, argue

Edwards and Scullion, is the claim that can be made that the 'new criminology' has ignored agents of control, especially 'given its central concern with locating deviance in a social and political context in which power is crucial. Yet detailed attention to the activities of controllers is rare . . . a new criminology is still a criminology' (1982: 321–3).

By the mid-1980s, it must be acknowledged, law and order and public policing (with regard to issues like accountability, racism, new police powers, etc.) were firmly on the agenda, but on the agenda of what is in danger of becoming something of a 'conventional criminology' in terms of its preoccupations. For, if attention to the activities of some of 'the controllers' is now more common, it none the less remains the case that the great diversity and breadth (not to mention importance) of private and informal dimensions of control, order and violence still remain neglected and marginal (see, for example, Cain, 1985, on informal justice; Gregory, 1986, on sex, class and crime; Henry, 1983, 1987a, b, c, on private justice; Scraton and South, 1983, on DHSS specialist claims control teams; Shearing and Stenning, 1981, 1983, 1987, on private security; and West, 1986, 1987, on forms of social control in Nicaragua).

Foucault: a new vision of social control?

In recent years the work of Michel Foucault, arriving from outside the boundaries of 'new' or 'conventional' criminology (or sociology, history and philosophy for that matter), has provided a major and significant stimulus to the study of systems of social control. But, importantly, Foucault's work offers several key themes which resonate strongly with some of the concerns that emerged out of the 'new criminology' debates.

For Foucault (1977) contemporary, complex societies are best characterised not in terms of their economic system, their political structure or their social composition, but in terms of the 'mode of power' which *pervades* and thereby dominates them. Hussein captures part of the thrust of Foucault's thesis with both clarity and brevity:

> the mode of action of power in disciplinary societies takes the form of the creation of a norm and the institution of procedures to rectify deviations from the norm. Therefore, 'At the heart of all disciplinary systems functions a small penal mechanism' (Foucault, 1977: 177). However, there are important differences between judicial penalty and disciplinary penalty. The former operates by referring to laws and judicial texts, the latter by referring to observable behaviour. (1978: 937)

The private security sector works precisely within a regime of, and with the *raison d'être* of, applying a code of 'disciplinary penalty'.

Revolving around 'protection' and 'surveillance' – and thereby also, and crucially, protection *from* surveillance and intrusion in numerous forms – its own mode of action must continually refer to 'observable behaviour' and, by extension and necessity, the detection and/or anticipation of the unobservable. Given this, the following chapters are informed not only by developments in the broadening of criminological studies and concerns but also by the suggestive work of Foucault and the debates it has generated and coincided with (see, for example, Cohen, 1979, 1985; Fine et al., 1979).

One key question for Foucault has obvious centrality here. Again, Hussein (1978: 937) summarises neatly: 'what *means*, Foucault asks, do disciplinary institutions employ to secure discipline?' It is not necessary to detail here Foucault's exposition of the three principal means ((a) hierarchical observation; (b) normalising judgement; (c) examination); in so far as they are central to the practice of the private security sector, their significance should shortly be apparent. It should suffice to emphasise here my shared conviction that the power of organised observation is crucial, by noting Foucault's contention that: 'The exercise of discipline presupposes a mechanism that coerces by means of observation' (1977: 170).

The private and the public: a blurring of boundaries?

The distinction between the 'private' and the 'public' spheres (and the implications of privatisation of arenas of production, exchange and governance, for example, health, justice, policing, the penal system, within the latter) is becoming increasingly complex in modern Western societies. Understanding where the public/private divide is clearly in focus or is being blurred is of considerable relevance to studies of social control (Bottoms, 1983; Cohen, 1979, 1983; Reiss, 1987).

As a starting point, Williams offers the following definition of 'the private':

> Private, that is, in its positive senses, is a record of the legitimation of a bourgeois view of life; the ultimate generalised privilege, however abstract in practice, of seclusion and protection from others (the public); of lack of accountability to 'them'; and in related gains in closeness and comfort of these general kinds. As such, and especially in the senses of the rights of the *individual* (to his *private life*, or from a quite different tradition, to his *civil liberties*) and of the valued intimacy of family and friends, it has been widely adopted outside the strict bourgeois viewpoint. This is the real reason for its current complexity. (1976: 204)

In the chapters that follow, it is worth bearing in mind the equation of 'the private' with 'lack of accountability'. However, of more specific concern here is the nature of the private and the public in relation to systems of justice and security.

In a slightly weary tone, the American political scientist, Hanna Pitkin has observed that:

> The prevailing disillusionment with established leadership and institutions produces not protest but withdrawal into privacy, yet privatisation manifestly is not providing the comfort and security we seek. And all that anyone seems able to muster for calling people back . . . is the familiar and incompatible pair of devices: the exhortation to civic duty, and the appeal to self-interest. Neither seems to be doing much good. (1981: 327)

Privatisation (in both commercial and psychological senses) promotes insularity and isolation, paranoia and prejudice, subverting any sense of 'social comfort' or 'comfort with society'. The policing institutions declare their limitations (and their own insecurities) and appeal to a *shared* civic responsibility for the management of the contemporary social malaise. At the same time, governments have been elected on the strength of comforting promises and strongly populist platforms; self-interest is taken seriously and the privatisation of services is embraced, resonating with criticisms of the public sector (see, for example, Frieden, 1986). Within, and reflecting, such changes, the police and their role are changing. As the French legal theorist, Gleizal (1981: 362) remarks: 'The police are being transformed. Their aim is no longer solely the maintenance of law and order . . . but also now to assure citizens' security. The police not only should exist but should also be liked.'

Both the police and the private security sector are increasingly 'image' conscious; they present themselves not simply as 'doing the job' but they also demand that they should be acknowledged for it – for their contribution; they 'care' and should be given some credit for it. Furthermore, the public should acknowledge their own responsibilities and contribute more to the policing and servicing of their communities. This is a further source of confusion around the boundaries of public and private arrangements for policing and security.

For studies of 'social control' agencies, approaching the concepts of the private and the public is evidently not straightforward (Cohen, 1985: 134–6; Shearing and Stenning, 1983: 493–506; 1987: 12). With slightly different concerns, Sennett (1977: 16) has presented a conception of the 'geography' of the public and the private. According to this view, the private is 'in here', personal, intimate, protected from intrusion by others – a space in which we are 'free to be ourselves' (Pitkin, 1981: 328). The public is 'out there', 'impersonal, distant, formal' – ready or liable for 'publication', for openness and exposure (Pitkin, 1981; Sennett, 1977). This sort of distinction certainly meshes with much that is common sense yet, as Pitkin responds, what then is to be made of that expansive, intrusive phenomenon at the heart of the capitalist economy: the 'private enterprise'? Within the equally common-sense frame of economic imagery, the ' "public sector" is divided from [the] private on the basis of ownership, and public means, roughly, government, the state' (Pitkin, 1981: 328). In terms of social interaction (and withdrawal from it), economic behaviour and the ordering of society through means of government and so on, there are ample sources of confusion about the boundaries and permeations between the private and the public (Starr, 1987).

Pitkin's erudite opening out of the private/public distinction also considers Hannah Arendt's (1958) conception of 'the public' as synonymous with 'political' public life in the sense of partaking in actions in a community of peers. While, here, 'the private' exhibits a tension between its historical connotation of the status of the 'deprived' (think, for example, of low 'rank') and its additional association with 'privilege' and the 'advantages of withdrawal'. The distinction drawn by C. Wright Mills (1959) between 'personal troubles of milieu' and 'public issues of social structure' offers a further valid and suggestive dichotomy.

Recent work in criminology has instructively contrasted 'public' or 'state' law and justice with 'private' control and justice. To offer just two examples, Shearing and Stenning (1984: 339) talk of criminal justice 'order' as being 'fundamentally a moral phenomenon and its maintenance a moral process'. The conceptualisation is of 'natural justice' and social order and its enforcement tend 'to be defined in absolute terms'. By contrast, private control 'rejects a moral conception of order' and the control process is a matter of instrumental intervention rather than moral reform. Henry (1987c: 90) also raises provocative questions in his discussion of the difficulties in equating private security with private justice.

The dilemma of approaching what is now obviously a difficult distinction cannot be resolved here by the offer of a 'correct' definition: a subject in itself for an entirely different kind of study. For present purposes, this broadening of conception, and its corresponding blurring of lines of distinction, is intended to forewarn and forearm in anticipation of the following discussions of the tensions, symbiotic relations and compromises between 'private' and 'public' institutions, actions and philosophies. Although the questions are not resolved, the focusing and blurring of the private/public spheres is central to the general account of private security presented here.

Less blurring, more focus: what the chapters cover

The observational fieldwork and literature review undertaken at the start of the research that has led to this book never resulted in the intended full ethnography of 'private security at work' (South, 1985). Instead, it raised new questions for me, significantly broadening the nature of my interests. Most importantly it suggested that the kind of medium-sized guard and patrol services with which I was familiarising myself were but one part of a much wider, though less visible, *range* of private security services. In retrospect, this strikes me as constituting seriously limited vision on my part; however, it is relatively under-standable if one considers the general myopia of the literature available on this subject in the late 1970s and early 1980s (for example, Home Office, 1979).

This interest in the range of services available suggested that, if the undercover activities of the 'ordinary', 'respectable' firms raised questions about civil liberties issues, then the activities of the less visible agencies might well raise even more. Thus questions about the accountability and legitimacy of the private security sector agencies generally, coincided and resonated with the recurrent public issues of licensing and regulating 'ordinary' private security firms.

In Chapters 2–5 I attempt to chart, on a broad but detailed scale, the activities and breadth of the private security sector in the United Kingdom (but also with reference to North America). In Chapters 6–8 I take up the matter of the accountability of the private security sector, drawing upon a variety of sources, and engage with past and current debates in arguing for a system of regulation and accountability for the private security sector. Chapter 9 reviews several recent developments which underline the arguments put forward in Chapters 6–8 and considers some broader theoretical and practical issues.

This book aims to present a more comprehensive and critically researched picture of the breadth and significance of the private security sector than has previously been available – at least for the UK. It still does not, however, definitively answer some of those 'basic' questions that I referred to earlier, such as 'How big is it?' This question could have been answered with cynical and polemical 'guesstimates', but such a resort would be both sociologically and politically dishonest and dangerous. Statistical information on private security in the UK is virtually non-existent, and even in other countries, where licensing and/or other registration procedures have existed for some years, information of this order is very sparse. As Shearing and Stenning observed in their major series of studies on private security in Canada:

> Despite serious efforts to improve matters in a number of jurisdictions (notably the United States) current statistical information on the size and growth of private security remains very crude. Estimates of expenditures on private security, for instance, vary wildly and standard categories for

determining the number of persons involved have not been developed sufficiently to support comparative analysis across national borders. (1981: 198)

Like Shearing and Stenning and others, I had originally felt that it
would be necessary to attempt some degree of international comparison. However, it quickly became clear that, unlike the comparison
of legislation, the information required for comparative analysis of
trends in employment, labour turnover, the expansion or foreign
ownership of companies and so on, was simply unavailable. Hence, in
discussing legislation, licensing and controls for private security
(Chapter 8), I have found it worth while to refer briefly to some
international models but, for the rest, the study *principally* confines
itself to the British experience (albeit with reference to North American
experience where parallels are evident and can justifiably be drawn).

This book does not attempt to cover the rich history of private
initiatives for protection and security that have generally thrived in
place of, as well as alongside, more clearly 'publicly' organised
provision. A cursory summary would do a severe disservice to such a
complex story (Radzinowicz, 1956a, b; Rock, 1983; South, 1987a;
Spitzer, 1979; Spitzer and Scull, 1977a). Nor does it seek to describe
those 'private' statutory forces which seem to operate somewhere
between the private sector and the public police, albeit usually bearing
some clear mandate from a public authority or agency. Whilst such
forces *have* been considered 'an alternative model at least for the
manned security services . . . organised along the lines of the ordinary
police forces, but employed and financed by a private or governmental
body other than the local police authorities' (Outer Circle Policy Unit,
1978: 11), for present purposes I must regard them as epi-phenomenal
forms of the system of *public* policing (although the work referenced
above describes the complexity of their lineage). Here I shall be
concentrating on those forms of policing, security and surveillance
where their functions and accountability are wholly privatised.

Conclusion: focusing and blurring

There are difficulties in delineating the divide between the private and
public spheres of modern life, and indeed this has been no less true in
the past. These difficulties carry over into the study of interlocking
systems of social control. The highly suggestive work of Foucault
(1977) and Cohen (1979, 1985) clearly influences my perspective here
and in what follows. But whilst some aspects of social control in
practice may seem self-evidently 'in focus', for example, the work of
the police, increasing the magnification with a view to seeing what else
may be happening can frequently produce an illuminating 'blurring
effect'.

Topically, for example, there has in recent years been much talk of inter- or multi-agency strategies in response to a variety of social problems. Commentary on these trends has almost exclusively focused upon the participation of public sector agencies, on aspects of their enthusiasm or resistance, and so on. This is a consequence of one particular sort of focus. But, with a different perspective, a search for some blurring of the boundaries between various agencies across the private/public divide would expect to find it in the development of the private security sector, if nowhere else.

Sir Kenneth Newman, former Commissioner of the Metropolitan Police, is a man who knows more than a little about strategies and deployment of resources. In a speech given at the opening of the International Fire, Security and Safety Exhibition at Olympia on 15 April 1985, Sir Kenneth stated that he was engaged 'in a long-term effort to promote police/public cooperation – cooperation that will be continuous, structured and effective'. This required a 'multi-agency approach. The security industry was one of the most important of these agencies' (Metropolitan Police, 1985: 2). I do not believe that in the immediately foreseeable future any Commissioner or chief constable will be seriously contemplating the wholesale turnover of their files and computer data bases to agencies working within the private security sector. (The less charitable, however, might draw attention to the implications of the number of very senior police officers, including apparently Sir Kenneth, retiring into senior posts within private security organisations; see Chapter 6, p. 111.) I do believe that whatever their differences in the past, as Sir Kenneth intimated, police, private security, other agencies and the public will have to learn to live together. However, what developments may follow can only be influenced if we keep them in full and accountable view.

Notes

1 Although I first used the term 'private security sector' in a paper delivered to the National Deviancy Conference in 1978 and at the time thought it a possibly original, though obvious, neat and accurate term, I subsequently found that it had been used in passing and without fanfare by Joseph Thurston, President of Community Guardians Association Limited in an address to a Canadian Security Conference in 1973 (Thurston, in Jeffries, 1974: 40). At the same time as I was writing that paper (which subsequently became South, 1984), O'Toole (1978) published a book with the title: *The Private Sector: Private Spies, Rent-a-Cops and the Police Industrial Complex*, which I only discovered a few years later. No doubt many others have seen the heuristic potential of this term and I make no claim to its originality, only to its utility.

2 I have, however, followed up some of these directions elsewhere. On matters such as

rule bending, cost cutting and occupational deviance, see South, 1983; for a critical analysis of the post-war growth of the private security sector, with reference to Britain and North America, see South, 1984; the history of private initiatives in 'policing' and social regulation in eighteenth and nineteenth-century England is described in South, 1987a; the concept of environmental security in relation to crime prevention and urban society is discussed in South, 1987b; models of the relationship between private security and the public police are outlined in South, 1988; and 'private justice' is considered in relation to the hidden economy in Scraton and South, 1981 and 1984.

2 The Growth of Private Security in Britain

One key legacy of the history of the arrangements that society has made for public order and social control is the enduring distinction between private and public policing as found in the institution of law. Considering the roots of this distinction, Stenning and Shearing have emphasised that:

> Police and law-enforcement powers, because they developed originally from the peace-keeping powers of ordinary citizens, have also evolved closely constrained by the legal recognition of the rights of private ownership. The legal concept through which this evolution was accomplished was the concept of 'the peace'. Essentially the 'King's peace' extended to the King's highway and other common lands not the subject of private ownership. In places which were the subject of private ownership, it was originally not the King's peace which prevailed but the 'private peace' of the owner/occupier. (1980b: 233)

This differentiation between public criminal law and private civil law persists today.

Throughout the twentieth century the 'private peace' of the owner/occupier of property has been a central point around which the developing relations among the police, the public and private security have revolved. Early problems in the establishment of the police and conflicts (overt and covert) over their control, as well as the activities and powers of private detectives and private guards, emerged out of the strength of this concept of 'private peace'. By the turn of the century the new national policing system had still not settled down (Radzinowicz, 1956a), but private guarding associations and agencies seem to have been having a leaner time of it. The private detective bureaux which had emerged were also having to cast around for a new approach and style of work as they faced a popular cynicism towards them born of their frequent malpractices in matrimonial cases. At the same time, however, the early decades of the century also saw the technical side of private security establish itself commercially in the United Kingdom with the installation of alarm systems, whilst in the USA the clearly recognisable foundations of the modern private security organisation were being laid (Draper, 1978: 16).

Private interest and the police

In the early years of organised policing of the new industrial cities in Britain, much power had accrued to the members of the overseeing watch committees. The private commercial interests of these members not infrequently enjoyed special protection and service and, where they involved dubious or illegal practices, occasionally enjoyed discretionary immunity from prosecution. Brogden (1981), for example, offers the case of the Liverpool Watch Committee of 1914, where the chairman was the attorney for major dealers in alcohol. After the introduction of beer-house licensing in the 1870s, small unlicensed premises not owned by the major interests were often hounded out of existence by the police. Another member of the committee was the physician to many of the brothels. Elsewhere, as in Romsey for example, opposition to outside inspection of the police as a body often came strongly from the brewers and publicans who had a near monopoly over the provision of the negligible town police (Critchley, 1967: 121). In the case of Liverpool, as Fosdick (1969: 53) remarks, 'needless to say, the activities of the police, in respect to liquor and prostitution were negligible.' The private direction of the new police in certain matters of commercial interest had clearly not disappeared by the First World War.

Private enquiry agents and private detectives

Equally unsettled as the Victorian era faded were the private enquiry agents who had flourished in fact and fiction – with the flamboyance of the former on occasion nearing the flights of fancy of the latter. But such flamboyance had encouraged dubious practices which the courts were increasingly inclined to view with disfavour. Whether it was the temper of the times or simply of the courts that was changing, 'evidence' that might previously have stood the test in matrimonial cases was now being rejected when its veracity seemed too easily challenged, especially where it simply looked like convenient circumstance or downright lies. The profitability of the divorce business was already in decline and instead a few agencies expanded or established new professional interests (Draper, 1978: 16). Multi-service firms, such as Garniers established in 1901, became the pattern for twentieth-century investigation agencies to follow. As Draper (1978: 16) puts it, 'the Victorian enquiry agent had matured into the modern private detective.' This is not to say, of course, that these early practices of blackmail and deception disappeared, but that is a matter to which I shall return in Chapter 5.

Clearly, as the turn of the century passed, neither the public police nor private alternatives could claim to occupy a wholly stable and unambiguous position in the history of the moment. However, my concern here has to be principally with those private options which persisted through this period, for persist they did despite their low profile (compared to the consolidation of the public police) and their varied manifestations.[1]

The persistence of voluntary policing

The concept of voluntary policing or, perhaps more appropriately at times, 'self-policing' has an interesting extension beyond the nineteenth century with the growth of the women police associations. Though not *strictly* privatised policing or policing on a commercial basis, their organisation and status as voluntary associations deserves mention here.

Their intentions were those of practical 'self-help' for women and the preservation of Victorian morality – a strange mix of assertion and denial of independence. Thus they were to protect women from aggressors and from their own occasionally unsound judgements. The legacy of the 'evangelical police' and the societies for the suppression of vice (Hall and McLennan, 1980: 64; Radzinowicz, 1956b; South, 1987a: 95–6) is discernible, as are contemporary fears over the white slave traffic (Garner, 1978: 43). The associations also owed much to the inspiration of the Suffragette Movement, encouraging women to assert their competence in traditional male occupations (Garner, 1978: 43).

Whatever their commitment and motivation, from the end of the nineteenth century to the 1920s:

> there were a variety of modes of service, some served the government while others were financed privately; some had specific duties, others had wide-ranging powers; most groups were shortlived but a few became permanent officers within the Metropolitan police. All the associations began as privately funded organisations trying to pressure the government into adopting the principle of women police whilst at the same time attempting to show why this was necessary by practical demonstration, such as setting up women patrols to guard the public spaces and parks. (Garner, 1978: 44)

The vigilance committees and similar private associations already relied on women as well as men to report unlawful and immoral acts to the police for prosecution (Garner, 1978: 45; Owings, 1925: 4). The use of the police against the suffragettes led many women to believe that the presence of women within the police force might result in a more sympathetic reaction to their cause from a male-dominated establishment, both politically and physically. The First World War brought a further rationale – patriotism and, significantly with men away at war, it also brought opportunities. Whilst many in the Women's Movement were strongly ambivalent about 'the war effort' and others highly critical (Rowbotham, 1973: 108–22), still others were eager to prove that women could do men's jobs. A large number of voluntary, uniformed associations sprang up, often organised by society ladies and, as Marwick (1977: 40) describes them, performing their roles as a 'not necessarily ineffective mixture of Girl Guides, County Charity and Territorial Army'.

By the 1920s, the Women's Police Service (WPS) operated in several major cities, and while their work was generally for the police or government departments, they also worked in commercial factories (for example, Nestlé and Anglo-Swiss Condensed Milk at Bromley) (Allen, 1925: 71; Garner, 1978: 51) and for private organisations such as the British Empire League Country Club: 'where they "removed the loose women of Richmond" and at the request of Vicar William Q. Amer of Holloway, N7 they cleared the neighbourhood of undesirable females in less than two months, no doubt being paid by the Church' (Garner, 1978: 51). At the same time, members of the WPS were also employed on a permanent basis by the makers of Maypole Margarine as factory police women (Allen, 1925: 150; Garner, 1978: 51). The WPS was shortly reconstituted as the Women's Auxiliary Service after conflicts with the new Metropolitan Commissioner, Sir Nevil Macready, in 1918, who, whilst forming the Metropolitan Women's Police, remained highly suspicious of the suffragette cause. Voluntary work, supported by donation and subscription, continued, as did commercial commissions for private security type work, as for example at the 1924 Wembley Imperial Exposition.

A further example of initiatives taken by women's organisations is represented by the 'moral policing' provided for by a convention organised in 1914 by the National Union of Women Workers. With the widespread movement of soldiers and male workers around the country necessitated by the war effort, concern arose over the 'dangers arising from the uncontrolled excitement which possessed much of the girlhood and womanhood of the country' (Garner, 1978: 54; Owings, 1925: 23). Initially paid for from voluntary funds, these moral police were subsidised by the Home Office after 1916 at about £400 per annum to train other women to aid police work in London. Police funds were then used to employ a private, secondary force of moral guardians who, for example, reported on the behaviour of the members of the audience in London cinemas (Garner, 1978: 55). At the same time, other sponsors and employers, such as vigilance committees, church organisations and the London Council for the Promotion of Public Morality, maintained an interest in the private employment of women patrols to encourage moral rectitude.

The fascinating histories of these women's 'self-help' groups, generally funded by private commissions, voluntary contributions and subscriptions or government grants, cannot be adequately or appropriately dealt with in a study of privately paid policing and security.[2] Suffice it to say here that the proliferation of women's private/ voluntary police associations, now largely forgotten, highlights one irregularity among many in the conventional unilinear picture of police history (South, 1987a). It also shows how quickly and effectively, private, trained, uniformed and equipped personnel can be brought together – and, in some cases, be absorbed into the public policing arrangements of the state.

Private security and the police in the inter-war years

Periods of conflict, oppression and victimisation invariably throw up examples of organised resistance and opposition. The General Strike of 1926 and the aggressive reaction, more particularly of the middle and upper class special constables than the regular police, led to the formation of defence corps by the workers. In some cases relations with the police were simply bloody. In others (whatever the truth of stories of friendly football matches), as at Willesden, with the 200 strong Maintenance of Order Corps and at Selby, apparently harmonious cooperation was established in a mixture of community self-policing and state policing (Garner, 1978: 62). But the response of employers in the General Strike actually highlights another facet of the privatisation of policing: the direct use of ordinary employees in a security capacity. *The Times* newspaper, for example, directed its employees to act as guards to protect the loading and delivery of newspapers (Garner, 1978: 63).

Most factories and warehouse complexes employed 'works police' for gate security work and to patrol for fire and intrusion. The outbreak of the Second World War in 1939 made such provision a more pressing problem, most acutely so where products, services and safe storage were essential to the war effort. Unsurprisingly, the state saw the need for the incorporation of such security responsibilities into its own general home defence strategy and these early in-house security arrangements were amalgamated into the Home Guard (Calder, 1969: 143, 379; Garner, 1978: 64). After the war, many large companies retained, and even expanded, these basic in-house security forces. Other firms felt the labour-intensive costs of such staffing (before the development of sophisticated security technology in the 1950s and 1960s) to be too prohibitive and instead opted for the provision of security by 'rental'.

Some sophistication in the sense of a 'technical' approach to security had already entered the commercial market place even before the end of the First World War, with the introduction of electrical alarms (see pp. 64–5). Other innovations followed. In 1926 an entrepreneur called Arnold Kunzler formed a company called Machinery and Technical Transport. As Draper (1978: 19) notes, 'the word "technical" in reality stood for "security" but the company believed then (as it believes to this day) that one of the secrets of security is anonymity.' Machinery and Technical Transport provided couriers to accompany and safeguard the passage of various goods, including cash, valuables and bullion by road, rail or air. Specially designed security vehicles were a later innovation but MAT developed with the times and is still operating as Brinks-MAT in the UK, a part of the international Brinks security organisation.

In 1935 a night watch patrol was offered as part of a limited range of guard patrol services run by Night Watch Services Limited on a commercial, rental basis. Night Watch Services was established by the Marquis of Willingdon and Henry Tiarks, a merchant banker, to protect the penthouse propertied set against East End undesirables and Moseley's Fascists who were drawing violence to their meetings wherever they were in London (Bowden, 1978: 253; Clayton, 1967: 12; Garner, 1978: 65). The pre-war complement of 15 guards on bicycles was reduced to two by 1945, but thereafter the firm grew, changing its name first to Security Corps in 1947 and then later, in response to Home Office concern that this sounded too military, to Securicor (Bunyan, 1976: 231). While the history of Securicor is therefore longer than commonly thought, elsewhere private policing and security is even older. Apart from the USA, Sweden offers a good example. The Group 4 Total Security Company today operates one of the major British security organisations, and may be the largest across Europe. Unsurprisingly, it is a grouped amalgamation of four companies, Cash in Transit, Securitas Alarms, Store Detectives and Factory Guards Limited. Factory Guards was the forerunner, established in the UK in 1952 as a subsidiary of the Swedish parent company, Securitas International, which has an even longer history than Securicor, being founded in 1913.

If the years immediately before the Second World War were formative for the organisation of the post-war private security sector and the type of firms that would emerge, so too was it a period in which the operational style and priorities of the police significantly changed in response to an apparently changing style of criminal activity. These last two related changes also had implications for the development of post-war private security. As Scraton (1982: 35) points out: 'well over a hundred years after Colquhoun's vision of a scientific form of policing there was little to recommend the service on this level. Classification systems were disparate and incompatible and communication between forces was sparse.'

In 1933 the Dixon Committee was appointed to assess the state of detective work within British policing. Critchley (1978) summarises the conclusions and recommendations of the committee, important as the blueprint of the organisation and practice of modern police detection work, and the system and standard against which so-called private detection should be measured. It should be remembered though, that the negative appraisal of the achievements of the British police was the result of comparison with overseas police systems, where one exemplar, the United States, had derived much of its original and imaginative approach to criminal investigation from private security agencies such as the Pinkertons. Reporting in 1934, the Dixon Committee concluded that:

> England lagged behind other countries in the use of scientific aids in the detection of crime, and the outcome of its work was the introduction of systematic training courses for detectives; the establishment of regional crime-clearing houses to assist in identifying convicted persons, particularly mobile criminals; the issue by the Home Office of instructions of scientific aids, drawing detectives' attention to the ways in which laboratory work could help them; the consolidation of a system of forensic science laboratories; and the provision of rapid, reliable and systematic means of collecting and communicating information about criminals between all police forces in the country. (Critchley, 1978: 210)

Far from resenting such criticism, senior police officers seem to have welcomed it. The modernisation of policing technology and need for sophistication in the approach to detective work was a paramount necessity in their eyes as they identified signs of the growth of 'organised crime' with another image imported from the USA, that of 'gangland'. The growth of inner-city gangs, born of the loyalties and fears of resistant community networks, depressed areas and depressing housing, provided, as they established themselves beyond street corner meetings and local prostitution and protection, the *basis* for more profitable forms of crime. These included organised robbery, burglary and the move from what McIntosh (1975) refers to as 'craft' to 'project' crime. The latter, in its turn, was a significant contributor to the growth of the private security sector, stimulating, in a relationship of assault and defence symbiosis, the development of alarm systems, armoured cars, guard services, camera monitoring and recording, investigation services, and perpetually more and more elaborate cash protection and dispensing systems.[3] These developments, however, were not the only major contributors to the dramatic post-war expansion of the private security sector (see South, 1984).

Contract private security today

The only consistent and reliable statement that is continually made about the size and scope of the private security industry today is that it is hard to obtain consistent and reliable information about it. One of the most recent surveys of the contract security field produced by its principal trade union, MATSA (the Managerial, Administrative, Technical and Supervisory Association, part of the GMBATU) notes: 'There are no reliable figures on the size of the security industry. It is rapidly changing, partly seasonal and, of course, there are a number of very small companies about whom it is hard to get any information at all' (1983: 3).

It is worth pointing out at this early stage that if this last observation is true of the most visible and familiar aspects of the private security sector, then it is even more true of the less conspicuous and more specialised aspects. And it is not simply that such information is unavailable to interested parties such as the trade unions. Until the Home Office produced its Green Paper, 'The Private Security Industry', in 1979, it seems to have been particularly underinformed about or just particularly uninterested in, the subject. In reply to a letter from Bruce George, MP, to the Home Office Crime Prevention Centre, Lord Harris, Under-secretary at the Home Office, wrote in March 1977:

> As you know, the Home Office does not keep a record of such organisations. In 1971, however, it did ask chief officers of police in England and Wales how many organisations were known to them which provided services for the protection of persons and property, including the installation of security equipment. The replies showed that 741 such organisations were known. This is the most recent information we have.

For some time this 1971 figure was the only vaguely official one to go on and yet many who knew the industry felt it a woefully inadequate estimate.

Before 1950, sales in the private security business, that is, contract security dealing in guards, armoured cars, alarms and so on, amounted to less than £5 million per year. By 1970, turnover had risen to around £55 million, employing, according to one estimate, around 40,000 men and women (Wiles and McClintock, 1972: 67–8). An estimate for 1976 suggested a much more sizeable set of figures: 7,000 firms, 250,000 uniformed staff and 10,000 armoured vehicles (Bunyan, 1976: 230). Whilst probably something of an over-estimate in 1976, the figure is certainly a reasonable one to consider in the late 1980s. If so, it represents a staggering estimate of the size of the visible dimensions of private security.

Such estimates were no better or worse informed than those which could be made by the police. Speaking in 1979, P.D. Knights, Chief Constable of the West Midlands Police, addressed the Association of Chief Police Officers/Association of Metropolitan Authorities joint summer conference on the theme of 'Policing – public or private?' and had to return to the 1971 figure, offering the following breakdown:

> no reliable up-to-date statistics are available. One writer has put the figure at 128,000 (*in excess of our total police force*). The 1971 census would show about 80,000 people recorded at that time as being occupied as security guards, patrolmen, watchmen, gate-keepers and in similar employment. Police forces in 1971 knew of 741 private security organisations in England and Wales. About a dozen operated nationally and 80% of the total operated in only one force area. 47% of the organisations installed intruder alarms, 39% guard dogs, 38% mobile guards and 32% static guards. A majority of firms (60%) offered only one service. 529 of these companies employed an estimated 26,000 persons (which might give a total of 30,000 all told), and of the 26,000, over 20,000 (or 84%) were employed by only nine firms. More recent estimates put the total at 40,000 employees. Their turnover, outside of manufacturing, is put at about £130 million annually. (Knights, 1979: 5–6; emphasis added)

More recently available information has not been exceptionally helpful. Sales turnover remains an indicator of growth which many refer to. Randall and Hamilton (1972) reported to a 1971 Cambridge Institute of Criminology conference on private security that annual sales turnover had risen from £5 million to £55 million in the period 1950–70. By 1976, this had increased to an estimated £135 million according to the 1979 Home Office Green Paper (Shearing and Stenning, 1981: 207). And again the 1971 figure recurs, as if it had been the product of some sound survey of the field originally, when in fact senior police officers had simply been asked to put together their locally available information, and had done just that.

With a commitment to unionisation in the security industry, MATSA has made as consistent and thorough an effort as anyone to chart the growth and size of the private security companies in the UK. In its 1983 report, *The Security Industry*, MATSA notes the 'best official estimates' starting with the Cambridge conference and the 1971 police figures. It also notes that in 1978 the British Security Industry Association (BSIA) claimed to have 63 member companies employing 32,063 contract security workers.[4] The report continues:

> As the top ten companies are all BSIA members and cover around 80% of the industry, total direct employment in contract security companies in 1978 may have been around 40,000. By Autumn 1983, the BSIA estimated that membership covered 26,500 contract security guarding jobs with a further 2,000 in ancillary occupations. Alarm maintenance and installation employment had reached 4,000 making an approximate total of 32,500

employment in member companies. Obviously, the vast majority of security companies are not members. (1983: 3)

This report also makes the critically important observation that contract security is only one dimension of the private security 'industry' which in wider terms includes specialised constabularies such as the ports police, parks police, transport police, the Atomic Energy Authority police etc.; in-house security; security equipment design, manufacture and installation; private detectives; store detectives; security consultants, advisors and trainers; and so on.

More recently, and with a focus on what is conventionally seen as the private security industry, a 1984 report, jointly produced by MATSA and the Low Pay Unit, suggests an employment level of 'up to 200,000 in total, with sales in 1982 of well over £400 million – equivalent [then] to 10 percent of the entire Government law and order budget' (Williams et al., 1984: 1). In terms of expansion, sales and profit, the industry enjoyed highly significant growth from the late 1950s to the early 1980s; there are some signs that in more recent years 'in real terms the industry has remained roughly stable', both in terms of sales and market shares looking at the four sectors of guarding, transport, alarms, and safes and locks (Williams et al., 1984: 2). (This is not, of course, considering the other dimensions of the private security sector referred to above.)

It should by now be clear, if it has not been all along, that it is extremely difficult (if not currently impossible) to give any guaranteed accurate estimate or assessment of the size of the contract security industry specifically or the private security sector as a whole. I have presented all the available major, reputable estimates and have been unable to gather any data which could generate any estimates which I could argue to be more accurate than those recently proposed. The estimate from the MATSA/Low Pay Unit (1984) report is one that I would certainly support, and if there were grounds for feeling that Bunyan's (1976) estimate of 250,000 staff in the private security industry was an over-estimate for the mid-1970s there can be far fewer reservations about its likely accuracy in the late 1980s.

Although the number of companies operating in the contract security field is unknown – though one estimate suggests that it is at least over 1,000 (MATSA, 1983) – what is striking about this particular growth industry is that it is so heavily dominated by just five companies.[5] These five now take up around 75–80 percent of the UK market. In terms of size they rank downward from Securicor, Group 4, Chubb, Security Express to Pritchards, with Securicor remaining the really dominant force in the UK market. There would be little point or value in offering here what would essentially be company histories.

However, there are a number of developments in the ways in which certain companies are diversifying their activities that are significant.

Reference has already been made to the pre-war establishment of the forerunner of Securicor and its post-war renaming and subsequent growth, expanding rapidly throughout the 1960s up to the present. However, within that expansion it has not merely sought the extension of established services but has consistently moved into newly developed areas. Thus, today it is clearly placing less of its growth emphasis on 'traditional' security services, such as the provision of static and armoured van guards etc., and has moved, for example, into the booming area of communications: the development and application of cellular technology used in mobile communications systems. In a major project in this area Securicor has entered into a partnership with British Telecom, known as Sectel. This venture has a 25-year operating licence to build up a national cellular radio network which will:

> enable business people to use a cordless telephone to make and receive calls while on the move. Major cities and their connecting motorways will be divided into small areas, or cells, each with its own radio transmitter and receiver operating on a unique frequency. As subscribers travel from one cell to another a computerised exchange switches frequencies automatically to provide a continuous link. (Golding and Murdock, 1983: 33)

Golding and Murdock's comment on this particular kind of enterprise, which in this case takes radio frequencies out of public access and privatises them, reflects an unsurprising feature of all the commercial activities of the private security sector: a 'tendency to put the demands and needs of business before the broader public interest'. Securicor is also involved in cash-in-transit operations (CIT), which are reported to be 'doing reasonably' (MATSA, 1983) and also has interests in alarms, cleaning services, hotels, vehicle dealerships and insurance and travel. Its parcels and courier services 'are expanding', including its data service delivery organisation.

In common with most of its major competitors, Securicor has been diversifying from a position of financial good health in an economic climate when many businesses have been simply consolidating or contracting. As the MATSA (1983: 4) report put it: 'Even in the depths of the recession with competition at its fiercest, the company is doing far better than the average UK business.' There is little point in noting similar details for other companies such as Group 4 which (alongside Chubb, is the next largest security company in the UK) except to observe that it is also diversifying from early concentration on property guarding, CIT and store detective work into other areas. Securicor and Group 4 do, however, raise one further point which has, in general, been more of an issue for American and Canadian commentators. This is the question of foreign ownership of security companies (Shearing and Stenning, 1981: 207). There are certainly now a number of foreign-owned (almost exclusively US-based) companies in Britain, but Group 4 is actually a Swedish company, and while Securicor is a British company it has sizeable overseas operations, with around 30 percent of its total staff working abroad. As Shearing and Stenning (1981: 207) have remarked, 'this suggests that foreign ownership is probably a significant factor in the European private security industry as well as in the industry in Britain and Canada.'

Chubb and Security Express are the next two really sizeable companies. However, smaller companies are still successfully fighting their way into the market and undergoing rapid expansion alongside the continued growth of companies which have specialised in the installation of security system and alarm technology. The MATSA (1983) report, for example, notes the expansion of companies like Security Centres Limited which 'buys up smaller, weaker companies turning them into local branches for hiring out burglar alarms' (MATSA, 1983: 5). Security functions are also taken on and commercially developed by firms apparently coming from a different direction. A clear example, over at least the past decade, has been the growth of office maintenance and cleaning service organisations which offer a complete package incorporating expertise in security and alarm systems as well as 'security-vetted' cleaning staff.

On a continuum of a whole range of commercial services, it is now increasingly difficult to say where the private security sector begins or ends. The 1983 MATSA report summarises what is still the current trend in the contract security business:

> The trend is therefore towards a multitude of small and medium-sized companies fighting for the patrol, guarding and cash-carrying contracts, with the very much larger companies tightening their hold on the technologically advanced end of the market. There may be a steady decline in CIT and pay-packeting as more companies move to cashless pay and plastic money becomes more widely used, but this may take a lot longer than is widely thought. (1983: 6)

Employee recruitment, turnover and training

One very significant consequence of this multitude of companies, of all sizes, is that, as Garner (1978: 96) has remarked, 'the multiplicity of sizes, resources and expertise in the industry makes it very difficult to generalise about recruitment and training and working conditions.' From the interviews I conducted with managers in manned security and alarm and lock-fitting companies, it was clear that issues of recruitment and training were fairly sensitive subjects that few people were totally happy with in the industry. For example, although the actual incidence of infiltration by persons with criminal intent or simply with a record of past offences which might make them inappropriate security employees is probably *relatively* slight, this is none the less an issue which security companies rightly feel is a public and police worry. It is hence a worry to them. The fact that there have been cases of people employed with convictions for violence, possession of stolen property, corruption and so on gives rise to considerable concern about the initial problem of selection of employees.

For many companies this becomes the key argument for greater recognition of private security's willingness to police itself if it were granted exclusion from the provisions of the Rehabilitation of Offenders Act 1974, and given the means to vet prospective employees more thoroughly (Chapter 7). There is also obvious awareness among employers of static guard and mobile patrol staff that given the low levels of pay – an issue which the Low Pay Unit has campaigned about (Williams et al., 1984) – and the antisocial and long hours of the shift system (usually 12 hours or longer), then this level of private security is unlikely to attract high-calibre employees. On the other hand, the companies argue, these conditions are forced upon them by the competitive nature of the security market. Rates of pay are kept low by the vicious circle of competition which exists in this highly labour-intensive sector of the industry where the major costs are the wage bills. The companies argue that if they paid more then they would have to charge more; they would then be undercut by competitors. Similarly, in a business which offers a 24-hour service, then three shifts of eight hours might attract some better staff, but cost considerations mean that two 12-hour shifts are more desirable. These factors, coupled with the generally boring nature of the job, contribute to a massive turnover of staff which, in turn, reduces the possibility of the services achieving the levels of efficiency that security companies claim (or would like to claim).[6]

The proceedings of the Cambridge Institute of Criminology, Cropwood Conference on private security (Wiles and McClintock, 1972) estimated that 25 percent of the labour force changed four to five times per year. Over 15 years later, with the massive growth that the industry has maintained but with little commensurate improvement in conditions or pay, this estimate should at least hold and the figure is probably considerably higher.[7] Most medium to small firms simply accept that they are employing a large percentage of casual, floating and part-time labour which will move on regardless; hence, it is viewed as a waste of time and money to try to offer any (or more than a morning or day's) training and orientation.

There are serious criticisms to be made of such disregard for the sensitive positions that guards will occupy and the information and skills that they will need (see Chapter 6). The level of preparation that is currently seen as 'better than most companies provide' need not be a sophisticated matter. One small to medium-sized company that I studied prided itself on its approach to training which, after some lengthy experience, tried to cover points of relevant law and safety issues. The management none the less insisted that in the contract security business training really does have to start with basics. This included ensuring that employees have the ability to read, write and speak English in order that they may write reports, read safety signs and instructions and communicate with anyone in or near the property or with the police or property owners.

In the field of manufacturing and installing security devices and locks, one manager suggested that the standard procedure for taking on employees would be very simple. Receiving the job application, checking the references and then undergoing 'on-the-job' training. Although work in this particular industry often calls for some qualifications, probably at least a higher education certificate in electronics (or equivalent), it is also acknowledged that anyone can set themselves up in business with no qualifications at all. Movement into the world of the locksmith, with its craft traditions, might more typically mean joining a specialist firm as a trainee at 16. Membership of the Master Locksmiths Association would then only follow after a series of examinations.

Growth, expansion, employment and prospects

Although the contract security field is characterised by the instability and high turnover of its labour force, it is none the less extremely important to consider this area in terms of it being a major employer. As a growth industry of some proportions, it is a large-scale provider of jobs. This is obviously a key issue for the trade unions as well as the industry itself. Drawing on the 1983 Economic Review from the University of Warwick, Institute for Employment Research (1983), the 1983 MATSA report predicted (in summary):

> That contingent upon the growth of trade, retail activity, distribution and so on, the security industry generally will experience continued overall growth across all regions of the country. (Predicted growth is *not* directly linked to any predicted rise in crime.)

> That the increase of 10,000 jobs in contract security companies which occurred between 1975 and 1982 is part of a continuing growth trend, which may even accelerate.

That the broad range of security occupations is the only area of manual employment which is *not* predicted to decline. By 1990 an overall gain of 100,000 jobs should take total employment in this area to just under half a million. This figure includes 'public administration', i.e. the police, but clearly non-public security occupations are a major percentage of the total. Within this sector both contracted security services and other security-type jobs in other industries are included. The industry is, as many have observed, 'recession resistant' and as unemployment ensures a pool of labour willing to accept low pay and increasing capital intensity of the manufacturing sector makes private security more cost-effective, it will remain so.

On the basis of these projections, both the public and the private security sectors are going to be of increasing significance on a range of criteria – not least size – for the foreseeable future.

The problem with such projections, however, is their vagueness and generality. On the scale on which they are calculated a variety of trends and indicators can be put together to produce a forecast figure for this or that. It is difficult, however, if not impossible, to break down the components of the projected future picture. This is partly because one can assume that general trends will have the impetus to carry the composite whole to its forecasted growth, but it is less easy to predict how individual components of the whole will fare. Where some may decline (for example, in static guard security) others may flourish and overtake in growth (probably electronic security systems). As indicated, the major companies in the contract security field are already seeking to diversify and make themselves less dependent upon business which is as labour-intensive, and hence competitive and costly, as guarding and cash-in-transit services. Hence, despite the sustained business activity and likely growth of smaller companies already in, and moving into, this area, there is unlikely to be major or rapid increase in the labour force here. As the MATSA (1983: 7–8) report notes: 'The "new" sectors like telecommunications, electronics, alarm systems and maintenance are less labour-intensive in themselves. However, a large organisation is needed to support such high technology, complex operations. It is these "indirect" jobs which are likely to continue growing.'

The other principal areas of the industry are also likely to sustain continued employment expansion. Courier, parcel delivery and security freight services will grow, cash-in-transit services will probably stabilise, contracting slowly in the future as electronic means of money transfer increasingly proliferate, whilst the 'traditional' areas of static and mobile guarding should enjoy continued if modest growth, especially with newer, smaller firms aggressively seeking their share of the market (MATSA, 1983: 7–8).

This picture for the UK in the 1980s reflects the 1976 forecast for the

USA put forward in the Federal Task Force Report on Private Security Standards and Goals which suggested that 'with the encroachment by electronic technology, growth rates for guard, armoured car and courier services will be modest compared to the . . . annual growth of the past few years' (Task Force Report on Private Security, 1976: 34). It should be noted though that, even given that the Task Force was considering growth in comparative and relative terms, it does seem now, for the USA and elsewhere, they may themselves have been too modest in their assessment of growth. However, it is true that it is these three areas particularly (within the contract security industry) which will be overtaken and, over time, see relative decline. Certainly, 'encroachment by electronic technology' is the significant factor in this crucial reorientation of the contract security industry and its activities and services.

'The classic nightwatchman is a thing of the past', observes the MATSA report. Closed circuit television, radio communication and electronic warning and sensor systems now work out cheaper and can certainly be more efficient and, more importantly, safer and more attractive to employees. The pace of development of electronics, the competitive nature of the market and the rising labour costs of guard and patrol services, mean that it is no longer just the sophisticated and up-market major corporations that can survey premises by camera and monitoring screens, staffed by a single guard. This is now an option open to an ever-increasing number of companies with physical plant or stock to guard. At the same time, it is perhaps disturbing that such technology lends itself on a 24-hour basis, not only to the overseeing of property by night, but also to the surveillance of that property *and of the work force* by day. But there is a further set of factors which makes electronic surveillance guarding attractive to customer companies and security firms alike.

As I have noted elsewhere (South, 1983) and as MATSA, despite its sympathy with security staff, concurs, 'guards can become frustrated or bored or suffer temptation as their employers make no effort to train or pay them adequately' (1983: 8). Fooling around, fiddling time or pilfering the protected goods can add interest to the job and the wage packet. Electronic surveillance technology, especially that which can record and can be subject to checking, therefore has several useful functions apart from its obvious contribution to crime and hazard prevention and monitoring. First, it is seen as a deterrent to fiddling, pilfering and other infractions; secondly, it also involves a higher degree of professionalism and interest than traditional guarding roles for the security staff (or so the theory goes); thirdly, it can be cheaper and more efficient for the employing customer; and, finally, it reduces the problems of rising labour costs for security companies.

Interestingly, despite the fact that this looks like a lucrative trend for the private security sector generally, the structuring of the UK market in this area means that the bubble already has limits set upon its expansion even before it bursts:

> In the UK a high price is charged for installation of alarms, closed circuit television etc., a relatively low hiring charge thereafter to cover maintenance (in the USA it is the other way round). This means big profits while the industry is expanding and selling new systems but the balloon will burst once the market becomes saturated. At the same time, since there is no money in service and maintenance, alarms have a poor reputation for reliability, to the great annoyance of passers-by, neighbours and police. (MATSA, 1983: 8)[8]

Practical and simple legislative intervention or concerted pressure from the insurance sector aiming to reverse this market trend and its consequences would make good sense for all concerned. For example, insistence on adherence to British standard specifications for the manufacture, installation *and regular maintenance* of alarm and similar security systems would not be unreasonable. However, in present and foreseeable circumstances, such a development is unlikely. None the less, as a recent survey of the industry by Jordan and Sons (Surveys) of London (1983: 5) observes, intruder alarms in total market terms are 'the most important sector by some distance'. I shall discuss the problems of performance of alarms and the stimulus to the market for them prompted by the requirements of the insurance business in Chapter 4.

Finally, in this survey of prospects, I turn to cash-in-transit (CIT) and Pay Pak services. As the MATSA report astutely points out, 'Cash-in-Transit is a response to whether people think crime is rising as much as whether it actually does. Hence the greater public presence of security companies itself generates trade' (1983: 9). The conspicuous movement of private security guards and armoured vans is commonplace on the streets and in operation on public and private property. Such a presence advertises the 'obvious need' for such services and resonates with public perceptions of the growing 'crime problem'. Continued demand for such services is hence encouraged.

Of course, there is a genuine commercial need for the protection of the increasing amount of cash and valuables in circulation. Despite the electronic transfer of funds, some decline in the number of workers who prefer cash in weekly wage packets, the rise in use of credit cards and so on, the move to the cashless society is making slow progress. The transport of cash for pay makes up about half of CIT trade and the rest is accounted for by bank business and shop takings. The latter are actually generating a greater volume of circulating cash and valuables than ever before. This is partly the result of the decline of the corner shop and small chain stores and the growth of larger superstores, multiple chain stores and shopping complexes which concentrate and multiply the generation of cash. Such developments have meant more business for CIT companies. Finally, the cash-only nature of transactions in the informal economy and 'off the books' arrangements in parts of the growing service sector, encouraged by the attraction of avoiding high VAT, National Insurance and income tax rates means that, as the MATSA report concludes, 'however much "plastic money" grows or bank opening hours become more convenient, there will always be a substantial demand for cash' (1983: 9).

The major security companies have been preparing for the move to the cashless society for years but their far-sightedness has generally been tempered by keeping an eye on how fast trends are really developing. Some of the security systems which companies like Securicor were beginning to develop in the 1970s have still not seen the light of day, at least partly because the computerised card systems of monetary transactions which they are posited upon have not arrived. Whilst property guarding, CIT services and other labour-intensive areas of operation still have so much commercial stability and some growth potential in them then, despite diversification and expansion in other directions, the major companies and their small competitors will remain in these areas.

Notes

1 I hope to examine some possible hypotheses concerning the relationship between the 'new' police and other private options around the turn of the century in a forthcoming paper. In particular, this will consider the implications of the statistical decline in theft, violence and civil disorder around this period (see Gatrell, 1980; Gurr, 1977).

2 Garner's excellent thesis, to which I am clearly indebted here, offers a thorough treatment of the subject (1978: ch. 3).

3 Of course, this kind of mutually shaping symbiotic relationship between criminal enterprises and innovative entrepreneurs in policing agencies can also be found elsewhere. For one analysis of this interaction in relation to illegal drug distribution and developments in law enforcement, see Dorn and South (1987).

4 The roles of MATSA and the BSIA, and other trade union and professional association bodies are discussed more fully in Chapter 7.

5 I shall describe here examples of security companies in the upper and middle ranges of the market, dealing with common aspects of, and problems with, the labour force that they employ (principally in the labour-intensive areas of guard and mobile patrol work) and then describing more broadly the range and nature of the services that they provide. Further description of two middle-range companies (one London-wide and beyond; the other more localised to the centre and south of London) is given in South (1985: ch. 2). I shall not describe the very small companies operating in this sphere, and can only deal cursorily with the common characteristics and problems of the employed (often marginal and casual) labour force found in private

security and mobile patrol work (although related issues are raised in Chapter 6).

6   I have discussed aspects of these issues, particularly the question of shifts and the boredom of the job, in South (1985: ch. 2).

7   Not surprisingly, given the international character of private security, similar problems are strongly evident in the USA and Canada. In 1972 Kakalik and Wildhorn observed in their Rand Report on private security in the USA, that: 'Turnover in private security work, especially guarding, is much higher than in public law enforcement. Lateral entry is rare in the public police; recruits generally enter when young and a substantial fraction remain until retirement. Precise, overall figures for turnover in the public police, however, are not available. In contract security work, especially in guard work, turnover is high, ranging from a low of about twenty percent per year for high-quality, more highly paid guards at government installations, to a high of 200 percent and more per year for the low-quality, low paid, hourly guard. The highest turnover rates are experienced during the first several months of employment' (1972: Vol. 2: 74; Shearing et al., 1980: 96–7). For Canada, the major studies undertaken by the Toronto Centre of Criminology confirm the same general picture. Shearing et al. were able to draw upon extensive survey data in their assessment of the high turnover characteristics of private security in Canada and found the same contributory factors: 'the American literature tends to identify poor salary as the principal cause of the high turnover within the security industry. Our respondents concurred that poor salary was a major cause of high turnover in Canada. Just over half of our respondents mentioned that low wages contributed to high turnover. Related to this was the response that the benefits offered employees were not attractive enough. This was mentioned as a factor by just over a sixth of our respondents. Further, agency executives commented that the absence of salary increases and chances for promotion contributed to the turnover problem. A number of the agency executives (sixteen percent) also pointed to the nature of security work itself as a source of high turnover. About ten percent mentioned the existence of shift work as a factor. Several pointed to the often boring nature of the work. In addition, several indicated that because many contracts were short-term, it was sometimes necessary to let employees go at the expiry of specific contracts. Another ten percent of the agency executives indicated that one of the reasons for high turnover was poor job performance, which resulted in a continual process of termination and hiring in some agencies. Another set of reasons offered for high turnover focused on the security agents themselves. Over ten percent of agency respondents indicated that security work was regarded by many as a stop-gap while employees looked for another job' (1980: 97–8).

8   The choice between employing patrolling guards and installing electronic surveillance technology is by no means a simple one. As Williams et al. (1984: 3) observe: 'More sophisticated and reliable devices would require better trained and motivated guards to monitor them, and the poor image of most intruder alarms may equally encourage the use of guards instead. On the other hand, a higher penetration of cheaper alarms might mean less reliance on relatively more expensive guards. In these ways the different sectors within the private security industry have a complex inter-relationship, and standards which operate in one sector may affect the performance of another.'

3 The Nature and Range of Services in the Contract Private Security Industry

The provision of contract security is the most visible private security activity. It covers a wide range of services and functions, including the provision of static guards and mobile patrols to guard and secure property and for the protection of persons; the transport of cash and making-up, picking-up and delivery of wages; other specialised delivery services; back-up communications networks, to assist and protect long-distance lorry drivers and their loads; tailored guard services for anything from race-horses to oil paintings and other special assignments; consultative work on maximising the efficiency and security potential of the work/business/ home environment; and various forms of investigative work from store detectives to shopfloor spies working undercover. Less reputable firms will also happily offer services which constitute the strong arm of private protection, providing 'guards' for use in evictions or the repossession of property.

For many years, and in the eyes of many still today, the static or foot patrol guard represented what the employment of private security services actually meant (or seemed to mean). Some description of the role and functions of security patrol staff is therefore necessary. The essence of the private security patrol guard has remained unchanged through history. The Pinkerton's bureau may have taken up the phrase 'The eye that never sleeps' to describe its private detective agents, but at least ideally the phrase describes the function of the security guard more accurately. The security guard is supposed 'to keep an eye out for potential security problems' (Shearing et al., 1980: 168). This involves the performance of tasks related to the safety and securing of property and the surveillance of persons within it. Checking on locks, doors, windows and gates, checking alarm and security systems, checking for fire risks and checking personnel, visitors and intruders are the basic routines. And such work is *highly* routinised, especially the core of tasks that fall into the 'housekeeping' category of duties, such as turning off lights and taps, shutting windows, switching off machinery, some maintenance and checking for fire hazards. Similarly, the checking of security guards themselves as they do their rounds is routinised, often using 'clock stations' located especially at vulnerable points where the guard must clock-in, inserting a key to have a ticker-tape marked at a specific time by the clock mechanism and telephoning into the control room as a back-up not only to confirm adherence to schedule but also as a check that the guard is all right.

Although in the past most patrolling was done on foot, and this is still generally the case, many firms employ mobile patrols not just to move between sites at unpredictable, irregular intervals (for obvious reasons) but also for the mobility of supervisory staff who can then personally check on guards and premises. As many commentators and security staff have observed, the patrol function of the security guard can be seen as 'very much like that of the traditional "cop on the beat"' (Shearing et al. 1980: 169).

Private beat patrols pre-dated public police patrols by centuries (Radzinowicz, 1956; South, 1987a) so it remains pertinent to keep in mind the question – which is the most traditional? Shearing et al. elaborate on the 'traditional' role which private security seems to have taken over from the public police:

> The modern public police have increasingly turned to the automobile as a means of transport, and have accordingly evolved into an emergency force which prides itself on its quick response time. While the public police continue to patrol our streets the traditional foot patrol function, historically regarded as the mainstay of the police role, is now almost the exclusive preserve of private security. (1980: 169)

Perhaps, however, a more 'dynamic' account of the *continuing* development of private security should be more cautious about this kind of 'static' pronouncement. Certainly, there has been some bifurcation of services – public and private – especially in the post-war period. But this has occurred within a continuum of policing services and functions which does not readily offer static and fixed positions or neat divisions. As at other times in history, there are familiar signs of overlap as well as of bifurcation. This has occurred in recent years as private security has offered mobile patrols of industrial and residential estates and the police have declared a desire to put more officers back onto foot patrols in the community. Equally traditional, but perhaps less routinised and certainly less emphasised, are security duties involving the searching of employees and, in some cases, visitors on the private property of commercial concerns and industrial plant, including their vehicles and those involved in delivery and distribution.[1] These latter duties relate to occasional mundane tasks taken on by private security such as the receiving and shipping of goods usually after ordinary working hours. In the USA and Canada private security is now also involved in the process of 'receiving and shipping' people as passengers. In their long-term study, Shearing et al. (1980:

170) found 'yet another form of access control mentioned, which because of its visibility has become associated with private security work . . . air craft pre-boarding checks'. Although a 'relatively rare activity', at least in Canada, and despite the fact that there is no precisely similar private security activity in the UK, given the use of private security to detain and guard people at the London area airports and the vague provisions of the Protection of Aircraft Act 1973 (see Chapter 6), such developments in the UK are not remote possibilities.

Remembering earlier comments about contract security companies' concerns about training, it might have seemed patronising to those unfamiliar with the industry to find such concerns starting at basic levels like literacy and communication skills. However, there are some essential semi-professional components of the security guard's work which in reputable firms perform several functions. The most obvious example is the writing of reports. These are important in terms of efficiency, communication and as an additional resource in checking up on the work of employees. They can also be important as an 'advertisement' and guarantee of good and conscientious service for the company in dealings with customers, police and others (for example, the media). Additionally, at the occupational level, they can offer a psychological boost to job satisfaction. Although almost inevitably regarded as an arduous task, staff *can* none the less see report writing as a professional commitment and, further, one which gives them a respectability and professional sub-cultural affinity to the broader law enforcement enterprise. Such feelings are naturally heightened and emphasised when a security guard is required to give evidence in court. This may not be a frequent call of duty but, given the nature of the job, it is not surprising that it is an occasional one.

While not wishing to sensationalise by veering close to military metaphors (although there is a strong validating historical lineage), the guard's functions can be seen as the securing of the internal security and safety of an area or areas, or of premises and persons on a route that the guard is commissioned to patrol and protect. Within the perimeters of their patrolled site or parameters of their mobile patrol, they must be alert for internal problems but, equally importantly, must also secure against, deter and detect unauthorised intrusion as well as noting authorised entrance. Such requirements necessitate alertness and, it is argued by many, a range of skills and 'a good deal of semi-professional knowledge' (Williams et al., 1984: 7). I am unsure about how widespread such skills and knowledge may actually be in the industry, especially given the lack of regard for training. However, it is certainly the case that there is 'little recognition of the danger or skills involved in security work in the pay received by security guards' (Williams et al., 1984: 7). Company expectations that guards be fit and alert may also be confounded by other demands placed on them. Whilst in some companies it can be a disciplinary offence for guards not to maintain a certain standard, as Williams et al. (1984: 7) observe: 'the company may not pause too long to consider the effect of a 12 hour shift on the average employee's alertness . . . When the system inevitably breaks down the failure will present itself as an individual fault on the part of the particular guard.' Thus, just as private security focuses disciplinary attention externally on individuals in breach of company rules, so internally it adopts a disciplinary code which blames individual workers for the deficiencies resulting from its own competitive practices in the market.

Whilst security is actually employed to provide a wide range of services, it should none the less be emphasised that the primary concern highlighted by private security in selling its services, and by its employers, lies with the concept of 'loss prevention'. This includes everything from discovering the results of the negligence, carelessness and incompetence of employees to detecting and protecting against minor and major theft. Here, as part of a system of surveillance and discipline (in the sense developed by Foucault, 1977) a primary aspect of what Shearing et al. (1980: 172) call 'remedial loss prevention work' is, as they observe, 'its supervisory and educative component'. In this respect written reports passed to the employing contractor are expected to indicate 'breaches of security' which Shearing et al. (1980: 172) found in their Canadian study 'were often used by clients as a means of increasing the "security consciousness" of their employees and as a basis for improving the security measures in force'. The same expectations are held by UK corporate and government employers of private security.

The private security tasks of patrolling, checking, housekeeping and itemising breaches of security are essentially the operation of a system of surveillance. Whilst police surveillance is directed to cover what Spitzer (1975) has termed 'problem populations', this is generally focused around actual or potential breaches of the law and public order. However, as Shearing and Stenning (1981: 214–15) suggestively argue, the emphasis of private security on 'prevention' means that the focus of its surveillance falls not so much upon 'breaches of the law' or even of organisational rules, but rather more upon the 'opportunities for such breaches': 'As a consequence, the objects of private security surveillance tend to be not just potential troublemakers but also *those who are in a position to create such opportunities for breaches. Thus, the target population is greatly enlarged*' (emphasis added). Surveillance is therefore brought to bear, not simply on the actual instances of rule infractions, but on the person or persons who have broken the rules or who may indeed merely be in a position to contribute to the conditions where rules are not followed strictly. As an example of the 'refinement' of such micro-disciplinary surveillance strategy, Shearing and Stenning cite the case of the use of 'snowflake' notes used to record and draw attention to violations of risk-reduction rules:

> In support of the project drive for theft reduction, Atlantic Richfield security instituted an evening patrol still in effect. For each risk found, the patrolling officer fills out and leaves a courteous form called a 'snowflake', which gives the particular insecure condition found, such as personal valuable property left out, unlocked doors and valuable portable calculators on desks. A duplicate of each snowflake is filed by floor and location, and habitual violators are interviewed. As a last resort, compliance is sought through the *violator*'s department manager. (Luzon, 1978, quoted in Shearing and Stenning, 1981: 215, their emphasis)

As this example illustrates, when the surveillance spotlight is turned from those who commit breaches of rules to those who create opportunities for such breaches a new class of 'delinquent' is created; the category 'offender' is expanded to include those who violate security procedures as well as those who commit traditional criminal and other offences. As the 'snowflake' strategy implies, the loss preventative role of private security, in creating a new category of delinquents, also creates a new category of person requiring information.

As should by now be clear, the invocation of Foucault's (1977) analysis of disciplinary surveillance is not simply a theoretical appropriation to offer theoretical perspective to this account of private security. The strategy of disciplinary surveillance makes sense in everyday empirical terms to the practice and practitioners of private security. It forms part of the programme of the private security enterprise which offers services to ensure the security of the conditions of production, exchange and reproduction (for example, maintenance).

Mobile services

Closely related to the service of static and patrol guards is the provision of mobile patrols. These offer irregular checks, to confound predictability, to be made on the external, and sometimes internal, security of premises, usually where a static or patrol guard is not felt necessary or is considered too expensive. Such a service is held to be particularly useful and important when covering property to which entry is forbidden under any circumstances, as for example where Customs and Excise forbid entry to bonded warehouses. Dog-handling services are provided by some companies at an extra cost if requested. From the interviews conducted with guards in the industry, it was evident that from the point of view of those who had worked with dogs, they can be of enormous psychological support when patrolling a large, dark, rambling building. Companies stress that the provision of mobile services and support is extremely valuable, if not absolutely necessary, as it enables random supervision to encourage efficiency, allows for the immediate replacement and transportation of sick or called-away guards and also enables the management of an efficient key-holding service so that clients do not need to rush to premises to allow police or other services access when an emergency occurs.

The other major mobile services are cash transportation and special delivery services. Before the arrival and expansion of these services, cash-in-transit (CIT) was carried in public on the street by employees, taken by taxi or, as in the case of banks, conveyed by special British Road Services vehicles with bank staff travelling with it (Garner, 1978: 91). In 1971 the Post Office changed its 'high value packet' delivery system, effectively making the banks search for an alternative to this method. Many banks and commercial concerns had, of course, already sought the services of CIT specialists and conditions for a boost to such services had earlier received favourable indications for future growth prospects when, in the wake of the 1962 Royal Commission on policing, the police service had withdrawn much of its back-up escort support for cash transport. The signs were right for investment in armoured van services and until the relatively successful raids on armoured vans began in the late 1970s, losses from CIT vehicles were slight and considerable confidence was generated about them (in 1975 less than £3 million was lost compared to total theft losses of £600 million). This confidence expressed itself in one unexpected way in a male-dominated industry. As Garner (1978: 92) reports, Securicor apparently at one time began to use women employees for the job of staying inside the van, operating the radio and pushing out the safe boxes, saying that they 'have clearer voices than men on the radio' and that the job was not dangerous – 'it's like sitting in a safe.' It is unclear but would seem likely that this practice has changed in response to the impact of more violent and successful attacks on CIT vehicles.

Undoubtedly, whatever the prospects for growth or (more likely) simple consolidation in the CIT business, it has been a development that matched its times and will not see contraction while we remain a cash-based society. Wage-packeting and distribution services ensure that a firm's wages office is not an attractive target on pay-day and the money is vulnerable for the shortest length of time. The employment of specialist services rather than use of a firm's own personnel took some time to be accepted by British managements but is now a well-entrenched orthodoxy which, as with special delivery services using fast delivery vans and courier staff working nationally and internationally, now justifies itself in terms of efficiency and competitive rates.

Related to the development of road transport services and an awareness of the threat of criminal attack on them, as well as the occurrence of other emergencies, Securicor in particular began to expand its radio telephone service. As a result, it established HELP, its highway link radio telephone service, to provide links between commercial transport vehicles on the road and Securicor's control centres spread across the country, with the aim of enabling drivers to summon help in cases of accident, illness or attack. Use of a radio link also enables employers to change plans, routes, schedules and so on in a secure manner. Such a service is not simply astute commercial opportunism. Though hardly a 'sensational' common crime, and hence not heavily publicised, highway robbery as a modern pheno- menon is not infrequent. In June 1962 the Vehicle Observer Corps was established as a voluntary organisation of around 700 firms involved in road transport and haulage. The aim of the Corps was to alert drivers on the road to common and frequent dangers and to the *modus operandi* of recent attacks on drivers and their loads. It also paid out rewards to drivers who spotted stolen high-value cargoes (Bell, n.d.: 22). As Garner wryly observes of this scheme, it is 'rather like the rewards offered in the 18th century for information leading to prosecutions' (1978: 94). As I have indicated elsewhere (South, 1987a), there should be little surprise in finding such continuities.

Security equipment and systems

High profits, low risks and a wide range of products and markets characterise the business of selling (and to a lesser extent manu- facturing) security equipment and systems. As noted above, patrol firms have diversified into this area traditionally dominated by expanded locksmith manufacturers (such as Chubb) because it is a logical extension and adjunct to their services. In technical and service terms, there are clear advantages in having alarms linked to the supplying security company's control centre in conjunction with its provision of a key-holding service. In recent years, it has certainly become apparent that aggressive entrants to this market do not believe that it is only the rich who can be encouraged to 'invest' in security equipment, alarms and safes. Such companies have not been neglecting their sales efforts in depressed social areas, particularly in the inner city. This is partly attributable to strong recommendations made by insurers of small businesses and shops, but it is not unreasonable to suggest that deeper insecurities and popular fears about crime and rioting on the streets are also being reflected and capitalised upon.

The often posited link between a rising crime rate and the growth of private security is a more contentious one than might at first be thought. The spur of insurance company encouragement to take security seriously certainly has had its impact, although the concerns here also embrace fire, flood and accident, and adjustment of premiums does not necessarily reflect the final cost of all security precautions taken. For example, effective alarm and other 'detection' technology might be frequently recognised in such adjustments, the employment of patrol guards less often (Williams et al., 1984: 5). Crime *per se* may be on the rise, but whether it is the kind of crime which private security services are generally employed to prevent (for example, the 'preventative' role of the guard patrolling a factory at night) is difficult to demonstrate. In some cases demand may be less to do with the actual likelihood of clients being affected by a rising crime rate and more to do with a climate in which subjective perceptions are that crime *will* affect them. The preventative security philosophy thrives on and contributes to a social and commercial *fear* of crime. There is something of an analogy here with private health care in the United States. Borna (1986: 330) considers the same parallel in discussing the rise of the private prison and quotes Kulis's observation that 'private health care practitioners funnel off the relatively healthy cases for whom minimum treatment can be profitably provided; but the less profitable chronically ill cases are left for the public sector' (Kulis, 1983: 14). In a similar way, the private security sector partly owes its significant growth to taking on many customers who, in reality, in terms of vulnerability to crime, are probably as 'healthy' as they could reasonably be, yet who fear crime. Thus, being able to afford it, and encouraged by popular imagery and hardline insurance recommendations, they pay for security to protect them from crimes that they may not actually be in significant danger of being victims of.

Armoured cars and cash-in-transit services

Although Allan Pinkerton had established his famous private detective agency in the USA in 1830 and moved into the provision of protective patrol guard services in 1850, 'secure', 'express' delivery services were developed by other entrepreneurs entering the nineteenth-century private security market. Also in 1850, Henry Wells established the American Express Company, which indeed 'did nicely'. Though not strictly the first (Draper, 1978: 16), Wells's operation, joined in 1852 by William G. Fargo, was a pioneer in its time. But, as in the security market of the twentieth century, rivals were quick to see that there was scope for competition. The Adams Express Company was established in 1854 and today's Brinks Incorporated (which operates in the USA and the UK) started life in 1859 when Perry Brinks established a company to provide secure transportation of valuable goods (Draper,

1978: 16). A huge market had opened up – even in the era of the stage coach.

The security transport business did not get underway in Britain for nearly another hundred years, in large part because, as Draper (1978: 16) observes, while the United States was, in the nineteenth century, a continent of 'migrating population and spreading towns', 'in England and the rest of Europe, a community existence remained', as did poor communications and, it might be added, other traditional notions about transport and security. Even the promise of the railways was not exploited to any great degree but found its significance and impact within a traditional perspective of what transport systems should achieve. In turn, therefore, the railways were seen as swift and secure and all that could be needed for security transport. Hence, it was not until the middle of the next century that the idea of the 'armoured car' found its moment in the UK.

In 1955, an entrepreneur named Winkelman, who had gained experience of the Brinks Inc. armoured car operation in the USA, established his own armoured car company in Britain. This service offered the security of a 'motorised bank vault' for transporting increasingly large amounts of cash in a society then particularly (as it is still to some extent) suspicious about moving money by means of paper (and now electronic) transactions between banks. Securicor established its own armoured car division in 1959 and eventually bought out Winkelman in 1964. Security Express was established in 1960 by De La Rue and Wells Fargo, with the former buying out the latter in 1965, finally selling the company in 1985.

Such entrepreneurial moves could, of course, only be successful where and when the market demand was influenced by conditions which encouraged the purchase of the services. In the case of armoured car services, other bank protection services and the related development and aggressive marketing of security hardware designed to protect cash and valuables, it is to the changes in patterns of post-war crime that we must refer.

Mack (1975: 59) argues that the organisation of crime changed significantly in the late 1950s with the development of 'commando-type' robberies. A graphic picture of some of the methods used in a bank raid, for example, can be summarised from the evidence of a bank-robber turned informer:

> bank ceilings blasted with gunshot as an effective form of 'frightener', till-drawers shot open, commando assaults by ladder over grilles, counter-doors sledge-hammered down, raids over in a minute or two, mounting hauls, people injured. A decade that had begun with the craftsman bank-burglar working delicately at the vault with a thermal lance had ended with the primitive sledge-hammer. (Mack, 1975: 60)

Such evidence of 'criminal organisation' found police organisation unprepared and inadequate to deal with such 'serious, specialist crime'. As Scraton (1982: 44) notes, the sense of outrage which such examples of the 'post war crime wave stimulated throughout Britain placed the police under immense pressure. The development of new technologies in response to the range of crimes was not sufficient to gain real ground in containing project crime.' While the police increasingly turned to the development of networks of informers to establish some system of surveillance over the potential and real sources of major criminal enterprise, those on the receiving end of project crime were, unsurprisingly, also in a mood to cast their eyes about seriously. Their commercial inclination, however, encouraged them to perceive that, in response to 'new' forms of criminal enterprise, there was much to recommend new entrepreneurial forms of security protection and crime prevention.

Shoplifting and retail security services

Shoplifting and dealing with it are emotive issues. It is an area of ambivalence: something about which in some respects too little is made and in others too much. Kenneth Robinson writing in *Punch* in 1977 observed that 'whoever the shoplifters might be, they are doing . . . well' before swiftly caricaturing the private security response:

> The job of catching shoplifters is becoming a lucrative industry. A lot of people are having a very good time because of the growth of petty crime. Men wearing steel helmets, dark glasses and striped pullovers can be seen hovering in the back rooms of large stores, playing sinister-looking roles they never thought a respectable community would give them. They don't have weapons – not yet – but it surely won't be long before they are given not only truncheon-vouchers but also their own television series. (Robinson, 1977: 377)

Ambivalence (to some degree) and dissonance is even evident among the interest groups where one might expect to find unity. But, as Henry (1983) has argued, the administration and exercise of private justice for the control of private loss problems can tend to the accommodation of plural perspectives. Since 1977, and alongside traditional interested parties such as the Home Office, retail stores and private security companies, the Association for the Prevention of Theft in Shops (APTS) has become a vocal pressure and coordinating group, representing various retail interests. The nature of this representation may have been a contributory factor in an interesting divergence of views among APTS, private security and the Home Office over 'who' it actually *is* that may be principally responsible for the majority of losses (theft, pilferage) from retail stores. The APTS Director, Baroness

Phillips, is unequivocal about the aspirations of the organisation, writing that: 'the Association is not merely a prevention exercise on behalf of traders but another agency to support authority in the fight against crime' (Phillips, 1982: 5). None the less, there seems to be some disagreement about the perpetrators of the crime in question, and this is indicative of uncertainty about the nature of the problem and hence about 'appropriate' responses.

The significance of the problem and the need for serious response starts, for most commentators, with its *size* and the subsequent breakdown indicating those responsible and against whom the response should be directed. According to the APTS:

> The figures of loss, 'shrinkage' as it is called in the retail trade, are given as a possible £1 billion in 1982 and although this covers bad stock control, back-door theft and employees' dishonesty, *the major loss comes from customer theft*, despite the declaration of various security firms who prefer to suggest that 60% of goods stolen from stores are taken by staff. (Phillips, 1982: 5, emphasis added).

It may be that it is a touching loyalty to shop staff on the part of APTS that leads them to assert that the major proportion of shrinkage is the result of customer theft, while security firms may have their own interests reflected in their emphasis on shrinkage as the result of theft by employees. It is perhaps unsurprising, therefore, that the Home Office comes down somewhere in between the two positions, though leaning slightly in favour of the private security view. Thus the Home Office and Police guide, *The Disappearing Profits: Pilferage from Smaller Shops*, suggests that shrinkage is made up of three elements:

> National averages show that of every £1.00 that is lost about 30 pence can be put down to error and genuine wastage, while of the remaining 70 pence that dishonest people are stealing from you, about 30 pence are accounted for by shoplifters taking your goods. This leaves about 40 pence which is stolen (in the form of goods or cash) by some members of your staff. (1973a: 1)

I shall return to more sophisticated estimates and arguments about the prevalence and significance of shoplifting below. However, it is important to set the scene with the appropriate backdrop of uncertainty because, despite disagreement about numbers, private crusades such as APTS and private entrepreneurs such as security companies can, in tandem, cooperation or competition, develop a very disturbing scenario around the appropriate responses to the problem.

To take a swift look at what could happen in the UK by looking at what has already happened in the USA, we could note the availability of a handy 452-page book called *Where's What* (O'Toole, 1978: 152–4). *Where's What* is a 'guidebook for a tour through 6,723 different record systems maintained by the federal government . . . [and] . . . personal data depots operated by the private sector' (O'Toole, 1978: 152). The handbook directs those interested in the past of any given individual not only to governmental sources of information but also beyond to the record systems kept on those who have passed through the private justice processing system – whether they know it or not. Shoplifting and store theft incidents – real, suspected or imagined – are grist to the mill of a system which can only thrive confidently if it feels it is working efficiently – that is, even when in doubt recording everything and everyone.

Obviously, there are specific conditions surrounding the response of US retail organisations to shop theft, a particular history and cultural set of commercial values surrounding the nature and seriousness of the problem, and hence legitimacy of response. The current organisation of security and response to shop theft in the UK seems far more ambivalent, inconsistent and, at times, apparently disorganised. But it is, of course, precisely these circumstances that private security services and pressure groups like APTS would like to see replaced by the more serious 'positive' and organised response common in the USA.

Ambivalence about shoplifting in the UK, why it occurs and what can be done about it is reflected in the fairly familiar attitude which has explained it as a side-effect of the attractive and accessible display of goods, bringing with it, as a necessary evil, the need to employ security staff. It is presumably this kind of attitude that prompted Robinson to write in his *Punch* article that 'a society that sells easy-to-grab sausages next to help-yourself panti-hose has reached such a point of decadence that it must expect fairly unstable behaviour from its victims' (1977: 377). In a more serious vein, though similarly touched by incredulity, other researchers (government and academic) have observed that commercial considerations and costs, not any sense of compassion, tend to govern responses to discovered shop theft and also to commercially motivated psychological enticement.

Thus, the 1973 Home Office Working Party on Shoplifting and Thefts by Shop Staff reported that:

> Most of the retailers' representatives with whom we discussed the matter agreed that lay-out could make a substantial contribution to the prevention of losses. It was agreed that those high displays and blind corners which impeded observation by staff, those unattended low counters and shelves which facilitated shoplifting, the stacking of displays close to, or in entrances and at exits were all to be avoided. It was also agreed that offices overlooking the shopping area and (in supermarkets) the check-out points were aids to security. Yet in every case we were told that management took little, if any, account of these points when planning the lay-out of shops and display areas. *The sole criterion was the effect it would have upon sales.* (Home Office, 1973b: para. 3.13, emphasis added)

Fifteen years later, changes have taken place. It is certainly the case that crime prevention messages and groups like APTS have had *some* impact. APTS now has over 200 affiliated groups around the country with members ranging from American Express to small shops (*Security Times*, 1986a: 14). Most medium to large-scale retailers have taken up a much broader repertoire of design initiatives to curtail store theft. Yet, apparently, the problem has not diminished. The mundane experience of going shopping now brings one under the observing eye of cameras and strategically placed mirrors, and the doorways of large stores are now frequently guarded not only by security staff but also by electronic sensors to detect tags fixed to goods. But the more recent approach to taking shoplifting seriously brings with it new problems as it shifts gear from lackadaisical prevention measures to more zealous approaches, whether disturbing ideas like subliminal deterrence messages or apprehension-orientated methods.[2] However, recent guidelines from the Attorney General on the handling of shoplifters and sections of the Police and Criminal Evidence Act 1984 have been clearer than ever before in setting out the limits of what companies and security staff may do in dealing with cases of shoplifting.[3] APTS and various retailers have apparently expressed some concern about such changes in the law which they view as making 'life easier for shoplifters' (*Evening Standard*, 1986).

Having outlined the 'problem' and noted the ambiguities contained in understanding its causality, control and component parts, I turn now to consider the application and practice of store security in this context.

According to the Home Office Working Party on store security (1973b: para. 4.14), there are two identifiable types of security staff who may work in shops and stores: first, security officers who deal principally with theft and rule-breaking by internal staff and the delivery of goods by other firms, and so on; and secondly, store detectives who are employed to deal with shoplifters. In practice, however, for all except quite large stores, such a distinction is unlikely to be precise or at all evident. There is in any case inevitable blurring of boundaries where both categories are concerned about 'undesirable-looking' individuals or groups in or hanging around outside the store.

There are no available figures relating to the gender breakdown of employees in these categories, but from interviews and the literature it seems safe to suggest that security officers tend to be male, for example, 'retired policemen supplementing their pensions in a time-honoured manner' (May, 1978: 139), whilst store detectives tend to be female and often employed part-time, whether working for security firms which train them and offer a vague semblance of career structure or for the retail organisation itself. Such workers can be sociologically described as marginal but none the less (or perhaps because of this) they assert strong group and occupational norms, claims for informal, if not formal, autonomy and negotiate their being on the periphery of the immediate working environment by suggesting loyalty to a higher authority in the form of the security company they 'really' work for or else the Chief Security Officer or Director of the retail organisation, remotely (and facelessly) based at head office (on the latter see May, 1978: 141).

The issue of the assertion of autonomy by store security staff has received attention from a number of researchers, most evidently because it is part of the discretionary basis of private justice so strongly identified with the decision to prosecute or not prosecute those apprehended (or simply observed but ignored) while shoplifting. In the UK, May's study of juvenile shoplifters and the organisation of store security in Scotland found that: 'In the organisation of their work security officers, both part-time and full-time, enjoyed a high degree of autonomy. Shared perceptions of what constitutes 'high risk' periods determine their presence on the sales floor' (1978: 140). In the USA, Rojek's study of private justice systems and crime reporting in a mid-western city found that:

> Discount stores had entrusted all security decision-making power to their private police employees to such an extent that the organizational structure of these stores had been redefined, thereby giving the security staff *complete autonomy*. The threat of employee theft had prompted major organizational changes, resulting in the security staff being held answerable not to the local retail store manager, but to a special security component within the overall organization . . . However, in all stores a pervasive sense of concealment and specialization tends to shield security personnel from company rules and regulations thereby ensuring them of a significant degree of autonomy. (1979: 109, emphasis added)

This autonomy works at the level of shopfloor practice; it can at this level guide and, to some extent, control, decisions about apprehension and movement onto the next stage of the construction of the statistics about shoplifting and impressions about the efficacy of security. For the next stage is generally notification to senior security staff or some level of management. This then opens up another arena of discretionary decision making about whether to notify the police and whether or not to seek to prosecute. As should be evident in this particular sphere, there is much similarity between the processes involved in the practice of security work and the eventual construction of criminal statistics, and the work of the police (see Hindess, 1973).

However, the nature and patterns of policies (such as are distinguishable) which stores have are clearly significant in terms of public perception of 'the shoplifting problem', commercial perception of the utility of security and the actual practice of security in this area. Interestingly, there are at least two consistencies identified by studies of 'policy' in this area in the UK, USA and Canada. These are first that there is a *variety* of 'policies', suggesting a circumstantial flexibility based on little real policy *applicable* to practice, whatever head office or deterrent signs may say. And, secondly, that the fundamental consideration of *cost* not compassion governs decisions and procedures.

In the UK, a recent report of a Home Office study on dealing with shoplifters found that, as had been expected:

> the shops included in the study demonstrated a wide range of policies for dealing with suspected shoplifters. In some cases all those apprehended were referred to the police, in others as few as one-third (contrary to the recommendation of the Home Office Working Party that all those apprehended should be referred to the police). (Murphy and Iles, 1983: 25)

This variation in actual practice needs to be examined further, however, for within it there are a number of factors related to the use of discretion in whether or not to apprehend suspects and then whether or not to report them to the police. Other research confirms the common nature of the factors discussed in the Murphy and Iles study: the very old and very young, and those with a particular physical or mental condition 'such as pregnancy or depression' might receive favourable consideration in deciding whether to apprehend or prosecute. Thus, although not formalised in any way, in many cases established practice was already moving into line with the recent guidelines, despite the consternation of retailers and APTS. Of course, the implications of various costs also play their part:

> many stores operated within cash limits; they would not contact the police if the offender had taken only one expensive item, when there was some possibility that it was a mistake, and where the costs to the store in terms of the lost service of the detective while at the police station or in court outweighed the value of the goods involved. (Murphy and Iles, 1983: 25)

Variation in security procedures relating to apprehension and prosecution of shoplifters is therefore pronounced, both between different stores and between avowed policy and the action taken.

As this same study notes, the variety of policies and practices has a number of significant implications.

> First there exists a large number of people who are apprehended and recorded by stores as shoplifters but not referred to the police. Secondly, the figures . . . for referral rates need to be interpreted within the concept of preventative action – the point being that there were known to be far more shoplifters than those apprehended. Thirdly, it appears that store detectives do more than apprehend suspects and refer them to police; they also operate in many situations where prosecution is not the aim and the strategies and

techniques they employ require a degree of tact and skill. Further, there does not appear to be any standard method of preventing shoplifting; the tactics used differ from store to store, and vary according to the time of day or year and the number of suspects. (Murphy and Iles, 1983: 27)

I have already emphasised the contradictions surrounding the position occupied by private security. The specific context of retail security provides a microcosm of some of the ambiguities which the private security function and private security employee must negotiate. This largely hinges on the paradox that private security is supposed to detect offences and hence deter by detecting, but is not necessarily supposed to deter by apprehending those detected. As May (1978: 156) puts it, 'apprehension is inherently problematic.' This assertion rests on three factors:

> Firstly, the security officer can never be certain of the suspect's response to intervention. For the first time she finds herself having to react to events rather than dictating them. Secondly, the limits to her authority remain unclear. While a security officer may regard her actions as morally justified, she cannot know that they are legally justifiable. Intervention must always proceed with the fear that one day this ignorance will be exposed. Thirdly, even if the security officer can show that her actions were both morally and legally justified she may find that the Company for whom she works does not regard them as commercially justified. That is, in the final analysis she must take care not only to avoid violating the law that remains unknown (and, until too late, unknowable) but also a Company 'policy' that is essentially ambiguous. (May, 1978: 156)

But beyond these problems in the practice of private security, the case of shoplifting (as opposed to the more difficult issue of shrinkage as a whole) also highlights two other issues central to an examination of the private security world. First, its contribution to the construction of official statistics and, secondly, the prevalence of what I call the 'security mentality' and its tendency to typologise and stereotype.

The official recording of the crime of shoplifting is suggestive about the contribution of the security industry to popular perceptions of the incidence of crime in society, in so far as, in filtered and digested forms, such popular perceptions are informed by reports of trends in criminal statistics. Shoplifting may, as most in the retail and security industries would claim, have indeed increased in incidence – it is likely in what are, for many, hard times, but still we cannot be certain by how much. We can, however, be certain that the growth of private security has 'inflated' the statistics by increasing detection rates, and, in many cases, by pushing for prosecution.

The fact that retail managements have unknowable and ambiguous policies about the apprehension and prosecution of shoplifters should not be confused with the inclinations of security staff. Similarly, identifying a system of private justice which employs security staff to detect and apprehend on occasion but which leaves the next stage of disposition of suspects to employing managements (to which security staff naturally ultimately defer) does not mean that there are not inclinations and structural pressures found in the position of security staff which disincline them wholeheartedly to go along with decisions not to apprehend or prosecute. Senior security staff at retail companies' head offices and security companies advising retailers will generally try to encourage a policy of apprehension and prosecution. Security staff on the shopfloor must mediate between the reasons for such an inclination and the store management practices which will often seek to discourage apprehension or at least prosecution.

May (1978) notes some of the factors that produce this dilemma, starting from the point of how the efficiency of store managements versus the efficiency of store security staff might be evaluated. For the store management, the overriding concern is profitability, and the possibilities of disruption in the store, mistakes in apprehension and bad publicity for being 'callous' in prosecuting those likely to arouse public sympathy mean that apprehension and calling in the police do not always seem self-evident contributions to profitability. For the security staff, on the other hand, whilst their success as a deterrent is difficult to measure (for how can one measure accurately what is *not* being stolen?), their success as apprehenders of suspects and offenders is easily quantified. A conflict of perceptions of 'success' therefore arises (see Home Office, 1973b for evidence of the use by some companies of apprehensions as a measure of security success). If this is a difficulty faced at the practical edge of store security work, there are also two broader considerations with relevance to private security work generally. As May neatly observes:

> Like all security organizations (e.g. police, army) security staff in stores find themselves on the horns of a dilemma. While on the one hand the elimination of the problem might be regarded as a measure of their effectiveness, at the same time this would remove their raison d'etre. The ideal situation calls for an expanding crime problem which security staff can show they are on top of, and this is most readily demonstrated through the volume of apprehensions.
>
> These situational pressures are reinforced by ideological factors. Security staff for the most part possess what I can best describe as a 'police mentality'; that is, they tend to see shoplifters as constituting a limited and readily identifiable group who sooner or later will find opportunities to steal. (1978: 148–9)

Such stereotyping was evident in my own research on security staff who also held a worldview similar to that which May refers to as a 'police mentality', although I will call it a 'security mentality' in order to distinguish it from the ideology and occupational culture of the police (South, 1983, 1985: 22–84). I conclude this review of the issues relating to retail security, which could form the basis of a separate study (see, for example, Murphy, 1986) by elaborating on the nature of security mentality stereotyping as illustrated by a quote from a popular *Handbook for Detectives* (Meek, 1967) and noting the important but neglected (here, as elsewhere) consequences of overzealous certainty about some people feasibly 'looking like' and therefore 'probably being' shoplifters: the case of wrongful apprehension and allegation.

The private security industry and the police typically assert that they seek to avoid prejudice and stereotyping in their occupational cultures, acting only on what they have *reason* to suspect, have observed, have evidence of and so on. Evidently, however, occupational practice (and its urging of short-hand and expediency), occupational experience and occupational folk wisdom, all combine to provide pointers, hints and warning signs. Up to a point this is understandable, common sense, even logically desirable in terms of capitalising on the value of experience. What is required at this point, however, is good judgement, not a good imagination. The place of stereotyping, and its ideological significance, in the operational security mentality is a cause for concern. It is disturbing in its tendency to separate the 'them' who are deviant, criminal and weird, from the 'us' who are upright, honest and clean-living. No matter how liberally coated, the underlying assumptions can be strongly discriminatory towards many social groups and, in particular, xenophobic towards those regarded as 'foreigners'.

Meek's *Handbook for Detectives* offers a good example. An experienced commentator, he uses a technique familiar in private security texts – the adoption of a 'liberal' pseudo-psychology to cover his prejudices.

> It is frequently found that arrested hoisters suffer from the loss of a limb deformity, or from some facial disfigurement such as a birth-mark; or they are hump-backed or have a cleft palate, or an uncontrollable nervous twitch, or extremely offensive breath, or some permanent complaint of which they are only too conscious though it may not be apparent to others. Such misfortunes can develop in their victims a mood of resentment against the world in general which they try to assuage by vengeful actions such as writing anonymous letters and stealing from shops. A cripple can always anticipate merciful treatment so has no need to put forward a complicated defence. Customers with ailments or disfigurements sad though it may be must therefore be watched.
>
> Foreigners, particularly hard-up au pair girls from countries where attractive goods are not so generously displayed fall easily for the temptation of shoplifting. Being a long way from home makes them reckless. (Meek, 1967: 50–1)

Not surprisingly, if this kind of advice influences or reflects the opinions and attitudes of security staff then in their practice they will inevitably not only apprehend people 'caught in the act' (who may or may not conform to stereotypes), but will also be encouraged in their belief that they 'know what to look for' and challenge a number of perfectly innocent parties. In some cases, where security staff have not detected any shoplifting at periods when they might expect to, it might be hypothesised that they will increasingly turn their attention to customers who 'fit' the stereotypes and perhaps, wishing to deter by indicating their interest and making their surveillance apparent, could encourage 'suspicious' behaviour on the part of worried and embarrassed shoppers. The consequences will be wrongful accusations, which are apparently increasing (King, 1983).

Notes

1   The legal status of any such 'powers' to stop and search people is open to dispute. On private premises the owners can invest their rights in their employed private security personnel but, as for example in the law relating to trespass, this would not seem to extend to providing for powers of search. To detain a trespasser, there must be grounds for reasonable suspicion that the person has committed the offence, then a lawful citizen's arrest may be carried out. Such an arrest does not bestow any powers of search. However, in some cases employees may find that their company regulations, which they agree to abide by in accepting their contract of employment, require their agreement to searches by security staff and/or management staff. In practice, even where such an agreement is not in force, as for example with non-employee visitors, a polite but official sounding 'request' from a uniformed guard that a person allows his or her vehicle to be searched will usually meet with compliance, even if this is accompanied by some reluctance.

2   A study conducted by Price Waterhouse in the USA assessing the use of subliminal messages in stores 'proved favourable in its impact on shrinkage although details are not conclusive'. In Britain, Subliminal Assistance Ltd has patented a system which it hopes to test in a large retail chain and introduce commercially. 'Subliminal messaging' is prohibited on television and radio by the Broadcasting Act 1981, part 1, section 4, sub-section 3. However, no similar legislation covers shops or the workplace. Fears have been raised that subliminal messages (repeated low-volume messages played at the threshold of conscious hearing) could be used to encourage customers to buy goods rather than discourage them from shoplifting (Pead, 1985: 1947).

3   The guidelines from the Attorney General covered 'the proper treatment for young people, pensioners, the mentally handicapped and others held for shop theft and gave police power to caution instead of taking them to court if they judged the case to be isolated or a moment of forgetfulness' (*Evening Standard*, 1986). In response to the Police and Criminal Evidence Act 1984, APTS has issued guidelines to its members 'setting out a Home Office statement regarding the powers of security staff. It stresses that they have no special power of arrest, search, entry or seizure and that if an arrest is made it involves no power of detention for questioning. Neither are security officers and store detectives charged with the duty of investigating offences. In

dealing with young and handicapped suspects they must be "most cautious not to overstep the clear limitations of their powers under the statute and under common law" ' (*Evening Standard*, 1986).

4 In-house Security and the Security Hardware Industries

Less visible than the 'open and above board' services for hire from the contract security companies, but none the less a major area of employment of security personnel, are the in-house security staffs and departments of business and industry. Although in-house security appears to employ more personnel than the (known) statistically enumerated staff of private security companies, this figure is inflated by staff who do a variety of duties which are not necessarily of a security nature – from the shopfloor to the upper reaches of the corporate environment (Shearing et al., 1985c). In addition, the range of actual security functions performed by in-house staff, while wide, is necessarily not as wide as the range performed throughout the private security sector as a whole. Thus most in-house security is of the mundane nature of patrol, gate-keeping duties, registering visitors and so on. There is, however, a relatively new specialism which has developed with particular regard to in-house security arrangements whether provided by in-house security managers or by contracted security consultants. This is the concept of risk management and evaluation, and I shall discuss some of its principles below.

From the point of view of purely cost considerations, then the widespread persistence of large-scale employment of in-house security staffs is odd. The commercial argument of those who proclaim the virtues of contract security usually emphasises that the attraction of hiring an outside agency lies most significantly in diminishing the added labour costs of in-house security staff. A proposition increasingly heard in relation to the privatisation of public services, this argument has long been around in selling the privatisation of security in the private sector. As Garner summarises:

> for round-the-clock, all year round protection, one needs at least seven men on the payroll depending upon the size of the plant, as each eight hour shift has to be covered and holidays or emergencies like illness need to be taken into account. National insurance, pensions, uniform, holiday pay and sometimes transport home after late shifts, all need to be included for the full cost to be ascertained. (This is of course before training costs are added.) (1978: 68)

Such requirements which in-house employers usually have to meet to bring their security staff into line with all other employees' benefits, hours and so on are not, of course, problems which the contract security employers tend to be overly concerned with. In interviews conducted in 1983 with representatives of MATSA it was suggested that in some companies security staff may be in a different union to the rest of the workforce which weakens their position whilst allowing management to suggest that this is best for industrial harmony. The major trade union on site will then be unconcerned about the conditions of service of the security staff and more interested in what they do. The security staff, if indeed unionised at all (something else which management *can* discourage on grounds of 'conflicts of loyalty'), will in any case be in the very weak position of the minority without allies.

None the less, in terms of strict numbers, in-house security (on the available statistics and consonant with trends in the USA and Canada) seems to employ more staff than contract security at a ratio by the late 1970s of 3 : 2 (Shearing and Stenning, 1981: 202–3) (see Table 4.1). This is because, for many firms, the additional costs are viewed as an investment with a return of loyalty and quality (Williams et al., 1984: 30).

Table 4.1   *Private security personnel: United Kingdom, 1971–8*

	1971 (000s)	1978 (000s)	Change (%) 1971–8	Change (%) Yearly average
Public police	97.3	109	12	1.6
Private security	80	100	25	3.2
In-house	50	60	20	2.6
Contract	30	40	33	4.2
Ratio police/private security	6 : 5	1.09 : 1		
Ratio in-house/contract	5 : 3	3 : 2		

Although not officially stated or broken down in available statistics, it seems that the category of in-house security is often a 'convenience' category for many companies, covering staff with multiple roles; the term 'security' adding a touch of company efficiency and employee status. Such additional roles would include responsibility for out-of-hours shipping and freighting, delivery, checks on health and safety regulations, maintenance of some items and areas, including for example cleaning duties and so on.

Sources: Reports of Her Majesty's Chief Inspector of Constabulary for the years 1971 and 1978 (app. 1, 'Total police strength not including civilians, special constables and staff'). London: HMSO, 1972 and 1979. United Kingdom, Home Office, 1979: 3. From Shearing and Stenning, 1981: 203.

As a general and standard definition of the expected activities of in-house security staff, I derive the following from a wide variety of literature originating from respondents in the research, from advice given by various business associations and government departments and from the writings of specialists on industrial security. The first two sources tend to emphasise the basic, the routine and the mundane, whilst the latter, principally US writers, tend to add an over-emphasis on readiness and capability for dealing with the exceptional, like industrial espionage and terrorism. Hence this 'definition of activities' is something of an averaging-out exercise. Perhaps as a result of this (although I think not), at this basic, standardised level of functions, in-house security comes out in formal terms as little different from contract security staff (patrol/static guard):

1 Control and direct and indirect supervision and surveillance of the workforce. Checking, for example, on clocking on and off procedures and working to formal and informal criteria for suspicion of personnel who may be absenting themselves from shifts or involved in pilferage, etc.
2 Control of access to site premises, both entry and exit, involving the recording of arrival and departure of vehicles, as well as ensuring that visitors are helpfully guided to their destinations (a function of diplomacy and company representation), whilst ensuring that intruders are discouraged (a function of security and company solicitude).
3 Finally, general responsibility to ensure the security, securing, surveillance and recording of the state of site premises.

I do not have the space here to go into the more rare and exceptional (and hence interesting) aspects of in-house security services and functions. However, having outlined the basic levels of in-house operations, it would be misleading not to stress that – corresponding to trends in the private security sector generally – in-house security engaged in both specialist operations and in certain industries can also, necessarily, take on specialist forms of organisation. To offer three examples, therefore, I take first the case of surveillance as an elaborate in-house security operation in an industrial concern, and secondly the development of airline security, as reported by one of its insiders in the 1950s and early 1960s. Finally, and briefly, I offer the example of how major economic developments – in this case the exploitation of North Sea oil – can open up new circumstances and responsibility for companies in their provision of in-house (and contract) security.

Specialist in-house security

In Britain, the surveillance of trade union representatives, their offices and meetings within companies is probably, *in general*, not a lot more sinister than actions that union representatives will take to keep an eye on what managements are up to: the significant differences reside in matters of power and resources. As Bunyan (1976: 252) observes, 'while bugging and tapping of union offices and 'phones is not unknown, the practice does not seem widespread. But surveillance could be carried out in other ways.' Bunyan reports that in 1973 equipment was installed in the office of the Chief Security Officer of Guest, Keen and Nettlefold's Birmingham plant which enabled him to eavesdrop on all calls made on the plant's internal telephone system and interrupt should he so desire! The equipment was removed when the workers at the plant found out about it and made protests. The explanation offered by GKN's Administrative Director was less than wholly convincing. The machine, he said, had been installed to allow the Security Officer to contact his staff: 'His men are trained in First Aid for instance. They might have been needed for that purpose. The fact that the 'phone enabled the security chief to listen in on all our 'phones was coincidental' (Bunyan, 1976: 253; *Sunday People*, 7 January 1973).

In the context of in-house security directly operating across international boundaries, Fish (1962) provides an 'insider', if exceptional, account of the overlap between private security (in this case airline security departments) and international civil police agencies. Such collaboration most commonly occurs in relation to terrorism (though this is a recent development) and smuggling. Fish describes how such cooperation was developing even in the 1950s. For example, in relation to drug trafficking:

> although Customs and police at Hong Kong were kept on their toes in an attempt to keep up with the increasing ingenuity of the smugglers, we all knew the grim facts. The seizures were no more than a minute part of what was getting through. Heroin had been discovered in a shipment of small pictures, neatly pasted in between the picture and the cardboard backing; also in a hidden compartment in the back of a wooden doll. On another occasion, the stuff had merely been mixed with a shipment of rice. Buchanan's [BOAC, now part of British Airways] private intelligence system went into action between Hong Kong and Bangkok. Security officers, in co-operation with the Hong Kong police, began a discreet watch on passengers and regular freight shipments in and out of the colony. (Fish, 1962: 162)

Although airports have at various times been 'policed' by the public police and at other times by locally based 'private' statutory police forces (usually run by the local authority transport, docks or port authority), private security companies have also been widely employed in various capacities, both generally throughout airports as well as in the employment of particular companies, for example, for the guarding of goods in transit. But the operating airline companies also maintain their own security staff. The first airline seriously to use its own private security department was BOAC, establishing it in 1945 under the direction of an ex-detective inspector from Scotland Yard, Donald Fish, who just before taking up the appointment was also on secondment 'for special duties' with M15 as well as being a captain in the Intelligence Corps (Fish, 1962: 52). Fish, writing of his career in 1962, recognised that international law was not then (nor is it now) prepared to deal with the sort of crime, liabilities and other problems which the post-war expansion of the air routes and capability of air technology would bring. His forecast of acceptance of the need for an international air security police has however (not yet) been realised:

> if the airlines are to meet the very real threat of highly organised air crime hanging over them at the moment, it is their own security forces who will have to do the work. Sooner or later, they will have to combine under some central authority to form the nucleus of a really international Air Police Force, with full legal powers to attack air crime wherever it occurs, irrespective of local laws and national boundaries. There seems no other way. (Fish, 1962: 26)

The cooperative vision that Fish tendered may be a little melodramatic; it was offered at a time when Interpol seemed a genuinely successful international force for the cooperative exchange of information about crime, and the contemporary feeling was that such an auspicious start could only be improved upon. Further, Fish had himself seen the growth of intimate cooperation between the security staff of various airlines, and not only among themselves but also with specialised police agencies of various countries: from CID and specialist drug/currency/fraud/forgery squads to intelligence agencies. However, it remains now, as realistically as it probably did then, extremely unlikely that any nation would give up the sort of sovereignty or legal monopoly which the establishment of an 'Air Police' would imply.

Nevertheless, although Fish suggests that 'there seems no other way', we might reasonably anticipate the continuation of changes in the coordination of airline security. Indeed, professional security associations, liaison between security staff and encouragement from bodies such as the United Nations are developments which have already led to greater coordination in air security, most obviously and explicitly as a response to air terrorism but in other areas also. Essentially, *de facto* extension and coordination of airline security 'authority', responsibilities – and legally granted powers – has occurred without recourse to the creation of a cumbersome but accountable bureaucracy or the divesting of any legal powers by any state to an external authority.

A third type of specialised in-house security can be given as an example of changes in law and policing resulting from extensions of property rights and the redefinition of private versus state jurisdiction afforded by the relationship between commerce and state after the discovery of North Sea oil. At a time when the energy crisis was underlining the true seriousness of deepening recession and rising inflation, the exploitation of North Sea oil was greeted as a saviour. However, the period of the late 1960s and early 1970s was also characterised by the growing tactical capability of international and indigenous terrorist groups. This development generated considerable concern about the security of North Sea oil and gas. There are now over 40 major companies involved in offshore production and development operations and probably well over 150 operational rigs. To provide constant security against capture or sabotage, a series of secret contingency plans was drawn up by the UK government and the Offshore Operators Association.

Offshore rigs are, of course, rather uniquely difficult to gain access to and this means that the first level of security is provided by nature. However, it also means that the provision of a permanent civil police or armed forces presence would be stretching the limits of the conventional brief of these forces as well as stretching their establishment numbers in terms of other commitments. Typically, then, the commercial compromise leaves the owners of the rigs responsible for 'structural and operational security measures on their installations' (Smart and Hodgson, 1979: 40). However, as Smart and Hodgson detail, there are two further levels of responsibility which neatly illustrate a tiered approach to provision of security by the state which now confidently incorporates (as indeed in many instances it always has) the level of private security.[1]

The police, by virtue of the terms of the Continental Shelf Act 1964: 'have authority to operate in the sea areas within a 500 metre radius of offshore installations. The Chief Constables exercise their authority under the Port of Operation rule and respond to incidents on platforms registered in the ports within their areas of jurisdiction' (Smart and Hodgson, 1979: 40). The third level of responsibility rests with the armed forces who 'have to be prepared to act in support of the civil power at offshore installations to contain urban guerilla action or threats' (Smart and Hodgson, 1979: 40), but who would (theoretically) be used under the direction of the civil power. This is a serious commitment by the state to provide back-up and rapid support; however, the absence of a permanent immediate presence necessitates placing great emphasis on sophisticated in-house security provision along lines worked out in negotiations between the Offshore Operators Association and government departments and agencies. This association also lays down guidelines for stringent safety precautions which health and safety officials are supposed to oversee with the cooperation of security staff and the police, though with a documented poor safety record in the North Sea, coordination at this level may leave something to be desired (see Carson, 1982).

Risk management

Mention of health and safety responsibilities is by no means incidental in this context, however. The specialism of risk management which is offered to commercial customers on a consultancy basis but which also has a primary place in any description of comprehensive in-house security, embraces, as one independent consultant observes, 'such a wide spectrum that one needs to start with some terms of reference. In this context, it ranges from the Health and Safety at Work Act, through the fire regulations, to measures against fraud, theft and terrorism' (Hasler, 1978: 45).

As an in-house security services manager makes clear, none of this is new. Risk management 'is simply a means of bringing together functions which have hitherto been conducted quite separately and, at the same time, enables the whole subject of the management of risk to be treated in a more sophisticated and orderly manner' (Bridges, 1978: 46). Indeed, the in-vogue status of risk management as a concept needs little further consideration except to emphasise that its significance is in bringing together previously disparate functions (although it is arguable how really separate they have been in the past). In terms of the development of private security, what should be noted is the emphasis on *programmed planning*, an idea well developed since the 1960s in the USA (Momboisse, 1968). Essentially, programmed planning (which can integrate highly sophisticated psychological approaches to critical, vulnerable and hazardous situations) boils down to 'a place for everyone and everyone in their place'. It is first and foremost directed at the total security of premises and plant. For example, in Momboisse's classic text, *Industrial Security for Strikes, Riots and Disasters* (1968), the two principal criteria for risk evaluation determining the degree of protection necessary are discussed in terms of the political geography of 'the facility'. 'Criticality', for example, is defined thus: 'The portion of the facility which is considered to be of high criticality is one whose partial or complete loss would have an immediate and serious impact on the ability of the facility to provide continuity of production or service for a considerable period of time'

(Momboisse, 1968: 8). 'Vulnerability' is 'the susceptibility of a facility to espionage, thefts, slow downs or work stoppage for any cause' (Momboisse, 1968: 9). But programmed planning is not parochial; it can also extend to the coordination of information and development of provision for mutual aid between companies and outside services, although recent research in Canada suggests that the police may not appreciate the scope – and implications – of the related concepts of risk management and loss prevention (Shearing et. al., 1985a).

Risk management and planning is not new. In many ways its in-vogue status, especially with insurers, is misleading in this respect. It is however clearly the line of development which corporate (and even small-scale) enterprise will follow with regard to the organisation of in-house security in the future.

Defence, deterrence and detection: alarms, detection devices, locks and safes

Although this section is principally concerned with the security hardware industries, it should be apparent, and borne in mind, that there is a crucial role played in the fortunes of the private security industry overall and especially the alarm and lock industries by the *insurance sector*. This is self-evident but no less significant for being so. After all, the major growth (in *value* terms) of private security has been in the commercial not the private (household) sector. Such growth is evidently not unrelated to where the influence and pressure of insurers is strongest (because of risk criteria and high premiums for plant and stock, etc.). The fear of crimes such as household burglary is very high among the general public, yet in the absence, until recently, of strong encouragement from insurers, this fear has not resulted in particularly significant investment in devices such as intruder alarms. There are evidently grounds for scepticism about the fear of crime being the *only* major push to the growth of private security. Hence the complex picture must also take serious account of other institutionalised economic forces.

The concerns of the insurance sector in relation to private security have always revolved more around the deterrence of crime than catching criminals. As the MATSA report notes, this can produce an odd conflict because insurance companies:

> prefer, and often stipulate, noisy visible alarms [; by] the time the police or guard have responded there is of course little chance of catching the intruder. This conflict of policy between insurance companies and security alarm makers on the one hand, and the police or Home Office on the other, is a running sore for the industry. (1983: 8–9)

The present unsatisfactory situation has its roots in the 1950s. Then insurance companies first seriously began to make it a requirement of commercial and industrial clients that they install alarm systems. Numerous policies were issued on this basis but without proper evaluation of the risks. In response, a major market opened up for cheap and frequently badly designed and inefficient alarm systems. These were generally installed without considering the implications of either the problem of who was to respond to them or the quickly apparent high incidence of false alarms – up to 90 percent. Relations with the police soured as their resources were stretched and the Post Office felt pressure on the telephone system from the installation of automatic dialling equipment that did not meet their specifications. Insurance company customers saved money on their alarm systems but as a result public services paid a high price (Williams et al., 1984: 46).

The insurance companies did, of course, come to recognise that it might be preferable if their policies were more closely based on tighter estimates of the risk that different customers represented. However, several problems militate against this: the difficulties of assessing and interpreting risk; the problem of getting accurate information about what alarm system suppliers are actually offering; the desire not to offend clients in a competitive market by demanding inspections; and the difficulties of carrying out such inspections if they were possible (they would need to be random, unanticipated and regular). Such problems would involve considerable expense, which presumably the insurance companies would seek to pass on to their clients – not an attractive proposition where other companies may not wish to be so scrupulous. Thus, the ability (or willingness) of the insurance sector to take measures to improve alarm system and installation standards is severely limited (Williams et al., 1984: 28–9).

None the less, insurance companies remain an extremely powerful influence on private security and the development of crime prevention policy. Reports of business consultancies make no mistake in emphasising that a customer's interest in security is still generally the result of his or her insurance company's advice about the unacceptability of the risk without some form of security cover. This has been the standard pattern. But in recent years some insurers have begun to offer discounts on premiums for customers installing alarm systems, and in 1986 the extension of this initiative to home insurance received encouragement from a joint meeting of the Home Office, police, trade unions, local authorities and the insurance companies' representatives (*Daily Mail*, 1986; see also *The Independent*, 1986). In some cases, insurers have linked directly with security hardware manufacturers. At the level of inter-industry liaison, limited formal links exist with the

British Insurance Association being represented on the National Inspection Board of the National Supervisory Council for Intruder Alarms (NSCIA). This latter body maintains a Roll of Approved Installers who are to adhere to the British Standard 5750 Quality Assessment Schedule covering the installation and maintenance of alarm systems.

While there are many who would argue that the NSCIA has been fairly ineffective as a regulator of the alarm and security systems industry, none the less membership of the organisation does bring the advantage that, theoretically at least, insurance companies prefer their clients to use such installers and some *limited* and indirect regulation of the standards of the market may follow from this.

Members of the NSCIA can also be members of the Security Systems section of the British Security Industry Association, which is concerned with the development of guidelines for standards and performance of equipment and alarm systems and which maintains a Security Systems Inspectorate to 'monitor quality'. Membership of this section in 1987 stood at 35 companies (though this figure may be slightly inflated by the listing of several regional limited companies which would appear to be divisions of two parent companies). The claims of either of these two organisations to be anything like fully representative of the security systems industry have always been challengeable, and in 1986 yet another 'representative' organisation, BASI (British Association of Security Installers), was established aiming to improve standards and service (*Security Times*, 1986b). The life of the BASI turned out to be rather short and it recently wound up its affairs. However, the IAIA (Intruder Alarm Installers Association) continues to attract a membership of small companies from outside the orbit of either the NSCIA or the BSIA's Inspectorate. Clearly, the model of self-regulation of the security systems industry is not working and has led to fragmentation among those concerned about standards and confusion among insurers and clients.

Despite significant growth, profits in the alarm and security systems business have not always been easy to come by. In value terms, the commercial sector of customers has been the most important, although this is probably now close to saturation, but the volume potential of the private household market still offers a great deal of scope for expansion. This will obviously benefit greatly from the encouragement to install alarms in households now being given by the insurance companies.

The alarm business is not, of course, by any means new. Electronic alarms were first used commercially in the UK in 1916 and, familiarly, were introduced as a result of pressure from insurers on furriers in London's East End, emphasising the deterrent value of alarms. But even then, the USA and Scandinavia had a longer history and more sophisticated use of alarms. The next technological staging post in the use of alarms in the UK did not come until 1936 with the use of Post Office telephone lines to connect alarm systems to a central alarm monitoring point, pioneered in London by the Rely-a-Bell company. This system was shortly extended throughout major UK population centres but despite its considerably greater efficiency it proved quite expensive. In 1938, a new system appeared based on the automatic dialling system of the telephone network, enabling a silent message to be sent over the 999 emergency lines and first used by the Burgot Alarm Company (Dring, 1972: 19). By 1971 one authoritative estimate of the number of alarms in use was set at around 110,000 of which 76,000 were directly connected to the police (Dring, 1972). However, it was still evidently unclear even in 1972, as it is now after years of growth, how many alarm firms were in business. In 1960, there were 11 known firms; by 1970 the Trade Directory listed 98 but it was accepted then, as now, that many more were unlisted.

It was hoped that coherence, standardisation and accountability could be brought to the alarm industry by the establishment in 1971 of the National Supervisory Council for Intruder Alarms, supported by the Home Office, the police, insurance companies and the security industry. The real effectiveness of the council's 'supervisory' role was, however, based on the willingness and voluntary cooperation of the firms in the market place to allow themselves to be supervised; unsurprisingly, such cooperation has frequently not been forthcoming. Further, as one media observer of the crime control scene has noted, 'in 1979, eight years after its formation, it was apparent that the general public was not aware of the Council's existence nor of the help it could offer either to those with alarms installed by Approved Installers or to those thinking of having one installed' (Burden, 1980: 113). Without formal, licence-based regulation, the watchdog will remain toothless and its bark ignored. The case for control is more serious when NSCIA, aware of its own limitations, none the less suggests that 'at least 750,000 alarm systems are needed in Britain' (Burden, 1980: 114).

Probably the most frequently cited problem with alarm systems is the extremely high rate of false alarms, and as a result the attitude among the police that the technology cries wolf too often (Matthews, 1972: 29). But there is anyway a general problem of speeding up the response time of the police as usually it is first a key-holding security company which receives the alarm and then has to notify the police to check the cause of the alarm. This fairly typical procedure occurs where the alarm is discovered by a patrolling guard on site or where the alarm is fed directly to a security company's central control. If the alarm is not wired to a centralised checkboard with a security firm then in the past it was either wired directly to the police (an unpopular practice no longer allowed by most forces) or else it simply rings in isolation until acted upon by somebody.

Not surprisingly, many in the security industry have argued that this is a serious problem area in which there is a need for much closer cooperation with the police on an operational basis. One suggestion, for example, has been to build private security alarm and guard control centres close to, or even next door to, police stations. Other members of the industry have, it should be noted, been very wary of such suggestions in terms of their concern for the industry's public image (a caution expressed in research interviews with both very senior and very junior employees in security companies). None the less, employment of new communications technology is being seriously exploited by the major companies in efforts to provide a more sophisticated and efficient service.

The relationship between the alarm companies and the police is clearly one that is often fraught with difficulties, and is founded, and occasionally flounders, upon tensions. The official police 'line' has some praise for the efforts made in the past 20 or so years to achieve a mutual operational accommodation, although the critical observation that still more needs to be done is consistent. But a different, unofficial, subcultural response can tend to view private security in general, and private alarm companies in particular, as close to parasitic. Other researchers in this area have also detected this sentiment. Shearing (1981: 290), for example, similarly notes that in Canada alarm companies are seen by the police as being among that section of the public which 'uses' the police 'exploiting their relationship as allies'. Whilst it is in the alarm company business in particular (at least in the UK – and I believe in Canada) that efforts have been made to simplify and synchronise police and security responses better, none the less a significant degree of resentment seems to remain. The feeling may principally be one of professional disdain for imagined (or real) negligence or incompetence on the part of alarm companies. As one West Yorkshire beat constable insisted to me: 'Of course they can do something about it!'

Whatever the persistent shortcomings, the development of security technology, and indeed of the private security sector as a whole, is strongly related to a competitive cycle not simply between customers demanding better security and their suppliers, but more importantly between security systems and those who attempt to neutralise them. Obviously, security technology has, in one sense, simply kept pace with technological developments generally. As the US Task Force on Private Security (1976) commented:

with the application of advanced technology to the security industry, even one of the oldest security devices, the lock, was subject to revolutionary changes: combination locks, combination time locks, delayed action time locks, combination locks with surveillance and electronic controls, and eventually access controlled systems that utilised the technology of television and mini-computers.

Professional competition nevertheless lies at the heart of this history of technological advance. Whether the professionals are designers of security systems or of organised crime:

> Edwin Holmes, who invented the first electric burglar alarm in 1853 put it this way: 'The whole history of bank burglary and vault building is competitive; and in the same manner that a new system is devised to protect armour plate, so the burglar finds or devises a new method of attack'. (O'Toole, 1978: 186)

As McIntosh (1971) has succinctly argued, advances in the organisation of thieving have generated a cycle in which the manufacturers of protective devices of all kinds have had to respond with their own increasingly sophisticated changes. McIntosh cites the example of burglary as a fairly routinised craft form of crime up to the industrialisation and urbanisation of the nineteenth century. Quite naturally, the great new buildings housing the new industrial wealth tended to be increasingly better protected. Thieves successfully rising to such a 'challenge' were met, in due course, by further improvements in protection techniques and 'an innovative cycle was under way' (McIntosh, 1971: 117). McIntosh presents the history of the safe since the nineteenth century as a good example of this process:

> Since Elizabethan days, strong-box locks with other locks had been vulnerable to the Black Art of skeleton keys and pick-locks. But this was defeated when the warded lock was replaced by the lever or tumbler locks. In turn techniques were developed for forcing locks off and for defending against this; for drilling holes in locks by various means and for defending against these; for dynamiting locks and defending against this, and so on. The technology of the 'peter man' (safebreaker) has by now moved through gelignite, oxy-acetylene or oxy-arc cutting equipment and even to the use of the thermic lance to cut through concrete to get at a safe, which puts some safebreakers at the forefront of technological advance. So rapidly is the technology changing in this sphere that leading safemakers are contemplating hiring safes rather than selling them on the grounds that, unlike most industrial or commercial equipment, an outmoded safe loses *all* not just some of its usefulness. (McIntosh, 1971: 118)

According to one professional 'heist' or 'hold-up' man, the improved security of bank safes, particularly the introduction of the time lock, and the tendency for ordinary safes just to carry non-negotiable cheques and securities, has prompted a move away from burglary and safe-breaking to hold-ups (McIntosh, 1971: 123). This kind of view is shared by other experienced commentators on crime and crime prevention. As Worsley (1983: 13) recollects of his visiting lectures at the Stafford Crime Prevention Centre, the 'most important "law"' he devised to provoke his audience was that 'security equipment and services do not prevent crime. They divert it to other targets and change its pattern, even producing violence, but in the national context they prevent nothing.' (For further comments on the 'displacement effect' and other problems in current approaches to crime prevention, see Lowman, 1982: 327; Reppetto, 1976; South, 1987b: 142–5; Weiss, 1988.)

Evidently, as is the case with other private security services, competing claims can be made about the technology and effectiveness of security devices and systems related to crime prevention. More disturbing is the efficiency – or inefficiency – of other forms of security hardware and this subject cannot be left without some brief description of technology less clearly designed for employment in the commendable, if ill-starred, pursuit of crime prevention.[2]

Security technology and issues of surveillance and privacy

This section explicitly moves away from a focus on crime prevention briefly to note examples of security technology designed with matters such as industrial espionage and personal information gathering, storage and retrieval in mind. An advertisement run in New York State newspapers in 1980 claimed:

> Now you can 'clone' your best employees and cut applicant screening costs to the bone. Do it with 'VAPI' Voice Analysis Personality Inventory. Generations beyond lie detection and psychological assessment.
> Fully validated and complies with EEOC and FEPC requirements.
> Rave reviews from users and labor leaders. Slashes recruiting and training costs, turnover and theft.
> Call collect.

The common version of the lie detector or polygraph monitors physiological signs of 'stress' such as heart rate and, retaining the stereotype of the culprit sweating while being grilled, the electrical conductivity of the skin (which measures a person's sweating). Perhaps the Voice Analysis Personality Inventory was inevitable as a development. Not because of any leap-frogging with the technological sophistication of organised crime, but because – even in the USA, the Disneyland of personality assessment tests and devices – scepticism about lie detectors and their effectiveness has been growing. As *The Sunday Times* (5 December 1982) reported:

Lie detectors are being seriously considered as a way of improving Britain's leaking security vetting system. But, according to a leading authority in America – where lie detectors have been widely used for years – they are almost useless. 'It is an insidious myth in the United States that lie detectors produce highly accurate results . . . In fact the best scientific evidence is that the polygraph produces a wrong answer about one time in three.'

The VAPI advertisement actually refers to a form of voice stress analysis. According to *The Sunday Times* report:

the original voice-stress analyser was invented and marketed by a former CIA man. Because it can be used without the subject's knowledge, even over the telephone, it is widely used for job-vetting in America. Voice-stress analysers are based on the idea that a natural, almost imperceptible, body tremor, with a frequency of about 10 cycles a second, is reduced by stress and that there are resultant detectable changes in speech.

According to Dr David Lykken of the University of Minnesota (the expert quoted by *The Sunday Times*), the results of four serious studies of the voice stress analyser 'were even worse than with the polygraph. They were no better than chance.'

Despite sufficient scientific evidence to encourage at least cautious scepticism, this area, as with others in the private security sector, attracts considerable research and development investment. This would seem a marginally less wasteful pursuit of the security equivalent of the philosopher's stone were it not for the fact that companies are already prepared to buy and use much technology which is effective only to varying and disputed degrees. The widespread use and acceptance of such technology has brought about a situation where, as Hougan (1979: *xx*) observes, 'surveillance has become such a routine of western life that we pay it hardly any attention.' Voice analysers, electronic eavesdropping and routinised camera surveillance may seem to reflect a picture of US commercial zeal and excess, but for the UK it is less a matter of 'it can't happen here' and rather more one of 'following the American pattern, one, ten or twenty years later'.[3]

What might also be noted is the peculiar vampiric thrust for immortality of the development of technology in the private security sector – feeding off its own life-blood: it is highly commercially competitive, insatiable in its efforts to prove itself outdated and in need of rejuvenation and further innovation. For, of course, once simple eavesdropping has become regarded as old-fashioned or impracticable, then the horizons of technological eavesdropping open wide – almost to infinity (see Wright, 1972: 223, on the so-called 'infinity transmitter' bug). Personal or technical surveillance devices are, as Campbell (1978: 600) has succinctly put it, 'generally used to attack personal or commercial security; sometimes they are used by those who claim to promote security by such surreptitious means.' In the absence of any effective regulation such irony is barely noted.

A full treatment of the technology of security and security systems would necessarily entail exploring the diversity of that market from the boring and mundane to the sensational and sinister. The point to be made here is that the significance of the private security sector today, and its antecedents in the past, cannot be really appreciated unless the tremendous influence on patterns of policing, crime and crime prevention – and indeed everyday life – which is made by the *technology* of security is emphasised.

There is much to consider with caution about the positive and negative consequences of developments that contribute to the security of people and their property whilst at the same time bringing closer the reality of a surveilled, overly security-conscious society. Deep ambivalence is perhaps the most appropriate response to such a contradictory history and modern development.

Notes

1   To give another example; in April 1984 the Conservative government, intending to privatise the ordnance factories, was considering arrangements which would also involve privatising the security of the plants, and was tentatively inviting tenders from reputable private security companies. The proposals were eventually dropped, but if they had been implemented these commercial services would, of course, have had the backing of the police and, in the last resort, the army. (The deliberations of the House of Commons Defence Committee were reported in the national press in April 1984.)

2   Beyond crime *prevention* concerns, one area of rapid technological advance is the design and manufacture of police and security equipment for *responding* to 'dangerous' situations: guns, equipment to disable assailants, riot equipment and so on. Such products are displayed and can be ordered from manufacturers and stockists at a variety of specialist national and international exhibitions and through specialist retailers. As recent concerns in the UK have reflected, controls over the sale of arms and other offensive weapons can be lax. The lethal nature of the products of this expanding specialist part of the security technology industry – and the relative ease with which such products can be obtained – demands scrutiny and serious regulation.

3   Two very different examples may be suggestive here. One response to increases in the cost of security guarding is the growth of access control systems, using electronically coded identity cards to gain entry. These can operate with a simple number code or, for greater security, employ 'biometric systems' relying on fingerprints, signatures, voice analysis or retinal patterns. Biometric cards have evolved partly in response to scenarios in which it is envisaged a holder may be pressured to reveal a simple number code. Access control is now predicted by some to be the next largest growth area in security technology, although it has already been recognised that such technology does not (at present) easily provide the kind of detailed information on physical movement that recording systems based on human observation can supply.

For the USA a major increase in this market is predicted and the UK will follow (Kidd, 1986: 11–14).

The second example is the manufacture and sale of electronic 'tagging' or monitoring devices used in 'home detention' alternative to prison schemes. When the British Minister with responsibility for prisons at the time, Lord Caithness, visited the USA in September 1987 to examine this system, he found manufacturers there were more than eager to try to develop a point of entry into the as yet untapped UK and European markets (Helm, 1987: 4). A recent Home Office Green Paper has now invited comments on a proposal to introduce such devices (Home Office, 1988).

5 Private Eyes: Private Spies?

While many forms of private security operation can be seen to work at a fairly visible level, and changes to our physical environment designed to provide better security also tend to be evident, at least to some degree, there is a further important dimension of the private security sector which has tended to adopt a very low profile.[1] Its existence and activities are no secret: its practitioners easily found in the *Yellow Pages* directory of virtually any town. But it is generally in the nature of the work done by private investigators that a low-key, frequently covert approach is demanded. Sometimes this is for relatively honourable reasons, like the good name of the client or subject of investigation; at other times, it simply facilitates dubious or dishonest practice, increasingly encouraged by some agencies' adoption of 'aggressive new tactics' (*Newsweek*, 1986: 40). In this chapter I shall describe the range of activities of this final, key dimension of the private security sector and continue to raise issues of concern which will be more fully taken up in later chapters which address the case for accountability and control of the private security sector.

To begin with, there is considerable definitional confusion in the area of private detection. Terms like private investigator, private detective or enquiry agent do not really reflect any precise degree of characterisation, and where some authors choose one term, claiming its particular appropriateness, this generally seems more a matter of whim and preference than taxonomic expertise. Enquiry agent *may* more commonly be a term used to describe the part-time amateur; private detective *may* be eschewed as a description by some respectable practitioners seeking to show they do not desire any confusion of their role and powers with those of the police; and private investigator sounds relatively unthreatening yet solid and professional. None the less, here I shall generally follow Draper (1978: 27) and use the terms interchangeably.

The public image of private investigators is also somewhat confused. This too, of course, is strongly related to the influence of the media, both in fictional depictions and in the occasional, usually negative, news report. Not surprisingly, the profession has been consistently concerned about the problem of image: 'The private detective works against cheats and bullies in the main, assists and often brings about the end of suffering and cruelties. Why does he not get due credit for his value to the community? The answer is simple – all our Public Relations have been negative and damaging' (Open Letter, The Association of British Private Detectives; quoted in Thompson, 1970: 141). Public relations efforts do not usually stress the saintly qualities of private investigators, but they do commonly emphasise the value of the profession to the community. According to one member of the Institute of Professional Investigators, for example, 'There is scarcely a field of modern day existence which does not at some time or another require the services of the Private Investigator' (undated document). Unfortunately, such statements may sound as much a threat of all-pervading intrusion as a confident professional claim. Certainly, private investigators are employed by clients who range across the economic scale from finance houses to ordinary families. Insurance companies, solicitors, large and small companies worried about internal theft, computer fraud or industrial sabotage, and interested parties like families or creditors concerned to trace a missing person who is not a priority for the police, may all employ private investigators. In recent years employee vetting and the compilation of personal profiles involving assessment of financial status and moral character has become a growth area of activity, especially as corporate expansion brings with it the commercial version of the 'need to know' principle of who should be told what in the company and the accompanying 'need to know' more about the person(s) being told. For the successful specialists, the investigation of 'white-collar crime' has replaced the investigation of adultery (*Newsweek*, 1986: 39).

Ever since the Victorian era evoked by Conan Doyle in his stories of 'the world's first consulting detective', private investigators have been fictionalised and their trade portrayed in romanticised or brutalised imagery. Needless to say, reality rarely conforms to such portrayals. It remains important none the less to look into the work of this rarely examined part of the private security sector, for the investigator represents the tendency within private security to be concerned both with *maintaining* the security of persons and property and with *penetrating* security in order to find, obtain or retrieve persons or property.

The private investigation business in Britain is diverse. This is reflected in the fact that since the 1960s there have been at least five professional organisations which have included private investigators among their members, although the status of all of them is unclear, as the Younger Committee (1972) found. These bodies are the Association of British Private Detectives, the Association of British Investigators, the Institute of Professional Investigators, the International Pro-fessional Security Association (discussed in more detail in Chapter 7), and the Institute of Industrial Security. On a wider international scale, the Council of International Investigators and the World Association of Detectives are apparently affiliates of similar organisations in other countries.

The impression of most commentators is that, however modestly, the investigation business is certainly expanding. Central to its development there remains (as always) a somewhat individualistic *modus operandi* which might take its actions well into the unethical and sometimes the illegal, yet at the same time claims have consistently been made since at least the 1960s, that it is striving as never before for professional respectability. The problem is that there is no widely recognised office or representative body for the profession. The competing organisations, with more or less unknown memberships, have presented a jumbled picture. In the past, the two organisations that seem to have made the strongest claims for representative credibility also did little to conceal the conflict between them. The Association of British Private Detectives (ABPD) was almost evangelical in its approach, publicising the integrity of the profession, apparently gathering evidence of malpractice and even threatening legal action against its perpetrators. Certainly in the late 1960s and early 1970s it was vocal in calling for higher standards and a sense of unity, pride and identity for the practice.

The Association of British Investigators (ABI) not only seems somewhat more moderate in its general tone but would also seem to be able to claim some legitimacy by virtue of its history. The ABI was originally known as the Association of British Detectives (formed in 1953), but changed its name partly because it did not wish to make claims for its members which might lead the public to confuse them with police detectives. It also seems very likely that it wished to avoid being confused with the ABPD. The Association of British Detectives was in turn an amalgamation of the Federation of British Detectives (founded in 1945) and the British Detectives Association (founded in 1919). All of these organisations represent only a minority of private investigators but their proliferation and lengthy history at least indicate vitality in a profession that has been around for a long time.

As with the estimates applying to the private security sector as a whole, it seems easier to count the number of supposedly representative associations than it does actual private investigators in practice. There are simply no wholly reliable sources of information, government or otherwise. As matters stand there are in any case very few estimates to collate and these offer a grossly inadequate basis for detailed discussion in this area or for related policy purposes. In 1970, Thompson suggested that 'if everyone calling himself a private detective were to be taken at his word, then the total number of operatives in the field might be set as high as fifteen thousand or so' (1970: 142). Both the ABI and ABPD disagreed with this estimate. According to Thompson, in 1970 the ABPD estimated that:

> there are probably no more than 2,700 full-time private investigators in the country, plus about 2,000 'status enquiry agents' and specialists in writ-serving. Of the 2,700 or so full-time private investigators, they claim that only about 1,000 are truly worthy of the name – and possibly as few as 500, depending on how strictly one interprets the qualifications needed for the job. (Thompson, 1970: 142)

The most recent 'statement' from the Home Office on this matter seems to be the five lines admitting the lack of information, in the 1979 Green Paper on *The Private Security Industry*. The best that the Home Office researchers could do here was to refer back to the 1972 Report of the Younger Committee on Privacy, noting that the committee, 'thought "that a reasonable estimate of the maximum number is of the order of 3,000", but said that it had not been able to obtain hard evidence (see paragraph 430 of the Report)' (Home Office, 1979: 5, para. 14). However, as Madgwick and Smythe (1974: 113) observed, this estimate, 'probably does not take account of the many people working on the fringe of the profession. One of the leading agencies estimates 15,000 as a conservative figure and the great proliferation of one-man businesses over the past few years inclines us to believe that this is no exaggeration.'

Clearly, alliances are at work somewhere here. Thompson was writing of the encroachment on privacy by 'Big Brother' (evoking the theme of Orwell's *1984*). The ABPD represented a view asserting the integrity of the profession and its ability to regulate itself. The Home Office has generally had much sympathy with this view. Madgwick and Smythe were writing from a perspective informed by many years involvement with the NCCL. The Younger Committee took its evidence on this issue from the few representatives of the profession that would present evidence. The picture remains as obscure now as in the late 1970s when Bowden (1978: 259), writing eight years after Thompson, suggested that the highest estimate might be around 20,000. On the basis of Thompson's and Madgwick and Smythe's estimates, the undoubted over-cautiousness of the ABPD and the Younger Committee evidence, I would suggest that Bowden's 1978 figure probably remains an acceptable 'high estimate' for the late 1980s.

One key issue around which this contention over numbers revolves, whether explicitly or not, is that of licensing or regulation of private investigators. I shall devote more attention to the arguments for and against licensing and regulation of the broader private security sector in Chapters 7 and 8. However, because private investigators have been the subject of *specific* attempts to legislate around them, I shall briefly fill in some of the background here.

As with much else in this area, the position of representatives of the private investigators' profession appears confused. According to Thompson (1970: 143) both the ABI and the ABPD have opposed legislation in the past. Presumably, the ABI (at least) changed its position in the early 1970s for in its 'Report . . . to the Royal Commission on Legal Services (1979)' (undated document, c. 1978) it stated that it had:

> for many years advocated that there should be some control of the Private Investigative profession, and strong support was given to the following:-
> Andrew Gardner, MP – Private Investigators Bill
> Norman Fowler, MP – Security Industry's Licensing Bill
> Michael Fiddler, MP – The Private Detective's Control Bill No. 1
> The Private Detective's Control Bill No. 2
> Bruce George, MP – Private Security (Registration) Bill.

It seems likely that the general trend in the profession has been towards favouring some form of licensing, though clearly this was at one time anathema to some. For example, the response of the ABPD to the news in 1968 that a Private Member's Bill proposed the requirements of a licence to practice and surety of £1,000 was that: 'If this was to reach the Statute Book, it would simply move us nearer the Police State and would eliminate our work as a field.' (Thompson, 1970: 143). At the same time, there were others who welcomed such proposals. Colin Finlay, a well-known private investigator and then Vice-president of the Council of International Investigators argued that: 'As the law stands at present, anyone can start up a private detective agency. Some of the many agencies that have sprung up in recent years have done untold harm. The people who run them don't really know what they're doing and are just getting money under false pretences' (*Evening Standard*, 27 May 1968). The law currently stands as it did in 1968 when Mr Finlay made his statement. Five years later, Norman Fowler, MP was commenting in the House, 'If a private detective here was convicted of the kind of offence for which the Watergate conspirators are now serving sentences in the United States there would be nothing to prevent him in this country recommencing work as a Private Detective on the day of his release' (*Hansard*, 4 July 1973: 538). Mr Fowler's statement topically reflected the feelings of many engaged in the debates and responses to the findings of the Younger Committee which had reported a year earlier.

When the Younger Committee had considered the possibility of issuing licences to private investigators it found, of course, that it could please no one. The ABI liked the idea of licences but when the committee felt there were grounds for over-printing on them that they carried no official authority and the public were under no obligation to cooperate, the enthusiasm of the ABI cooled. It apparently felt that in such a format the licence might actually discourage public cooperation, and likened it to a dog licence. At the same time, the reservations of the Committee were being prompted by the police and government who saw dangers of abuse of the document and misleading of the public.

The government subsequently rejected the proposals and reasons (Younger, 1972: para. 445) put forward by the Committee for favouring licensing of private investigators, but suggested that it might be possible to introduce a 'disqualification scheme'. This would entail anyone seeking to work as a private investigator undergoing a criminal record check carried out by the local police station. Disqualification from practising would follow if the check showed that the applicant did have a criminal record. Part of the thinking behind this suggestion was presumably that those who were aware that they did have a record would not try to obtain clearance. However, problems would have resulted from attempting to police this system if no resources were committed to it and the provisions of the Rehabilitation of Offenders Act 1974 (about which more later) would have had to be carefully considered. Nevertheless, as Draper (1978: 151) observes, this idea 'bears some resemblance to the Continental approach and, although it represents the very minimum form of checking, it would at least be a step in the right direction.' To those familiar with Home Office lack of interest in this issue, it is no surprise that the step was never taken.

Today, support for some form of regulatory legislation is probably still widespread among the more professional agencies. However, the reasons for this coincide with those of the reputable security companies that favour licensing. Not least among these is a desire to drive out of the market, by stiff licensing procedures and heavy financial security and insurance requirements, those smaller, less scrupulous firms who are seen as capable of undercutting prices by doing a shoddy job, and thereby bringing the business into disrepute. Such concern about competition is made the more understandable when it is realised that the private investigator business is not really one of glamour and plush office suites. Rather, in general, it is dull and drab, basic and frequently boring and, most importantly, routine. Obviously, the large and successful practices have grown by virtue of having something special about their services, their contacts and clients. But most of the work done by private investigators can as easily be done by small firms.

Most agencies, small and large, depend upon solicitors' offices for the bulk of their work. Despite advertising, few agencies receive anything like a majority of cases or enquiries through direct client approaches. It is far more likely that a person with a problem will approach a solicitor who may then refer them on to one of the private investigators that they know of and deal with. Importantly, for the investigator, client referral through solicitors means that they can be fairly sure of genuine cases. Further, contact through the solicitor can make legal aid available to the client if eligible (Draper, 1978: 28). Most investigators therefore need to build up their contacts with various solicitors' practices. Similarly, contacts in local Chambers of Commerce, among Rotarians and so on can provide the difference between a bread and butter practice and one which gets the jam of more prosperous clients who will pay for discretion, and of business clients who may even put the investigator's office on a retainer basis to handle all their company's enquiry work.

The use of the term 'practice' to describe the investigator's work is not intended to confuse their image with that of solicitors or doctors and the like. Rather, despite the continued strong presence of lone detective operations, there is a trend towards more organised, multiple staff offices with all the accompanying resources of a well-run business. Such practices are fairly evidently modelled on those of solicitors, with senior and junior partnerships and younger apprenticeships. Over time, such a development may serve to improve the image of investigators quite considerably.

Certainly, given their close working contact with solicitors, it is unsurprising that they should emulate the model, and also do so in the hope of attracting further business from reputable sources. The point about this search for business is that it is not necessarily the sort of work that private investigators are commonly thought to do; it is legal 'dogs-body' work, like process-serving, passing writs and summonses into the hands of those required to be party to legal proceedings. This task can be a simple matter of straightforward delivery or involve making enquiries in order to trace an elusive defendant. Such legal-servicing work may lack glamour but has the virtue of being a steady trade. In hard times another detective agency service can flourish: that of acting as bailiffs. Focused principally at the lower end of the profession, among what may be called enquiry agents (and carried out in Scotland mainly by estate agents), such work can also be relied on for its regularity (Draper, 1978: 30–1). Other consistent sources of work may be 'tracing' enquiries about a missing relative or stolen property, for example, or the gathering of evidence in a variety of circumstances:

> The private detective may be required to find and interview a witness to a road or industrial accident who has not been forthcoming with his evidence. He may also be employed by a party to civil litigation to find evidence supporting his case – evidence, for instance, as to the nature of the whereabouts of a defendant's assets and his means generally, or proof that one party has not been telling the truth under oath in the witness box. (Draper, 1978: 31)

Thus, genuine investigative work – in the real world as opposed to that of the media – plays only a small part in the work of private investigators. Involvement in criminal investigation may account for only about 10 percent of the investigator's workload (Draper, 1978: 31). This may be a slightly low estimate according to one police source (personal communication) but at the same time the police are not necessarily the best judges as, relatively speaking, they are likely to come into contact with more private investigators involved in work related to criminal offences than is perhaps representative of the average. Usually this work involves being retained by the Defence to check up on aspects of a case, trace witnesses, look into alibis and cover the ground gone over by the police to get an idea of the Prosecution evidence.

Investigators may, of course, also be used on occasion by the police themselves, either officially or unofficially, sought out because of their good reputation and perhaps because of some particular expertise, line of contact or to bring in a fresh face or perspective. Where the police have not conducted an investigation to the satisfaction of some party, then investigators may be employed to add to a Prosecution case. This is not common, but it does occur and, as Draper points out, 'it is likely to arise more frequently as the police find it more difficult to keep pace with the increasing numbers of serious crimes' (Draper, 1978: 31). During any investigation related to a criminal offence, and even in the course of an ordinary, routine kind of job, there is the strong possibility that the investigator will discover evidence of some criminal matter. The investigator will (or should) then discuss the issue with the client, recommending that the police be brought in. It should be noted, though, that this relationship leaves a great deal of room for discretion, and for a variety of motives!

Private detectives have something of a 'snooper' image. This may be due in part to the enquiries they undertake in criminal cases, but it is likely that much of the disapproval surrounding their image and profession – in the real world – arises from their past heavy involvement in matrimonial divorce cases. In the past 20 years, however, the Divorce Reform Act 1969 and subsequent amendments have diminished the importance of cases of adultery for private detectives. Generally, there are now easier ways to secure a divorce by establishing 'irretrievable breakdown' of the marriage. Additional provisions for 'postal divorces' by mutual consent accompanied by sworn statements have also removed some of the need for the employment of private detectives in those adversarial contests where a divorce action was defended in court requiring the submission of evidence. Having made these points, however, it should be noted that observation to prove adultery is still very much a part of the business of many agencies, perhaps taking up around 5 percent of their business (Draper, 1978: 34). Typically, such a case might arise where a husband fears that divorce by mutual consent could lead to him having to make a substantial settlement on his wife. Proof of adultery is apparently often sought by husbands in the hope that the divorce settlement will somehow be affected and reduced.

Adultery in such cases is proved, according to one private detective, by the 'eternal triangle': opportunity, inclination and association. For example:

> Take an instance of a man and woman who go into an empty house together at night, at say 10.30 p.m. At midnight the lights go out . . . we would be standing outside watching . . . and would keep observation perhaps all night . . . and you would see them come out the following morning. That means they've had the opportunity, you've proved the association and to spend all night together they certainly must have the inclination.

Such an account might form the basis of a courtroom statement, especially the emphasis on maintaining surveillance all night. But, of course, like any occupation, private detectives have their 'tricks of the trade' which are employed to ease their work. One security consultant with some experience of investigation work told me of one classic trick. Staying at an observation post all night, for example in the case of an adultery investigation, may be both unattractive and thought unnecessary. So, to check that those under surveillance have not moved during the period of absence or sleep, age-old techniques of 'marking' are used. These are anything from simply pushing a matchstick in a door which should be still there on return if the door has not been opened and marking the position of car tyres with chalk on the road, to placing pressure pads which are linked to a paper-tape time-recording mechanism. (Apparently the name of the 1960s television private eye, Frank Marker, was a small in-joke in the private investigation business.)

The private investigator as undercover agent

Whilst much of the investigator's mundane and routine work now comes by way of referrals from solicitors, there is one area where increasingly their services are sought by direct approach. This is in their employment as undercover agents at all levels of industry (Draper, 1978; Lipson, 1975). The direct approach is justified on grounds of secrecy and security, though on the other hand, in the UK at least, some client companies and investigative agencies will seek the cooperation of trade union representatives over the matters being investigated rather than risk discovery and the possibility of industrial dispute over the protocol of consultation and so on. Such work is, of course, highly sensitive in its nature and can range from the investigation of fraud and embezzlement at the top of the company hierarchy to large-scale pilferage at the bottom. In some cases, 'troublemakers' are being sought out, personal profiles compiled; even information on the habits and opinions of spouses can be the nature of an assignment.

Though some agencies have offered these services in Britain since at least the late 1950s, the increase in demand for them seems to have only slowly followed the boom in private security services generally, probably gaining some sense of legitimacy as a commercial option in the wake of broader acceptance of the place of principles of security in modern management. Such practices have been used extensively in the USA throughout this century and earlier, and often with little regard for ethical investigative practice. This can mean that they are viewed without great sympathy even by security professionals like Lipson (1975). According to this author of a well-known security text, undercover agents are usually put on a company's pay-roll as an ordinary employee, paid the full salary for the job they have been hired for and in addition receive a sum from their agency. They are mostly employed in relatively unskilled positions, such as shipping rooms, stock rooms and so on (but presumably this does not mean that some are not also deployed in the higher reaches of organisations).

> Their job is to infiltrate existing cliques and strata of companies ... Some of the techniques used can be said to border on entrapment, or the actions of an *agent provocateur*. Many make it known that they are interested in 'making a fast buck', placing a bet, obtaining marijuana or more potent drugs, joining the union – whatever it is that their assignment encompasses. (Lipson, 1975: 121)

It is unknown how far the *agent provocateur* approach has been adopted in Britain, but as the *Daily Mirror* reported on 23 November 1982 the idea of planting spies in the workplace is certainly becoming increasingly familiar.

> More and more firms – insurance companies, stockbrokers and supermarkets – are planting 'moles' to check on thieving by staff. The move is worrying union leaders who are virtually powerless because the spies are necessarily known only to top company executives. Though they appear to be on the payroll, they are employed and trained by security companies – and paid by results calculated in arrests or a cut in the firm's losses. [As one] union official complained ... 'This sort of thing must harm staff morale ... *Company detectives are known and accepted as part of life.* But how can bosses expect a happy atmosphere with the thought that there could be a spy on the next desk or counter. (emphasis added)

For the USA, Lipson suggests that investigation agencies and security staff follow up such undercover operations with trained interrogators who will question 'those "fingered" and obtain confessions and restitution. Cases developed in this manner are seldom referred to the criminal justice system' (1975: 121), but are part of the private justice system. This observation is at odds with Draper's contention that the police are unlikely to object to undercover investigations carried out privately in companies because 'in all probability, if the offenders are found out they will be handed over to them, making a welcome improvement in police detection statistics' (Draper, 1978: 32). Draper is probably being generous here in her estimation of the regard for legal process necessarily held by private companies or investigating agencies. There probably is higher regard for traditional referral to the police in the UK than in the USA, but it is also true that Draper's study, written from the point of view of a practitioner at the bar, is generally blind to the concept of private justice as embracing forms of social control which run to the side of the formal legal system (see Henry, 1983). On the other hand, writing with direct experience of work in the security world, Lipson is explicit about the implications of such a private justice system for the private security personnel involved.

> The private investigator is deeply involved in this practice of private justice. He often combines the function of investigator with that of prosecutor, while his business colleagues sit in judgement. The operation of these private, kangaroo 'courts', of course, means that the crimes they are dealing with are unreported and that justice has become a private affair. In this area the function of the private investigator represents a challenging and disturbing problem in criminology. (Lipson, 1975: 120)

While many private detective agencies will be in a position to attract reputable local and legal business and others will have a 'name' as specialists in certain kinds of investigation, many others must seek the basis for a steady living elsewhere. One avenue of work is supplementing the strength of the investigation departments of insurance companies, usually when an enquiry is being pursued over a lengthy period of time and is exhibiting some complexities requiring extended enquiries (for example dubious fire insurance claims).[2] But perhaps the area which has seen the most expansion for private detectives in recent years is the boom throughout the 1970s in credit-rating and referencing agencies. These agencies themselves pursue enquiries of a private investigative nature and hence, in some respects, the line between the two can become almost indistinguishably blurred.

Credit as a routine matter of commerce is by no means new, of course, and assessment of credit worthiness has always been an associated problem. In the nineteenth century, trade protection associations and private registers of bad debtors arose to formalise some degree of protection and means of investigation for those giving credit. But the twentieth century, and in particular the affluent decades of the 1950s, 1960s and early 1970s and the credit boom of the 1980s has seen the credit-investigation agencies flourish as an expansive and profitable area of business in itself. The promotion of a consumer-credit society, embraced in the 1950s and 1960s by slogans like 'live now, pay later', inevitably meant a boom in work for credit-reference agencies, first in vetting customers and then in reclaiming goods and payments when 'living on the never, never' proved too much for household budgets. In the 1980s the proliferation of credit cards has brought similar problems for the many households that have had to face massive reduction in family income through sudden unemployment.

Briefly, the credit-reference business falls into two areas. First, is the less intrusive (relatively speaking) credit rating of commercial businesses. This tends to be simply a matter of compiling a detailed report from the variety of available sources about the standing of the company financially, as a trader and customer and so on. There are, for example, registers of businesses with established credit ratings, such as the *White Book* published by Dun and Bradstreet of London (Draper, 1978: 35). Such profiling-type investigations rarely involve any intrusion into the personal lives of members of the company. Secondly, and of more concern, are those investigations pursued by agencies supplying credit references on individuals. Well-established organisations exist providing such services, usually regarded as reputable and of high standard, but there is little serious regulation in this area and, as Draper observes, 'one mistake on the part of the credit-reference agency can bring untold misery to an individual who gets blacklisted as a result of it' (Draper, 1978: 35).

Within the credit industry, then, the small private detective agency can really be small-fry indeed. However, as Draper (1978: 36) notes, they have their significance here for two reasons. First, they provide, and are used as, an '*alternative* source of credit reporting for traders and finance houses'. On a localised level private detectives prove useful for gathering information in those less serious cases which perhaps do not merit the time, trouble and cost of resorting to specialised agencies employing computer time and correspondingly trained and expensive staff and investigators. This division is emphasised further in the second important role of private detectives in the credit field. This is their function as a source and conduit of local information about private individuals and traders passed on to larger credit organisations. The use of such private detectives is probably diminishing and, in reality, they were, in any case, less professional investigators than casual amateurs. They were usually employed when the larger agency had no local office or representative and, appropriately, were generally called 'correspondents'. Their stock in trade was simply their knowledge of the locality and willingness to approach potentially unreliable sources of reference: neighbours, acquaintances and shopkeepers, etc. Part of their bad name, therefore, followed from the sort of information they tended to gather and their inclusion of it in written reports.

Some of the most dubious practices have, however, seen a degree of tightening up in the wake of the Consumer Credit Act 1974, particularly with regard to verifying accuracy of information. This follows the opening of access to personal credit-reference files provided for by the Act. Economic factors have also affected the business, as when the demand for personal credit seemed to reach its high point in 1973 and then declined, mirrored by a diminishing of the demand for credit-reference enquiry work (Draper, 1978: 37). Some of the smaller agencies could not survive without such work, whilst others geared their services more to the needs of the commercial business world in relation to credit investigations. A number of credit and private detective agencies have, however, simply shifted sideways into the area of debt collecting and 'counselling', and in the circumstances of the late 1980s it is likely that many are flourishing as never before. It should be noted that the clients who hire such agencies are not necessarily just businesses with an eye to the balance sheet: they are also hired on the rates by councils concerned over levels of bad debts.

Despite the protection offered by the Administration of Justice Act 1970 to debtors subject to harassment, some agencies employ distinctly unsavoury techniques in trying to extract repayment. While here, as in other areas of private detective work, these may be the minority, some attention should now be paid to examples of dishonest and corrupt practice.

Private detectives, professional abuse and civil liberties

There may be many private detectives who fit the seedy, down-at-heel image, but the majority make a reasonable living from their trade. There are, of course, an additional few for whom the business can be very lucrative. As Draper (1978: 30) observes, 'Any who are prepared to resort to unlawful methods, or indulge in dishonest activities such as industrial espionage, will find that some people are ready to pay a lot of money for their services.' In general, the profits to be made depend upon the character of the agency and of its cases. They can thus vary widely, and it is by no means a necessity to engage in unscrupulous practices in order to build up a highly profitable turnover. However, the private detective business can be insecure, competitive and highly opportunistic – indeed, successful and honest detective work can make relative virtues of these factors. But the scope for unethical, corrupt or illegal practice is none the less evidently large, especially given the absence of any serious official regulation – and denial of the repeatedly proved need for such measures.

Following an editorial in the *Guardian* (11 May 1970), the Central Office at Scotland Yard was encouraged to take a token sweep through the private investigator business. The editorial followed an interview by one of the *Guardian*'s reporters with a private detective who had boasted that he could easily obtain details of Inland Revenue status, criminal records, bank account details, debts and so on. Under various charges of 'demanding money with menaces', 'conspiracy to pervert the course of justice', perjury and under the Wireless Telegraphy Act 1967, nearly 20 private detectives were subsequently taken to court. Nearly 20 years on, a response from the Secretary of State for the Home Department to a Parliamentary Question stated that the Attorney General was conducting enquiries into 'allegations of abuses of the Police National Computer (PNC) by private detection agencies' (*Hansard*, 1987: 342), and in 1988 *Police Review* (1988: 212) reported the appearance before Winchester magistrates of five private detectives and three police officers on charges involving allegations of misuse of the PNC.

The comments of Thomas Beet, while perhaps a little extreme, may none the less remain an apposite caution, despite being written in 1906:

> I am convinced that fully 90 percent of the private detective establishments, masquerading in whatever form, are rotten to the core and simply exist and thrive upon a foundation of dishonesty, deceit, conspiracy and treachery . . . Thugs and thieves and criminals don the badge and outward semblance of the honest private detective in order that they may prey upon society. (Beet, 1906: 444)

Certainly, the infamous upholding in November 1974 of the appeal by the Withers brothers, a private detective partnership based in Brighton, casts neither private investigators nor the capacity of the law to protect the public in a good light. The Withers brothers had dishonestly obtained information of a confidential nature concerning private individuals by misrepresenting themselves to councils and government departments. This led to a charge and conviction for 'conspiracy to effect a public mischief'. However, at an appeal before the House of Lords, the Law Lords, Lord Dilhorne, Lord Diplock, Lord Simon and Lord Kilbranden, ruled that there was *no* offence at law of conspiracy here. It is sadly ironic that there have been so many other cases involving issues where legal dispute has arisen on points of law and where the Law Lords have displayed a ready inclination to discover 'conspiracy'. In many such cases civil liberties groups and legal commentators have criticised the judgement strongly. Yet here was a case which seemed one of blatant conspiratorial and dishonest mis-representation where a ruling in favour of breach of the law of conspiracy should have satisfied the principles of justice and the interests of civil liberties. The ruling of the Law Lords here did a disservice to the cause of civil liberties and potentially still leaves disturbing loopholes in the law.[3]

Not surprisingly, even before the law was found to be so seriously inadequate as a regulator of abuses by private detectives, the issues were a strong source of concern to civil liberties bodies. As the NCCL put it in their evidence to the Younger Committee:

> It is the NCCL's view that all forms of intrusion into people's private lives are inherently undesirable. Some of them may be necessary, and in an industrial society we have to concede more than we would readily wish. But we find it wholly deplorable that there should be no control over who can carry out these tasks and under what conditions. (reprinted in Jones, 1974: 135)

Such concern is justifiable. Unlike the situation in many other countries, barriers to entry into the commercial business of being a private detective are non-existent. The aspirant needs little more than the basics: one of the many popular guidebooks or short correspondence courses, a telephone, maybe a car and a fair degree of audacity. But this point should not be allowed to diminish the seriousness of some of the activities that private detectives become involved in. As a growing number advertise services such as pre-employment checks and lie-detector tests, they must increasingly run foul of those limited legal safeguards that *do* exist. For example, to take the case of the Rehabilitation of Offenders Act 1974 (discussed in relation to private security employees in Chapter 7), there will be times when there is inevitably a clash between the intentions of the Act which *should* restrain a private investigator telling a client about, say, a prospective employee's past minor conviction and their feeling of duty to that client. Commercial considerations and the need to display competence as an investigator would, in most cases, one suspects, override the principles and intent of the Act. Existing legislation to protect and safeguard the rights and privacy of individuals is in any case inadequate. When it is considered in relation to how it can be abused by agencies in the private security sector, then it is disturbingly so.

Conclusion: blurring the lines of definition

Quite rightly, Hilary Draper has argued that 'the line of definition between detective agencies and security companies is becoming somewhat blurred, making it more difficult to deal with their respective problems in isolation from each other' (1978: 47). While Draper does not discuss the broader division of private security services across the spectrum that can be identified, none the less, at this core, there is some sense in which the wheel is turning full circle and some investigating agencies are offering security consultancy and guard services while security organisations are offering investigatory services. The blurring of boundaries here and elsewhere in the private security sector (and across the private/public divide) is not a sign of confusion or imminent commercial collapse. The private security sector is expanding and will continue to do so, in varying ways, to varying degrees, for the foreseeable future. As it does so, the need to ensure that it is strictly regulated grows. It is to this issue that I turn in the following chapters.

Notes

1 Parts of this chapter draw on Hilary Draper's thorough and concise account of the private detective business (Draper, 1978: ch. 2). This account remains a significant contribution to what is generally an unresearched area. Although I do not have the space here to detail their range and activities thoroughly, there are other significant sections of the private security sector whose concerns and dealings are less with people in the flesh and rather more with people as data subjects. This occurs at levels from the routine of credit referencing to the high-tech levels of international commercial intelligence gathering and industrial espionage. While credit-reference agencies use their own and hired private investigators, they can generally be excluded from this survey of the private security sector (except that legislative measures designed to ensure probity of commercial agencies and civil liberties of citizens should affect them). Information about international computerisation of personal information and its use is, by its nature, difficult to come by, but in any case properly belongs to a different study. There is an intermediate arena for the collation and private transmission of personal information, that of privately subscribed agencies like the Economic League. However, these are more in the nature of private information agencies than private security or detective operators and hence deserve separate consideration elsewhere (Labour Research, 1987; South, 1983). None the less, the acquisition and collation of personal information is central to, and a significant part of, the work of many components of the private security sector.

2 Insurance companies in the UK usually have efficient investigation departments of their own but are quite willing to resort to outside help from private investigators or police fraud squads. However, developments in the USA should always be noted. There the establishment of in-house fraud investigation units is becoming common. As Guarino-Ghezzi (1983: 321) observes 'because fraud cases are rarely brought to court, these units operate as a kind of private police.' In a personal communication, Guarino-Ghezzi confirms that there seem to be striking similarities between the way that these private fraud investigators operate and the way that the DHSS Specialist Claims Control teams have operated in the UK (Scraton and South, 1983). It would be interesting and informative to explore further those constants and similarities which exist between public and private agencies of investigation adopting 'principles' of 'private justice' and resorting to civil and criminal law only secondarily.

3 I am grateful to Robert Reiner for his comments on this particular point – and many others.

6 Private Security: Causes for Concern

The private security sector is already a major area of commercial and industrial growth – and it continues to expand and make substantial profits. Its activities touch, directly and indirectly, upon many aspects of ordinary and extra-ordinary everyday life. It has now been widely recognised in Britain and abroad as a service sector industry of some special significance and there have been several attempts to introduce some form of official overview of the industry in Britain. All such attempts have, however, failed. But serious attention *must* be paid to what private security organisations do, how they do it and the implications for the changing division of policing labour and their place in society generally.

Two considerations should be borne in mind throughout the following discussion. On the one hand, concern is expressed that private security can be overly intrusive, less than scrupulous in its adherence to self-imposed guidelines and, on occasion, the law, and threatening to civil liberties. On the other hand, problems undoubtedly stem from the inefficiency of some private security operators, low pay, inadequate training, poor standards, cut-throat competition which leads to cutting corners on contracts and so on. The situation is somewhat paradoxical. Both of these sources of disquiet are indeed problems; however, if the solution is seen as improving the efficiency and effectiveness of private security, does this not bring with it the increased threat of more efficient and effective intrusion, surveillance and non-accountability? The key to the problem lies with the issue of the accountability and regulation of the private security sector.

In this chapter and in Chapters 7 and 8 I shall discuss the wide range of issues and arguments surrounding the case for or against licensing and regulation of private security (see, *inter alia*, Draper, 1978; George, 1984; Outer Circle Policy Unit, 1978; Stenning and Shearing, 1980a). However, it should be stressed, if it is not already apparent, that I am not presenting an attempt at neutrality in the debate. I am in favour of regulatory control of the private security sector and would support an effective model of licensing (for some parts of it) as a step towards ensuring public accountability and control of the security world. Whilst licensing alone is not an adequate 'solution' to the private security problem, none the less it does seem the only viable first step.

This and the following two chapters are therefore concerned, in a realistic[1] sense, only with those issues relevant to providing for the licensing and accountability of the private security sector. However, a broader approach to providing a genuine sense of *social* security must go beyond the common focus on policing and crime prevention and also consider how this can integrate with a broader *social* service providing crime prevention, insurance, victim support and other services. I shall make some suggestions about this more ambitious *second* step in Chapter 9.

It should be emphasised, of course, that there are powerful barriers to change. The occupational culture of the private security sector reflects a generally conservative worldview which permeates from the boardroom to the guardroom (see South, 1985: ch. 2 for case studies describing aspects of this occupational culture). The picture presented below is not therefore one that can be criticised for ill-informed optimism! It is nevertheless drawn from a wide range of sources from the literature, academic and media commentators, government and private security itself, as well as from fieldwork interviews with a variety of other interested parties, including MPs, private security managers and workers, police and ex-police and others.

Inefficiency? Who really pays for private security?

Many concerned with the future of private security, whether working within it or outside it, express a desire to see standards raised, to improve pay and conditions, offer training to workers and so on. However, the realities of the highly competitive market seem to militate against such improvements. This means, as is widely recognised, that services offered to and paid for by customers are usually (invariably?) not of the quality that they might be. In some instances, those concerned with civil liberties might initially feel that this is no bad thing if it means, for example, that surveillance services are not as efficient as claimed. However, as the NCCL and others have agreed in the past, it is far better to have responsible and trained personnel working in sensitive security positions than some of the inappropriate staff who *have* been employed and who would be of far greater concern. And, of course, private security is not simply going to 'go away', so such accommodations must be made and thought about.

The arguments of the supporters of self-regulation are confounded as soon as it is recognised that the need for companies to cut costs to stay competitive actually *restricts* freedom of choice in the market – the choices are limited in terms of the level of quality of service. Moreover, as Williams et al. (1984: 35) point out, 'many of the costs of the private security industry are being passed on to the public and taxpayer. The industry affects the police, the insurers, the client, local authorities, National Health Service, employees' families and the general public. Everybody pays a price.' Low pay, poor conditions and high turnover make for 'cut rate efficiency' (Williams et al., 1984: ch. 2). I have covered some of these issues earlier (in Chapter 2) and without going into detail about them and other social and economic costs related to the current organisation of private security (for example, costs to employees and their families; to industrial relations; those resulting from claims on police time; inefficiency in being able to deal with fire, serious theft and crime and so on), I can here only emphasise that low pay and all these related issues have in fact proved expensive not primarily to private security but to society.

A system of licensing could be the basis for setting minimum standards of pay, conditions, training and other matters, (possibly regulated by a voluntary or statutory National Joint Council) (Williams et al., 1984: 37). Indeed, given the support for this proposal among groups like the Low Pay Unit and the principal trade unions in security (MATSA and the TGWU) there would be strong impetus to ensure that licensing worked for the private security labour force just as much as it did for the respectability of the companies licensed and for society. Such developments will, of course, be closely followed by the trade unions, not least because in this field they are caught particularly uncomfortably between their efforts not to upset conservative managements and to increase their membership and obtain good agreements for them. They might also be wary about how negotiations for better conditions could be blocked. The following exchange at a workshop in Canada (Jeffries, 1974: 48–9) is suggestive. A representative of the Canadian Guards Association 'expressed his conviction that better working conditions in the industry would result in a higher quality work force'. A reply to this point argued the employers' line 'that higher pay should be dependent upon better training'. Although he agreed with the Canadian Guards Association's objectives, he said that 'improved qualifications must precede increased salaries'. This naturally prompts the question: who is to encourage or provide such training and relevant qualifications?

A system of licensing must ensure that companies are responsible for providing or sponsoring at least basic (and opportunities for more advanced) training. What needs to be avoided, of course, is a situation where companies which have for years relied upon and encouraged the recruitment of a low-qualified workforce, prepared to accept low wages and poor conditions, are able to turn around and say that prevailing standards are the fault of poorly qualified staff who do not merit better.

Training provision for security occupations has been extremely patchy and undeveloped in Britain (especially by comparison with other countries), and where claims about the satisfactory standard of training *are* made, as for example by some members of the BSIA, these too may be called into question (MATSA, 1986: 22–3). Yet training is an area which must be integrated into any strategy to improve the industry in its service delivery and inform its workers about their own rights and duties and also the legal and ethical constraints upon them. Whereas in the USA, training for security occupations has been a growth area in higher education (at least at Community College level), there has been little movement into this market in the UK and training in the college sector remains virtually non-existent. This only really leaves the courses, conferences and seminars run by the security industry itself. These may be offered under the auspices of representative organisations, like the International Professional Security Association or by individual companies, the larger of which (such as Securicor, Group 4) have their own training schools. Such limited availability means even reasonable standards of training, let alone high standards, are spread thinly.

Regulations could in future set minimum standards and periods of training. At present the only area of training that has attracted legislative interest is that concerned with the handling of guard dogs. The 'dogs issue' has long been an emotive one in the security business with some fearing it gives the industry a bad name. Hence, Group 4 long ago phased out its dog-using operation, but because other major voices in the British Security Industry Association continue to use dogs there can be no united disapproval of the practice. None the less, concern in the industry did lead to the establishment in 1974 of the British Institute of Professional Dog Trainers to represent dog trainers and handlers, but even with stipulations of examinations for handlers and tests for dogs on obedience, scent work, criminal work (chasing and catching) and so on, as prerequisites for membership, the Institute has no special powers to improve standards. It did, however, join in exerting pressure for legislation in this area and the 1975 Guard Dogs Act provided some legal basis for standards, following a number of serious cases of children and adults being mauled by guard dogs. Under the Act, from 1 February 1976 guard dogs have to be either under the direct control of their handler or else secured so that they are not free to roam premises. Additionally, warning signs should be clearly posted at all entrances. The Act was also supposed eventually to provide for local authority licensing and hence inspection of guard-dog kennels, but these provisions have never been brought into force, apparently on grounds of expense. The BSIA endorses those rules and regulations which therefore do apply, and can point out that member companies that use dogs have in fact improved standards quite voluntarily. So who needs statutory intervention?

Lack of public control over the range of activities in the private security sector

Most of the points dealt with above apply principally to the case for licensing and regulation of the main body of private security organisations and their activities: what is usually referred to as the private security industry. But, whether within the boundaries of this main dimension of private security or elsewhere within the broader private security spectrum, there are various other services and activities which must be noted and brought into the case for regulation. This includes apparently mundane services, like security-vetted cleaners, dubious practices of otherwise ordinary security companies as well as some of the services of specialist agencies and freelancing 'heavies'. Even in the innocuous case of cleaning staff, if a security-vetting system is felt to be desirable – for example where a cleaning company is under contract to a prison – then a system which can be bypassed by simply giving a false name does not seem to be strikingly effective (Hanna, 1987).

In 1978 a report from the Outer Circle Policy Unit pointed out that,

> where the security industry defines its role as the protection of profits (and therefore the process of production as well as property) then it extends into areas which are politically sensitive, such as strikes and picketing, and its activities are likely to be in conflict with the rights of employees. For instance, the *Handbook of Security* includes go-slows, strikes and picketing in a list of the most important *crimes* which a commercial manager of today must protect against. (1978: 8, quoting Hamilton and Norman, 1975, 1.1.02)

Importantly here, the rhetoric of private security redefines and reclassifies legitimate actions as 'crimes' offending against the private justice of commercial interest.

Unhappily, the *Handbook* does not simply reflect its authors' opinions, but practices and attitudes which have wide currency and high demand. In 1969, for example, the head of one notorious security and detective agency, Barry Quartermain, explained to a *Times* reporter that industrial 'counter' espionage essentially meant 'investigating agitators and finding the real motive behind a strike' (*The Times*, 28 June 1969). In the 1960s particularly, but through the 1970s and 1980s as well, specialist agencies opened up providing services like 'pre-planning for action in riots and other disorders . . . and penetration tests and how to apply them' (INCOMTEC, n.d.). Given the lengthy history of private security's involvement in 'emergency planning' for strikes, riots and disasters in the USA (see

Momboisse, 1968 and the discussion of risk management in Chapter 4), it is not surprising that many agencies there have boasted ex-US marines, police and secret service personnel on their staffs. But such services are homegrown as well, as the *Guardian* reported in 1972 (13 July), when a firm set up by ex-RAF security officers identified the shop stewards involved in the 1972 London docks strike.

Perhaps such fringe operations would be marginally less disturbing if the people involved in them did not seem to have such evident crossover connections with the world of state law enforcement and security, connections which in practice begin to 'interweave' (Marx, 1987). It may also be that such connections make article titles like 'Nuclear attack – there's a job for private security' (Evans, 1980) less far-fetched, the idea being that in the event of nuclear attack private security could be a valuable disciplined force to aid in civil defence organisation, especially in and on behalf of industry. Whilst a rather gloomy scenario, this is not an entirely fanciful one and indicates the kind of serious roles that some commentators feel private security could fill.

These points cannot be dismissed as if they had relevance only to some exceptional or possible reality. Private security already – and indeed for a long time – has been of serious relevance to those grand issues which exercise minds normally dismissive of the agitation of the civil liberties lobbies. One recent example is the case of the plans of the 1983 Conservative government for the privatisation of the ordnance factories and, initially with them, the arrangements for security at the plants. The withdrawal of the Ministry of Defence police and their replacement with a private security firm slowly became a proposal which alarmed the House of Commons Defence Select Committee. 'While nobody is going to steal a Challenger tank,' they argued, 'the [Royal Ordnance] range of arms, explosives and ammunition offers immense attractions to terrorist or extremist organisations' (*Evening Standard*, 26 July 1984: 1–2). According to the *Evening Standard*, 'the committee took "some very scathing evidence" about the private security industry and doubted the government's wisdom in including Ministry of Defence police in spending cuts if they were to continue effectively guarding weapons factories.' It should not, of course, be taken that effective licensing and regulation should ever be assumed to be a mechanism for 'improving' private security so that it could take over such roles. The important point here is that privatisation of an important military police function was confidently proposed by the government, which had informally, but none the less actively, considered tenders from various companies.

No doubt in this case the *bona fides* of the wholly British-owned company expected to get the contract had been well checked. But such assurances about the ownership and respectability of a company are an index of another serious consideration about control over private security, one which has already attracted some attention in Canada. In a report on contract security in Ontario, prepared for the Office of the Solicitor General of Canada, Shearing et al. (1980) observe that private security clearly raises very important questions about the administration of justice in terms of whether it is being defined and maintained fairly and equally or whether, in certain circumstances, the conflict of interests between corporations and government, and the resources that they control, means that justice can be skewed in the interests of the corporately blessed few. Of further importance, however, as they go on to argue, is that:

> This issue of private versus public interest takes on a new complexion . . . when the multi-national corporation as a provider or consumer of security services is introduced into the picture. With this development, the issue is no longer simply one of the public versus private interest, but of the possible conflicts between different national interests and the interests of the multi-national corporations that straddle continents and nations. (Friedenberg, 1975). (Shearing et al., 1980: 72)

Nationally and internationally, private security has grown to provide in-house services for commerce and industry as well as being stimulated by the international expansion of 'mass private property' which is open to the public although owned by corporate enterprise (shopping complexes are the prime example) (Shearing and Stenning, 1983). As Cohen (1985: 136) observes, with such expansion has come the shifting of a 'degree of sovereignty from state to capital, which is an authority far less subject to regulation and scrutiny'. If this is true in a national context, it is even more so on the international stage.

As yet, the case for the regulation of private security in Britain has not taken on board the issue of private security operations being allied to the 'sovereign states' of international corporations, rather than being accountable to homegrown authorities. But it seems unlikely that the matter will not have future importance. What *is* currently understood is that certain elements of the private security sector in Britain inhabit very murky waters with regard to identifying what they do – let alone to whom they feel accountable.

Who pays wins

In a Parliamentary Question (written: 1 August 1978) to the Secretary of State for Foreign and Commonwealth Affairs, Bruce George, MP, asked for a list of those private security companies hired by the department in the past five years, details of their responsibilities, the expenditure on them and the criteria for choosing companies for hire.

The details of the Written Reply are now outdated though, along with questions to and replies from other government departments, they did confirm widespread use of private security companies by virtually all departments. This remains the case, perhaps with some expansion of the heavy use of private security by government departments in Northern Ireland (George, 1984). What was of special interest about the brief reply from the Foreign and Commonwealth Office was its even briefer note on the employment of private security agencies abroad: 'Abroad, guards have been obtained through one private firm (KMS Limited) to protect Ambassadors at a very few particularly exposed posts.'

It is perhaps no surprise that KMS should be favoured by the Foreign and Commonwealth Office. Many of its requirements in different parts of the world call for highly trained security staff with a working familiarity with use of arms and with terrorism, insurgency, counter-insurgency and so on. KMS undoubtedly has considerable expertise in these fields (Campbell, 1978b). The only element of surprise should perhaps be around the fact that, as with the rest of the private security sector, there is no degree of control – other than contractual – over this specialised 'top-end' of the private security market.

According to one report (Campbell, 1978b: 7), KMS is an 'undercover mercenary recruiting organisation' with strong links with past and present members of the Special Air Service (SAS) engaged in 'a private army service, supplying bodyguards, troops and invasion parties to despotic rulers and other wealthy interests'. The arrangement between the Foreign Office and KMS was apparently described as 'a "normally budgeted" arrangement for a specialist British company to send visiting teams to a small handful of embassies to train locally-based staff in security practices' (Campbell, 1978b: 11). But, nearly ten years later, as the *London Daily News* (6 March 1987) reported in the wake of the 'Irangate' Tower report, 'KMS is no ordinary security company' (Davies and Edwards, 1987: 18). In the Irangate investigations, the company was shown by 'secret White House documents' to be 'involved at the highest levels in trying to land US contracts to give military training to the Nicaraguan Contras' (Rusbridger, 1987a) and, according to other evidence before the Congressional hearings, 'had a contract . . . to supply air crews to fly . . . arms to Nicaragua' (Rusbridger, 1987b). Unsurprisingly, such revelations led to questions being put to the Prime Minister in the House of Commons (which received evasive answers) and to representations to the Foreign Secretary from the Nicaraguan Ambassador in London (Davies, 1987).

Whilst involved in other clandestine mercenary operations around the world – at various times in Afghanistan, the Middle East, Africa and Asia as well as South America – often with the sponsorship, direct or indirect, of the Foreign Office (Davies and Edwards, 1987: 18), the company operates, recruits and trains in the UK, keeping its finances in Jersey and cultivating its contacts in Whitehall. The case of KMS also illustrates the specialisation and diversification that can occur in the private security sector. KMS was originally set up as a subsidiary company of another 'top-market' company, Control Risks, which specialises in kidnap insurance and negotiations. According to a Control Risks source, 'KMS was set up predominantly to handle Government work' (Davies and Edwards, 1987: 31). Directors of KMS also sit on the board of Saladin Security, headed by a former senior police officer in charge of the Special Branch, Rollo Watts (Davies and Edwards, 1987: 31).

The KMS story involves mercenary assignments with implications for diplomatic relations, close links with government departments and the interlocking of different private security companies and personnel (including ex-senior police officers with the contacts established in their years of service). Scrutiny of an area such as this would undoubtedly be unpalatable to the Home Office, but that does not diminish the case for its desirability, especially when other private security companies (with National Front connections) have been linked with the recruitment of mercenaries to work in either the Philippines or southern Africa (*Searchlight*, 1987: 3–4).

Given the nature of the activities of KMS, and other agencies involved in the recruitment of mercenaries, it is doubtful that any system of licensing and regulation could control them without very strong powers and the ability to enforce them. But such powers are necessary for, quite apart from the immorality of mercenary work abroad, there is little to prevent such agencies offering their various services in the UK. And, indeed, some agencies do specialise in offering 'elite' bodyguard and protection services in the UK. Regulation and a system of accountability must therefore take very seriously the range of activities in the private security sector as the following two sections also illustrate.

Bodyguards and minders

The spate of kidnappings in the late 1970s, which targeted senior business executives and wealthy families, led to a spurt of growth in the bodyguard business. At the prestige end of this market, the expensive services of such companies have partly been sold on the basis of drawing on the expertise and contacts of personnel who in the past have been senior police or intelligence officers, as in the case of Saladin Security. Many of Saladin's recruits are ex-SAS or Royal Marine commandos and their previous experience and training raises important questions about some security company's ambiguous relationship with firearms and the authority their personnel assume. Ex-Commander Rollo Watts, formerly head of the Special Branch and now with Saladin, naturally emphasises that what he calls 'protection officers' must remember that their activities are limited by the law. However, as one report (*Now Magazine*, 1979: 23) has pointed out, 'this comes hard to some of his recruits, many of whom have served in Ulster, where the army can stop suspects and search them and their cars. Although they may now be doing similar jobs they no longer have those extra-legal powers.'

The use of firearms is legally proscribed but, according to several informants, is certainly informally condoned at this end of the market. As far as can be ascertained, no bodyguard agency in Britain has personnel licensed to carry guns whilst operating in this country. Police guards for foreign statesmen may be armed and, by arrangement with the Home Office, personal guards may also be authorised. Some private figures who may be at risk may be granted firearms certificates to carry a gun for their own protection. However, many agencies operate abroad with armed personnel who move around the company internationally. Even the 'ordinary' guarding companies (such as Securicor) arm their staff abroad, and many senior personnel are trained in arms use. Like many of the specialist agencies, Saladin send their personnel abroad on assignments and it is acknowledged that on such occasions they will be armed, often with a mixture of weapons (*Now Magazine*, 1979: 23). It must be presumed that there are at least some occasions where the laws of other countries are therefore breached unless in all cases firearms permits are obtained for every country where such agencies may operate.

Agencies like Saladin are also prepared to act as initial consultants on a security 'problem' and carry through their service to the provision of guards, security systems and a 'security plan' to minimise risk. Other specialists, such as Zeus Security (previously run by Peter Hamilton, one of the major security theorists in the UK; see Hamilton, 1967, 1968, 1972, 1974) act as advisors both to potential targets and to other companies offering protection services. In the past, the Cititel offshoot of Consolidated Safeguards has also offered advice on vetting, industrial counter-espionage and building security to protect against bombs, sabotage and so on (*Now Magazine*, 1979: 25). The activities of these – and other agencies like them – at the specialised elite end of the market are all but invisible. The task of an adequate licensing and regulatory authority would be to bring them under public scrutiny and control.

Down-market: strong-arm security

Unfortunately, I do not have space here to cover a wide range of examples of dubious down-market practices. However, some mention should be made of the kinds of activities which can and do routinely involve violence. Some security firms happily undertake work involving the eviction of squatters. Over the years, numerous cases of this type of work have gained private security some notoriety in the media, although it is usually made clear that it tends to be the 'cowboy' type of agency that takes on such work. Less concern seems to have been demonstrated by the courts and the police, however, even though many such evictions probably contravene Section 6 of the Criminal Law Act 1967 which makes it an offence 'to use or threaten violence to secure entry into premises where another is present opposing your entry'. Somehow squatters seem exempt from the protection of the law, whilst private security, here as elsewhere, benefits from some purposefully turned 'blind eyes'.

The attitudes underpinning this kind of security work are neatly indicated by the office manager of Omega Security Services of north London, reported in *Time Out* in 1979 (16–22 February):

> This is just one of the little services we do for clients – it's just a job . . . We don't go in for crossing t's and dotting i's so long as we know where to send the bill . . . We're filling a vacuum in the security market. We're doing the sort of things Securicor wouldn't do – they're too establishment minded after all.

Evidently intrigued by the work of Omega Security, *Time Out* followed up their February report with a further one in March. This report highlighted how people with a perhaps dubious past can succeed in the security business without really trying. There is, after all, no test of integrity that needs to be passed. In Omega's case the head of the security guards was known as Barry Evans, an alias for Roger Gleaves, the former self-styled 'Bishop of Medway', 'who was jailed for four years in 1975 after a television documentary *Johnny Go Home*, claimed he corrupted young boys in hostels run by him'. Gleaves subsequently served less than half his sentence and has been attempting to prove his innocence.

The point with regard to the operations of a security firm is not whether or not Gleaves was innocent or guilty of what he was accused and convicted of. It is that there is no control over or means of officially checking on the *bona fides* of those who run and work for private security firms. It is arguable, of course, that the use of an alias should not in itself necessarily arouse concern. However, many clients and the general public might reasonably be alarmed about the ease with which someone with, for example, convictions for serious assault can establish a security firm, as has happened. Similarly disturbing are connections between the extreme right and private security agencies willing to accept assignments to intimidate (or worse) journalists (*Searchlight*, 1986: 3) and cases of others with a history of membership of far-right groups who offer bailiff and other security services such as 'instant response' teams, apparently including trained soldiers, to evict trespassers (*Searchlight*, 1985: 3). What should be of serious concern is that this issue is simply one small part of the consequences of the present absence of control over who can run a security firm and the services that it can offer.

Omega, for example, sent out standard solicitations for business offering to remove 'anti-social parasites' (that is, squatters) from property:

> Instead of wasting weeks or months in getting trespassers evicted, why not call us in to act on your behalf. We act strictly within the requirements of the Law (although we pay no attention to the 'rights' that are claimed but have no foundation in law) . . . we find that once our Repossession Officer and his staff, accompanied by the owner of the premises or his legal representative arrive at the house . . . then the people soon decide it would be more advantageous to them to reside elsewhere. (*Time Out*, 16–22 March 1979)

What is being sold here is not security but 'repossession' of property by use of threat and physical force. Perhaps such services *are* carried out within the (vague) letter of the law. But the approach and attitude of this and similar security firms is surely disturbing; and the conclusion must be that the (vague) letter of the law in this and other areas where security services are offered demands some amendment.

Of course, threat and physical force *are* resources in the world of security: not in the respectable, 'establishment-minded' world of Securicor, Group 4 and their like, but at the up-market end of the military-trained bodyguard and also at the down-market end of the gym-trained bouncer. The case of the death of Henry Bowles in November 1978 brought some attention to the frequent circumstances in which bouncers employed in bars and clubs use considerably more than what might be regarded in law as 'reasonable force' to evict people from premises.

After a firework was let off in a King's Cross pub, Bowles was pointed out to the bouncers as the person responsible. He was thrown out despite protestations. As *Time Out* reported, outside he was then 'kicked and punched unconscious. He died in hospital on 4th November, a fortnight later, without regaining consciousness' (*Time Out*, 8–14 December 1978). The subsequent court case at the Old Bailey found one of the pub's bouncers guilty of manslaughter and another guilty of common assault. The case did little to bring the casual employment of private strong-arm security under the scrutiny of the law, law-makers or public. It did establish that bouncers are entitled to use reasonable force in removing people from a place though, as the judge said in summing up, 'once the customer has been ejected, the licence to use reasonable force ceases because the object allowed for by the law has been attained.'

Subsequently, Bowles's brother, Matthew, started a campaign, CURB, to draw attention to a variety of cases where bouncers had been responsible for carrying out serious assaults, some of which (in Scotland, Liverpool, St Helens and London in 1978 alone) led to deaths. CURB sought to introduce some form of licensing or registration for bouncers as part of, or alongside, proposals from Bruce George, MP (and others) for regulation of a broad range of security-related occupations.[2] However, even without association with this broader campaign, Matthew Bowles had two particularly sound points to make. First, he had lost a brother as a result of wholly unnecessary violence; secondly, as he pointed out to the BBC's *Tonight* programme (12 March 1979), if his wife who worked as a child-minder had to be registered he felt there was undoubtedly a case to be made for some similar scrutiny of those who could be employed as bouncers. However, bouncers, like bodyguards, specialist agencies, the disreputable and the respectable 'establishment-minded' companies, did not become, and are not now, a source of official concern. Despite the range of activities across the breadth of the private security sector and the serious issues these raise, lack of control, accountability or even scrutiny is not a popular item on the agenda at the Home Office.[3]

Insider crimes and fraudulent practices

> All we are saying here is that the constraints of the rule of law, while accepted by the security industry, do not have the same inexorable and sometimes ironic centrality to its activity as in the case of the police. Hence, there is at least a greater potential for those constraints to be set aside in the course of activities based on entrepreneurial enterprise. (Carson and Young, 1976: 48)

The conventional view of private security is that its activities are related to the protection of property and the prevention of crime. However, such significance can be double-edged, for clearly – to any but the naive or wilfully blinkered – such tasks can give rise to a series of circumstances and contradictions conducive to their possible corruption. In this section I can only give some selected examples of the consequences of petty and substantial corruption of trust and ethics in the private security business (but see South, 1983). It is admittedly unlikely that licensing and regulation alone would eradicate all these problems. But, on the other hand, a wholly unregulated private security sector is certainly inviting abuse. Private security agencies and personnel are in fairly unique positions. They are, after all, invited by others to watch over their property, personnel, families, private information and premises. As the most desirable 'insiders' imaginable in the perpetration of a neat crime, 'the protectors' themselves are prime targets for corruption. This would seem to be a source of concern across a fair range of opinion. As Kerr (1979a: 123), writing for *Police Review*, observed, while the:

> apparently inadequate set of safeguards has proved pretty effective so far . . . there are [firms] who have no declared allegiance to any code of ethics or practice. In 1974, Sir Douglas Osmond, then Chief Constable of Hampshire, speaking at a fire and security conference said: 'Some three years ago, in one police region alone, no less than 69 persons with criminal records were identified as working as patrol guards'.

In 1982, the *Daily Mirror* (1982: 6) reiterated its concern (shared at various times by the press of all political shades)[4] that 'crooks are setting up their own security companies to help them pull off robberies from the inside – and possibly to make industrial espionage easier.' The same report expressed the concern of Derek Hunter, Regional Officer of the (then) General and Municipal Workers Union, who stated that 'we know of men who walk out of an employment exchange in the morning and are on duty in security guard uniform in the evening.' It seems reasonable to assume here that the union was not objecting to people finding a job within a day but rather to the impossibility of employers checking references or providing adequate training or briefing within a day. Both the union and the independent Low Pay Unit have called for the government to introduce an effective licensing system (*Daily Mirror*, 1982: 6; Williams et al., 1984).

The concern of the Low Pay Unit is, and has been for some years, the low levels of pay in private security, partly reflecting a suspicion that very low pay for a job giving access to other people's property can lead to temptation. Even the supposed 'rotten apples' who provoke this unifying moral horror seem to agree with such a proposition: 'One guard asked to be taken off a cash run because he had a conviction and had been jailed for robbing a security vehicle' added Mr Hunter (*Daily Mirror*, 1982: 6).

Some of these issues are also recognised by various representatives of the private security sector. However, such recognition is usually to be found in the arguments that they have continued to put forward in campaigning for exemption from the provisions of the Rehabilitation of Offenders Act 1974 concerning the law against disclosure of certain past criminal offences. While maintaining agreement with the fair and laudable principles of the Act, aspects of the argument for exemption maintain that it is unfair and a misjudgement to allow ex-offenders to be employed in the private security sector: unfair to customers and unfair to ex-offenders faced with the temptation.

At a potentially more costly level of the 'insider problem' – the easing of industrial espionage mentioned in the *Daily Mirror* report – the private security sector is less concerned with such charitable understanding and more with the weakness of available legal recourse. The British Corruption Act 1906 provides one of the very few legal bases for attempting to secure prosecution against in-house industrial espionage. Insider industrial espionage perpetrated by an employee is usually untouchable as trespass and if information is copied rather than being stolen in the form of tangible documentation, then there is no crime of theft. However, 'if the company can show that the source of the leak was a bribed employee . . . the British Corruption Act 1906 provides for a maximum penalty of £500 fine and/or imprisonment for two years' (Draper, 1978: 112). Trespass or breach of contract remain the principal grounds for legal prosecution in cases of industrial spying, though prosecutions have been brought employing the breadth of conspiracy law, successfully as 'conspiracy to obtain confidential information by corrupt and other unlawful means' and unsuccessfully as 'conspiracy to defraud' (Draper, 1978: 112).

It is undeniably the case that forms of criminal infiltration and corruption are well evidenced in various areas of the private security sector, and fairly liberally sprinkled throughout even its more creditable and reputable representatives. As it is principally these reputable representatives that seek official support for the principle of self-regulation, it is not surprising that their vantage point leads them to attempt to preserve a case for the integrity of the 'profession' of security. The result is reliance on the old 'rotten apple' theory. This is the explanation invariably put forward in most conventional discussions of police corruption, and is indeed best summed up in the report of the Knapp Commission (1972) on police corruption in New York: 'According to this theory . . . any policeman found to be corrupt must promptly be denounced as a rotten apple in an otherwise clean barrel. It must never be admitted that his otherwise individual corruption may be symptomatic of an underlying disease.' Given the peculiar and anomalous sense in which private security/investigator work can be one of the 'fiddle-prone' (Mars, 1982: 136–59) occupations *par excellence* (especially given the almost universal levels of low pay and low standards of qualification, training and incentive), then the confinement of criminal activity to the single individual who realises that he or she is 'on to a good way of making a bit (or lot) extra' seems a doubtful proposition. The general acceptance of the 'rotten apple' theory, however, functions in a not dissimilar way for the private security sector as for the police, as an attempt to preserve the public image of the private security sector as a whole.

Competition, cutting corners and sharp practice

The private security sector is heavily competitive. However, there is not the space here to consider the consequences of this across the full range of its activities; instead, I can only offer examples of deception and cost-cutting within the largest and most visible area of private security, that of provision of guarding services.

Few business concerns are interested in personally involving their own management in the supervision of safety of their premises and property outside normal working hours and are content to leave such matters to the police and private security. Hence, opportunities for short-service are numerous and are fully exploited by some companies. Some customers will pay for all-night guards who leave the premises as soon as they are deserted and return shortly before work commences the following day. Visiting patrol services often have such long lists of calls that they are physically impossible to fulfil. On one occasion, one of the directors of a firm interviewed in the course of this research had a case of a guard from a competing company offering a job to one of his staff, saying 'you come on at six, you go home at eight, and you get paid for four hours'; the contract to the company was actually for eight hours' guarding. Obviously, such arrangements increase profits for the company, keep wages low, and enable cut-rate charges to be offered to the clients employing the company, clearly an asset in undercutting private security agencies that genuinely try to fulfil the terms and obligations of their contracts.

The prevalence of cost-cutting practices is substantially dependent on, and partially the reason for, the employment in private security of an abnormally high proportion of part-time and casual staff. Moonlighting from another job or taking on this kind of part-time work while formally unemployed are common in private security and employers knowingly exploit this. Unrecorded work and unrecorded payment are familiar in certain areas of the private security business and, obviously for the firms themselves, employing staff on this basis produces considerable savings of outlay on insurance, pension contributions and other expenses, allowing a lower tax-free rate of pay and lower charges in the undercutting of competition.

In these sections I have only had the space to cover some of the areas of petty and serious malpractice. However, if there is any validity in applying the 'tip of the iceberg' metaphor to private security then the little that is known about 'insider crime' and fraudulent practice throughout the private security sector can be seen to offer substantial further evidence of the need for some form of regulation and scrutiny.

Intruding on privacy

In discussing the history of the concept of privacy, Shank (1986: 9) observes that despite the momentous nature of past social movements and conflicts with individual rights at their core, 'the right to privacy was not generally one [of these rights], except as might be inferred from the manner in which the other rights were to be protected.' Today, an individual's right to privacy is still a fragile thing and indeed, among Western democratic societies, Britain has consistently been one of the most grossly negligent in promoting the legal protection of individuals with regard to the personal information that can be gathered about them and the use to which such information may be put.

This state of affairs has been of strong concern to a variety of interests for many years, but government action from any political party has been minimal. The two most significant recent developments are the passage of the Data Protection Act 1984 and the Interception of Communications Act 1985. The former sought to bring Britain into line with the terms of the European Convention on Data Protection, but in practice the safeguards are limited and the powers of the office of the Data Protection Registrar seriously inadequate. Private companies can be taken to court and severe penalties imposed, but the largest and most powerful data user in the country – the government – is exempt from prosecution under the Act (Sullivan and Warren, 1987: 1). In the private sector, of course, prosecutions can only be brought where it is known that an offence has been committed, and as there is no effective monitoring or inspection of the private data being collected any serious regulatory role cannot be fulfilled. Dangers remain, for example, of private companies seeking and obtaining private information gathered and held by the state (Sullivan and Warren, 1987: 1).

The lack of effective controls over telephone tapping was made notoriously clear in the Malone court case of 1978. Here the judge was moved to comment that not only were there no *effective* controls over police telephone tapping (because with a warrant from the Home Secretary the police can tap telephones perfectly legally) but that also there were no effective sanctions against the private individual tapping telephones. In this regard Britain failed to meet the requirements of the European Human Rights Convention on the right of the individual to privacy. It is most likely that it is this criticism – made by many – rather than profound commitment to the principle of a right to privacy, that led to the Interception of Communications Act 1985. This Act was in large part the result of pressure from Labour and Alliance peers to add amendments on this issue to the 1985 Telecommunications Bill. However, the provisions of the Act are limited and while some specific rules and procedures have now been legislatively formulated the gesture still seems a rather cosmetic one.

The Act makes an *interception* of *specified* communications an offence unless a warrant has been issued by the Secretary of State. The Act does not cover what the Home Secretary at the time called 'surveillance', which would include use of electronic bugging devices. The distinction being made here is between 'unlawfully intercepting communications in the course of their passage through the post or public telecommunication system' (Hilliard, 1985: 577) and surveillance techniques and equipment which might enable the overhearing of a telephone conversation but which are not (for some reason) covered by the new offence of interception (Hilliard, 1985: 577). So, whilst it would seem that the latter practice remains legal (unless, as with some devices, it involves 'stealing' electricity from the telephone company), the Act does therefore make it illegal for a private individual, such as a private detective, to intercept a communication covered by the Act if no warrant has been issued by the Secretary of State. The Act makes no specification about who may be authorised to intercept communications or to whom any intercepted material or information may be passed. However, section 2 (2) of the Act does stipulate that 'The Secretary of State shall not issue a warrant under this section unless he considers that the warrant is necessary – (a) in the interests of national security; (b) for the purpose of preventing or detecting serious crime; or (c) for the purpose of safeguarding the economic well-being of the United Kingdom' (p. 2). As it would seem unlikely that a private detective or security agency would be granted a warrant in any of these circumstances then, in this respect, some controlling legislation over telephone tapping by private individuals is now in force. But the failure of the Act to cover electronic surveillance is a serious omission.

The government argues that the UK now complies with the relevant requirements of the European Convention on Human Rights but with the disturbing loopholes that remain this may be questionable. It should be noted, of course, that the illegal nature of an act is, in itself, no bar to its practice, as was evident in one recent Old Bailey trial where a private detective bugging the telephones of Seychelles political exiles in London claimed that 'the Foreign Office was aware of his unlawful surveillance' (Bailey and Leigh, 1987). Given that the area of telephone tapping and electronic surveillance is one in which the overlap of public and private security agencies is not unfamiliar, then the effective application of the 1985 Act may encounter some difficulties not readily acknowledged. As *The Sunday Times* (10 February 1980) reported on its front page:

> Army officers in Ulster, frustrated by official restrictions placed on telephone tapping, have been buying their own personal tapping equipment so that they can carry on their activities unhindered by the law. A *Sunday Times* investigation shows that the officers are among a rapidly expanding number of clients using private security firms to tap telephones. Other targets for private tapping have included – political activists in a key constituency; employees suspected by their employers of theft.

Given such established practices, the test of the effectiveness of the Act (and the Tribunal it establishes) will lie in the rigour with which it is enforced.

Powers of detention

In 1983 an *Observer* (27 March 1983: 3) report, 'Anger at Securicor guard on migrants', noted that 'the use of Securicor . . . to guard and escort immigrants is being examined by the Commission for Racial Equality.' Before and since then a number of MPs and civil rights and immigrant welfare organisations have expressed concern over the contract that Securicor holds from the Home Office to guard suspected illegal immigrants at Heathrow (Harmondsworth) and Gatwick, and escort them as they are moved about for detention and questioning.

The legal position occupied by Securicor here certainly needs to be clarified. In the *Observer* story, 'the National Council for Civil Liberties, pointed out that Securicor's legal position was curious. "They have only the power of an ordinary citizen making an arrest." ' Physical force can only be used for self-protection according to the relevant Home Office rules covering Securicor's work on this contract. This makes it difficult to understand how Securicor can detain those who are unwilling to submit to detention. This is not a problem of powers available at most other ports of transit in Britain where, at least in the past, official policing bodies have generally been responsible for performing such duties. It is odd then that the Home Office justifies the use of Securicor on the grounds that they 'considered that the use of police to control people who were not criminals would be too oppressive and because it was felt that immigration officers, who are civil servants, could not be asked to perform such tasks' (*Observer*, 27 March 1983: 3).

The real point of the story, however, is that it is not new. It quickly blew over as it has done many times in the past. In 1970 (28 August) *Police Review* carried a report attempting to clarify where the Home Secretary (then Reginald Maudling) derived his authority for employing Securicor at Heathrow and other airports. A Home Office representative was, at that time, apparently only able to quote section 13 of the Commonwealth Immigrants Act 1962 as authority: 'Any person required or authorised to be detained under this Act may be detained in such places as the Secretary of State may direct.' However, as *Police Review* commented, 'whether Parliament ever intended to permit "private gaols" is unlikely because nowhere in the Act does it confer powers of detention on anyone other than an immigration officer or a constable.'

However, in the summer of 1973 the Protection of Aircraft Act was introduced to comply with the provisions of the international Montreal Convention on hijacking and aircraft safety (Bunyan, 1976: 244). The Act was passed, with minimal consultation with interested parties, by both Houses without a division. As in other cases concerning the anomalous nature of private security, the unconsulted opposition to certain provisions of the Act were a strange alliance. NCCL and several Labour MPs spoke out and so too did Reg Gale, Chairman of the Police Federation, objecting to the powers extended by the Act to private security to search and detain airline passengers and ultimately, some feared, to bear arms. Under the Act the Secretary of State can require airport management to provide sufficient and adequate personnel for searches of site, aircraft and persons. Such personnel need not be police officers and under a (deliberately?) general description in the Directive private security can clearly be used. The Act now provides a firmer legal basis for the state's commercial compromise in the employment of private security staff in roles fulfilling public security and public immigration service functions at airports. As the *Daily Telegraph* (October 1977) noted, the work that Securicor undertakes 'for' the Immigration Service comes out of the budget allocated to that public service.

Such questions as those raised in 1983 about this private immigration service have therefore been around for some time – and they have certainly not gone away. Recent developments suggest that the privatisation of detention services are a reality on the current political agenda. The Home Office presently has contracts with four private security companies to provide detention and escort services under the authority of the Immigration Service. The relevant legislation now cited is the Immigration Act of 1971 (Williams et al., 1984: 42). It is not apparently known how much the contracts are worth or how many private security staff are employed in such roles (*Labour Weekly*, 1986: 7). The running of the detention centres has been of some concern to prison welfare organisations, such as the Prison Reform Trust who point out that facilities such as Securicor's Harmondsworth centre have no Board of Visitors and have received no visits from the Prison Inspectorate. Estimates suggest that this service costs three times as much as it would if carried out by the prison service, yet MPs seeking information on costs and other matters are told that it cannot be made available for reasons of commercial confidentiality (Hyder, 1987: 8).

A more recent development, the use in 1987 of a converted passenger ferry as a floating detention centre, attracted considerable attention. The ferry was moored at Harwich and again staffed by Securicor (who were responsible to a Chief Immigration Officer). Up to 80 detainees refused entry to Britain, many of them political refugees, could be accommodated on the ship at any one time. Although the ferry is no longer in use (having broken loose from its moorings after a night of heavy storms), a precedent has been set and if continually tightening immigration restrictions put pressure on the private detention facilities attached to the airports it is probable that a similar operation may be undertaken again (Campbell, 1987; Nelson, 1987: 7; *Policing London*, 1987: 30).

Whether an experimental idea or the basis for future policy, such a precedent reflects the thinking of other influential sources of opinion on the future privatisation of prison facilities. The recommendations of a 1987 House of Commons Home Affairs Select Committee Report (1987a) included the suggestion that the government consider privatising some prison services by contracting them out. The Home Office rationale for considering such a possibility is to see 'whether, by using the private sector and its techniques more intensively, we can accelerate the provision of prison places and thus ease, as rapidly as possible, the overcrowding with which we are concerned' (*Police Review*, 1987: 968). Contracts would be issued to private firms such as Securicor which, as described already, has a close relationship with the Home Office, 'to build, refurbish and manage prisons on behalf of the State' (*Police Review*, 1987: 968). Concerns raised by the Prison Officers Association that such an arrangement would require private security staff to have more coercive power than they should be entitled to were dismissed by the Chair of the Home Affairs Select Committee, Mr John Wheeler, MP. According to Mr Wheeler, the private security staff would be civilians and would not need the powers currently at the disposal of prison officers. 'Architectural design' and the avoidance of confrontation would be the means by which control was exerted. This may be a humane or naively optimistic vision, but it is also possible that Mr Wheeler's enthusiasm for the Committee's recommendation is influenced a little by his roles as Director General of the British Security Industry Association and as a director of the National Council for Intruder Alarms (*Guardian*, 1987).

Certainly the interest that the Home Office has displayed in developments in the United States has been strong. There, the best customer of one of the major 'prisons for profit' companies, the

Corrections Corporation of America, is the Immigration and Naturalisation Service. In response to 'the influx of illegal aliens from Caribbean and Central American countries who have filled the agency's detention centres, the INS has turned to the private sector . . . to build and operate facilities for the agency' (Borna, 1986: 325–6; see also Weiss, 1987). Several private security organisations have quickly sought to diversify into this new area. For example, Borna (1986: 326) notes that 'Buckingham Security Ltd [of Pennsylvania] . . . is attempting to make a niche for itself in such "special services" as protective custody, older prisoners, female prisoners, and the emotionally disturbed and physically handicapped.' Other private security operators, including the nation's largest, Wackenhut, are also actively interested in the construction and management of medium-security facilities (Adam Smith Institute, 1984: 64).

The 1984 report of the Adam Smith Institute, which examined a variety of aspects of the criminal justice system, unsurprisingly supported the idea of privatising prisons and similar institutions by contracting out. What was at least commendable about their observations on the subject was that they did raise the issue of the monitoring of standards. Implementation of such proposals would, they suggest, 'require government (or independent) monitoring to ensure that agreed standards are kept to, *but this would not be difficult* (Adam Smith Institute, 1984: 66, emphasis added). The problem with this happy optimism is that it is unrealistic. To monitor and regulate such new regimes effectively *would* be difficult – and expensive. At the very least new resources would be required to facilitate any accommodations that Boards of Visitors and the Prison Inspectorate had to make to the new system. But serious cost-effective implementation and running of the system would require an equally serious commitment to evaluation. More importantly, such a profound shifting of what are traditionally seen as the responsibilities of the state to the private sector must surely demand the establishment of mechanisms of accountability, regulation and appeal for prisoners. Legislation that might be developed now to ensure the accountability and regulation of the private security sector could be a basis for subsequent extension to the reality of 'prisons for profit'.

Private security and the police: links and networks

The crossover of roles and blurring of boundaries are also acutely evident when we consider the nature of the professional and personal networks that exist linking the public and private services.[5] The euphemism of the 'old-boy network' is a common and cosy metaphorical way of side-stepping issues that can often touch upon the corrupt abuse of personal position and privilege. Of direct concern here is the passage of information between private and official channels of information: the unchecked 'cooperation' between private and public sector from local private security agencies feeding 'observations' and 'hearsay' to the police at local collator level, through checks run through police criminal records as favours to ex-police officers now in the private security sector, to other outcomes of the familiar pattern of crossover employment from the police and military to private security. All of this constitutes a significant system of violation of the security of personal and official information. The existence of such informal networks also underlines the like-minded worldview shared by police, military and private security personnel. The up-market end of the private security sector, dealing in commercial intelligence and industrial espionage, also makes use of the advantages of crossover employment and old contacts, and in many cases has some considerable disregard for either the ethics of the profession or the laws of the land, or both.

The link between private security and the police at local collator level is of obvious mutual and reciprocal advantage where the police can help out with the vetting of prospective employees, and anyone else of interest, in return for the security companies' own local information gathering. Obviously, such arrangements largely depend upon the willingness of the police to cooperate and indeed it would appear that they rarely cooperate with very small, inefficient or particularly dubious agencies. Despite the fact that a small firm need not necessarily be justifiably regarded as dubious, nevertheless it could be denied this sort of cooperation, which simply means that in many cases (for there are many small firms) the claimed vetting procedures for hiring staff are either ineffective or non-existent. In the 'big league', however, as long ago as March 1971, J. Philip-Sorenson, Managing Director of Group 4, acknowledged to *The Times* that 'there is no doubt that there is an old-boy network which helps us to discover whether a man has a criminal record.'

Such crossover connections are, of course, by no means unique to Britain. The same phenomenon is clearly evident in Canada and the United States and almost certainly in every other country where the private security sector has developed. In one recent Canadian survey, for example, nearly half (48.1 percent) of the police respondent sample 'indicated that in their experience there was informal cooperation between police officers and security personnel "which is facilitated by personal acquaintance or contact, rather than by department policy or procedure"' (Shearing et al., 1985a: 145). Such cooperation primarily involves the passage of information between contacts, usually from the police to private security personnel (Shearing et al., 1985a: 145). As is the case in the UK, this process is explained by some as resulting from the senior positions of so many former police officers in private security organisations. This employment crossover is clearly commercially extremely useful; indeed, some respondents in a related survey of clients of private security – security managers and corporate executives (Shearing et al., 1985a: 146; 1985c) – suggested that without such access to information from the police, private security agencies could not hope to work effectively or even remain in business.

Not altogether surprisingly, such relationships and their nature are usually denied by the police, for obviously they are extremely sensitive and difficult to verify (Shearing et al., 1985a: 146). Further, they are not necessarily easy relationships for former police officers with years of commitment to one particular model of policing to accommodate to. As Shearing et al. (1985c: 374) report, many security directors with previous extensive experience in the police service 'were not comfortable with a shift from retributive sanctions based on guilt to a system based on economic pragmatism'. As with unease about the mechanics of the private justice system which private security is a part of, so is it the case that, at least some, ex-police officers are uncomfortable about a situation which promotes breaches of confidence – and the law.

None the less, there is presumably some degree of 'economic pragmatism' involved in the decision of so many former police officers, particularly those who have served at a high rank, to take up a second career in private security. This drain of experience and expertise from the public sector represents a serious loss, not least in terms of the public money that will have been expended in developing the talents of a senior police officer (Stevens, 1987). But the attractions of a second career and good salary to supplement an index-linked pension are strong. When the press reported in 1987 that the retiring Commissioner of the Metropolitan Police, Sir Kenneth Newman, was to join the Control Risks security company, it was noted that directors of the firm already included General Sir Frank King, a former commander of the army in Northern Ireland and another former Police Commissioner, Sir Robert Mark (Penrose, 1987). As, apparently, only a year before Sir Kenneth had 'warned such companies' that they 'were operating "at the very frontiers"' of official tolerance' (Dobson, 1987: 31), the contemplation of such a move surprised many. One senior police officer, for example, pointed out the obvious potential conflict of loyalties that such an appointment would bring: 'Newman will face the inevitable dilemma of whether information should be handed to Scotland Yard or kept confidential within his new company' (Penrose, 1987). Such concerns are by no means new, yet there is no official recognition of them.

As Stenning and Shearing (1980a: 265) observe with regard to the Home Office Discussion Paper on private security (1979):

> No one who has any familiarity with the world of private security could take seriously the Paper's claim that what is involved in this regard is really no more than an 'occasional transgression' (para. 67) of confidentiality rules by the police, and on this issue the credibility of the Paper's authors is sorely strained. The fact that widespread practices of this kind are hard to prove – and security officials, being the kind of people they are, go to great lengths to ensure that they will be hard to prove – is no justification for ignoring their existence and the important implications for public policy to which they give rise.

Evidently, public policy and clear legislation *must* address the implications of this system of frequent transgression of confidentiality and abuse of privilege.

Notes

1 A number of debates and exchanges has recently developed around the emergence of a left 'New Realist school' in British criminology. One unfortunate consequence of this (among others) is the distortion of discourse, such that even the use of a word like 'realistic' somehow becomes emblematic. Here, I merely take a position which I see as realistic and hence actionable in policy and practice terms.

2 The difficulties with including bouncers and minders in such legislation are readily acknowledged. That does not mean that they should be simply left out of any calls for regulatory mechanisms. CURB drew up a code of practice which included guidelines for the running of night clubs and other places of entertainment covering, among other things, the employment of bouncers. Such guidelines would offer a starting point for raising standards. CURB unfortunately failed to secure funding for its work after the demise of the Greater London Council which had given support (interview with Bruce George, MP, November 1987).

3 I have discussed elsewhere some of the background reasons why successive governments may have been reluctant to redefine legislatively the commercial compromise that they have established with the private security sector (see South, 1984).

4 While the research reported here is not centrally concerned with media images of the private security sector, this was an early interest and in the initial stages of the research the cuttings libraries and back issues of leading daily and Sunday newspapers were searched and documentary and magazine reports collected or abstracted. I am grateful to Sue Harris for discussions on the differences in media reporting of private security versus the public police.

5 The following draws in part upon South (1983: 49).

7 Self-regulation in the Private Security Sector

The British Security Industry Association

The BSIA was formed in 1967 by eight of the major firms in private security. The idea was to create a body which could claim to be a representative voice for the industry, act as a pressure group and generate for private security an image of responsibility and integrity. To this end it sought to persuade the government and, in particular, the Home Office, to recognise the industry as a force to be treated seriously in the field of crime prevention (despite the fact that, as I have described, crime prevention is but one aspect of the business of private security). Today, the BSIA can reasonably claim that it plays 'a consultative role between Government and industry' (BSIA, 1987: 1).[1]

The Association makes much of the fact that it represents between 75 and 90 percent (the estimates have varied over the years) of the trade of the main areas of private security, by annual turnover. It is, however, difficult to obtain any certain figures to support such a claim given that it is virtually impossible to determine with any accuracy the number of medium to small-sized firms operating and which are not BSIA members. Indeed, the question of the Association's representativeness has recently been challenged further by the formation of a new body, SIMSSA, specifically seeking to attract those companies that are not members of the BSIA (*Security Times*, 1987: 58). SIMSSA (the Security Installers – Manufacturers – Suppliers – Services Association) is concerned about a situation in which they see the small independent firm as having no part or voice in the making of standards produced for the industry by bodies such as the BSIA. This is a clear criticism of the BSIA as representative of some of the large security companies but remote from the small ones.

The objectives of the BSIA, as laid out in their 1987 introductory brochure, are, of course, highly laudable. They aim to be able to assure 'all customers that a BSIA member company is synonymous with standards of excellence and reliability' (BSIA, 1987: 1). Members must satisfy the Association and its two Inspectorates that they are 'soundly managed', 'their directors and senior executives [are] of good repute', that they have 'adequate financial backing', integrity with regard to 'advertising and selling practices', are 'appropriately insured' and treat 'security information relating to clients . . . in the strictest confidence' (BSIA, 1987: 1).

Until very recently, with the appointment (in 1982) of staff to its Manned Services and Security Systems Inspectorates, the BSIA operated on a rather modest basis with just the Director General and administrative and secretarial support. It none the less put some considerable public relations effort into creating the impression that it was a well-resourced, sophisticated and formidable organisation. Over the years, however, it would seem that some of the insecurities displayed by the Association in its infancy have been outgrown. Today, with Home Office endorsement of the self-regulation model for private security in the UK (see Home Office, 1979), the credibility of the Association seems much enhanced – at least to those who are convinced of the effectiveness of this approach. It can therefore, and does, make much of its representation on the Home Office Standing Conference on Crime Prevention and several sub-committees. Representatives have also served on other (official and non-official) committees and working parties concerned with technical aspects of security and crime prevention. There is indeed, then, a considerable degree of liaison between the Home Office, the civil policing network and the private security industry, but this does not really warrant the BSIA's sense of self-importance nor support many of the claims that it makes for its effectiveness. As Bruce George, MP, has observed,

> The BSIA is essentially a professional body. The words of L.C.B. Gower (1984) in the *Review of Investor Protection* are relevant to its role, 'A professional body originally established to protect the interests of its members cannot readily convert itself into one which also protects the public against its members. Independent lay members on its governing body may help – but may merely be window dressing' (Command 9125, 1984). (George, 1984: 49)

According to the rules laid down by the BSIA, the criteria for membership are quite stringent. However, requirements relating to methods and periods of screening of employees and to training are essentially hollow as the Association still has no really effective means of checking the veracity of information supplied. Their small staff of inspectors cannot realistically claim to be able to cover all the numerous offices which a membership of companies claiming to represent 90 percent of private security industry business inevitably has, especially when spread all over the UK. The BSIA none the less remains confident of its ability to regulate its members and hence a large section of the industry. It is therefore seen by many within the industry as viewing the other principal representative body, the International Professional Security Association, as very much a poor relation – if any kin at all. The BSIA has, on the other hand, been strongly enthusiastic about the degree of dialogue it has established with the Home Office, especially on matters of training, licensing and safety, costing and efficiency standards.

At the same time, the BSIA has generally (and understandably) been quite uncomfortable about admissions by some senior figures in private security that the extent of use of channels of dialogue with the police includes gaining access to privileged information in, for example, the vetting of prospective employees. The BSIA grudgingly acknowledges that such practices may indeed be 'a fact of life', but as Director General John Wheeler, MP, added in a personal interview in 1978, 'we wish it could be otherwise and look forward to a time when proper . . . procedures will make some of the Criminal Records Office data available to us, in some form.' Giving such access to an unofficial body would raise many objections not least related to how account-ability and confidentiality could be assured and monitored. However, the most recent Home Office endorsement of the adequacy of BSIA vetting, from a Working Group on Commercial Robbery (part of the Standing Conference on Crime Prevention, 1986) effectively dispensed with this issue in one paragraph:

> 12.8 The Group also considered whether there is a need for any exemptions in the Rehabilitation of Offenders Act, 1974, in order that commercial cash carriers might probe more deeply into the background of new recruits. However, having noted the considerable periods which must elapse before a conviction becomes spent under the Act, and recognising that the absence of a criminal record is no guarantee of future behaviour, it has been concluded that the existing vetting undertaken by BSIA members is adequate without the need for changes to the Act. (Home Office, 1986: 27)

At the same time, the Working Group also acknowledged evidence submitted by MATSA suggesting that the fierce competition in the industry leads to some firms cutting corners in their selection and training procedures. Conceding that this point is 'clearly a very important one' which they did not have time to pursue, the Working Group 'recommended that a detailed study of this important area be undertaken' (Home Office, 1986: 27). This recommendation does not seem to have elicited any particularly energetic response from the Home Office.

The BSIA agrees that there are undoubtedly abuses within the security business and that some form of control and accountability is desirable. However, its position on such control is in line with the views of some members of the Home Office Working Group referred to (which included a BSIA representative) that higher standards are best achieved by persuading 'customers to use only those companies conforming to BSIA standards' (Home Office, 1986: 27). Not everyone associated with the industry is as sanguine about the prospects for success of such an approach. In particular, trade unions which have organised in the private security field have stressed the need for standards to be set by legislation.

Unionisation has slowly, but in the past decade more surely, begun to take a hold within the major security companies. As described earlier, MATSA has organised in several of the larger companies as has the Transport and General Workers Union, whilst MFS (the Manufacturing, Finance and Science union, formerly ASTMS) has also moved into the managerial grades of some companies. A number of firms have entered into closed-shop agreements which will, of course, be affected by any legislation designed to end such agreements. Any really fundamental attempt to break away from union represen-tation in these companies is, however, relatively unlikely given that the unions have shown themselves willing to accommodate to the particular structures and needs of the security companies. The unions none the less remain vocal in their support for measures which could lead to improved conditions for their members and hence would favour licensing and regulation where this could serve as a means to improve levels of pay, benefits, status and other conditions. Of course, it is not difficult for the BSIA to suggest that it already demands high standards or that it encourages a minimum wage on which to build. But at present there is little incentive for everyone in the industry (whether BSIA members or not) to meet high standards and the minimum wages that have been prevalent throughout the industry have indeed been the minimum.

Obviously, the key issue for the BSIA with regard to its status as legitimately – and powerfully – representative of private security companies is whether it can deliver an effective system of self-regulation or whether some form of public licensing and regulation should take over. In general, but with some inconsistency over time, the BSIA has been highly sceptical of various proposals for licensing measures, although until the late 1970s it was not wholly opposed to the idea (Williams et al., 1984: 8). One recurrent point of debate has been the problem of whether and how to renegotiate the provisions of the Rehabilitation of Offenders Act 1974. The opinion of the BSIA, some others in the industry and, no doubt, the Home Office is that amendments to the Act would take such a great amount of consideration and negotiation that the process is not worth initiating.

Probably the most substantial criticism that the BSIA has been able to level against the pro-licensing proposals has been that there would be problems with the extended bureaucracy which would be required; for any regulatory board is envisaged as being unlikely to have sufficient staff to justify in practice setting high standards for the granting of licences which it would then be unable to inspect and police. The contention here is that the inevitable outcome of this practical dilemma would be that the standards and requirements set by the board would tend to be low enough for just about all firms to fulfil them and gain their licence. This seems a slightly extreme caricature in so far as there would at least be legislatively embodied minimum standards and requirements to fulfil so some positive contribution would still emerge, even from such a bleak scenario (and the problem of having insufficient staff to monitor and ensure compliance is one that the BSIA itself faces). The criticism really highlights the BSIA's reservations about *any* form of statutory intervention which in some respects is surprising, for the market leaders would remain in their positions of dominance and respectability but with added government bestowed status, at least within this weak licensing vision. The fear then is probably of enforceable minimum standards being the 'thin end of the wedge'. At the same time, it must be acknowledged that the criticism – as addressed to such an under-resourced regulatory board – is not without foundation. For example, in the USA, Scott and McPherson's study of licensing in Minnesota found that:

> The licensing agent (the State Crime Bureau and Director of Public Safety) feels that present statutes, court interpretations and shortage of manpower for enforcement (one part-time crime bureau staff person has total responsibility for private police licensing and regulation) restricts its discretion in granting or denying a license and in regulating activity once a license is granted. Indeed the operative Attorney General opinion requires that every applicant fulfilling the minimum requirements must be granted a license. (1971: 274)

In the case of the UK it remains unclear whether any licensing and regulation arrangements would benefit most from local accountability and knowledge, although local authorities would lack expertise and could not ensure uniformity of procedures, or perhaps from some of the strengths to be obtained from centralised coordination and inspection. However, the possibility of the bureaucratic reduction of licensing requirements to the lowest common denominator of standards occurring is not a remote one.

It *can* be argued in fact that a licensing programme would require a flexibility of standards. Unreasonably restrictive legislation would obviously limit such flexibility as is necessitated by the very momentum of private security's expansion and development of new areas of work. The standards and operational potential, as well as the activities of companies and arenas of activity within the private security sector, are constantly being updated and changing in scope – albeit not always as its respectable representatives would hope.

The model of self-regulation is not adequate to deal with such development and change. Despite the assurances of the BSIA that it is improving as an effective watchdog and disciplinary body, it inevitably lacks the legal teeth which an *independent* adjudicating body created by statute would have in order to enforce its decisions. Neither the BSIA nor its new Inspectorates are independent bodies and they could not therefore legitimately be vested with such powers. Similar points have been acknowledged even by members of the BSIA's inner circle. For example, in 1975, Peter Smith, of the Securicor group and then chair of the BSIA policy committee, argued that professional bodies considering issues which might lead to the expulsion of a member must adhere to the consistent expectations of the courts that they would adhere to the rules of 'natural justice'. Hence, where potential future litigation might follow concerning, for example, claims for damages, the 'private disciplinary court' of such a professional body would have to: 'be prepared to bring to the sifting of evidence, and to the deciding of issues of fact and law, all the skills, procedural and otherwise, which a competent judicial body would be expected to have, and to make available the necessary time required. Plainly this will generally be impractical' (Smith, 1975: 382–3). The real impracticability, however, resides in the nature of the existing ineffectuality and partiality of self-regulation.

It should not be thought, however, that Smith was advocating an alternative system. Rather he eloquently argued the case against the need for increased regulation and monitoring. For example, a common concern raised by critics is that bogus security companies are frequently able to defraud customers buying their services in good faith. Smith argued that this presupposes a naivety on the part of business managers which is simply wrong. Successful businesses check the suppliers of their services through their bankers, the Company's registry and, especially in the case of security services, they will usually require evidence of insurance cover. This sounds rather more like an account of how Smith *wishes* employing companies would act, for it remains the case that there have been, still are and will doubtless continue to be security firms which defraud their clients, albeit to varying degrees and with varying degrees of impunity.

Most of the pro-licensing lobby also points to 'criminal infiltration' of otherwise respectable companies and argues that regulation with access to criminal records would allow for a thorough screening out of would-be 'infiltrators'. Smith's response is characteristically concerned with a sense of 'moral fibre', which the absence of a criminal record will still tell the security company nothing about: the likelihood of succumbing to temptation, 'likely sobriety, reliability as a time-keeper, amenability to discipline or general maturity and stability as an individual' (Smith, 1979: 29). According to the BSIA, it is as likely that an individual's record of previous employment for the past 20 years or back to school leaving will provide an indication of character and suitability for security employment. But the real stumbling block for even this reference only system remains the provisions of the Rehabilitation of Offenders Act 1974.

The central principle of the Act, as relevant here, allows for convictions for offences which have resulted in sentences of up to two and a half years imprisonment to be 'ignored' if the offender successfully stays out of further trouble for a specified period of time after the original conviction, determined according to a sliding scale. Such a 'spent' conviction can then be ignored by applicants and past employers for the purposes of giving references. For a variety of independent commentators and industry representatives, this has seemed an absurd situation. Smith (1979: 29) points out, for example, that in relation to a probation order the rehabilitation period can be just one year from the date of conviction or the date of the expiry of the probation order, whichever is the later. 'So it would appear', observes Smith (1979: 30), 'that an individual convicted of theft and put on probation for twelve months can apply for security employment the day after his probation order expires and can entirely conceal the fact of his conviction from a prospective employer.'

Whilst in the main the pro-licensing lobby – including in the past the National Council for Civil Liberties – has supported the exemption of private security from the working of the Act if this were accompanied by statutory registration and regulation, representatives of private security have principally called for exemption from the Act as another aid to putting their house in order without considering how they could ensure that such provision could be used effectively, fairly and with due regard for civil liberties and personal privacy throughout the private security sector. A number of other industries and professions are exempted from the Act, and at first sight it does seem reasonable therefore to argue that private security is as deserving of exemption – at least in relation to some offences – as the majority of the others. However, successive Home Secretaries have rejected or ignored calls for private security to be similarly treated as a special case. (I shall return to the role and position of the Home Office later in this chapter.)

The International Professional Security Association

Whereas the BSIA represents security organisations that favour self-controlled self-regulation, IPSA represents individual security professionals as well as companies and has generally taken a policy stance favouring some form of government licensing. Formed in 1958, the Association issues an Ethical Code of Conduct and aims to 'establish, promote and encourage the science and professional practice of industrial and commercial security'. Its membership is open to all employers of, or employees engaged in, private security work on a full-time basis. It has a wide membership which can include private investigators and others working in the private security world – even internationally with its status of overseas associates.

Uniquely, it has consistently addressed the issue of the need for training in private security in a positive way by offering courses and conferences aimed at basic, intermediate and advanced levels. These courses have been recognised in the past by various government-appointed training boards, a factor of importance in encouraging the take-up of basic training opportunities particularly because it meant that the costs could be reimbursed by the sponsoring company. Enthusiasm for the provision of basic training, however, should not go untempered by reservations about the course content of advanced and managerial training.

In 1968, IPSA established the Institute of Industrial Security (now the International Institute of Security). Membership of the Institute requires membership of IPSA for one year and then the achievement of a certain standard in an examination. This covers questions on crime prevention, fire prevention, alarm systems, powers of arrest and search, theft, trespass, evidence and procedure, reporting and industrial relations (Draper, 1978: 128). The Institute offers correspondence courses which are widely taken up and IPSA's outreach activities also include the arrangement of seminars for management in industry and commerce. It is, however, at the level of 'advanced training' that cause for caution about the promotion of 'advanced standards' in the private sector should arise for this again highlights the conflict between the undesirability of untrained security staff being involved in sensitive work and the equally undesirable scenario of highly efficient and sophisticated but non-accountable private security services being on offer to anyone who can afford to pay for them.

Other associations: locksmiths and alarms, private investigators

Changes in the lock-making industry throughout the post-war period have severely reduced the specialist craft section of the trade, and most locks today are mass-produced and then fitted by the private purchaser or by anyone advertising their services as a locksmith. Although Codes of Practice produced by the Master Locksmiths Association have been supported by the Office of Fair Trading and the police, the Association itself has argued in the past that these can be ineffective and slow mechanisms for redressing any malpractice. As with other branches of the private security sector, locksmiths are concerned about the uncontrollable growth of a potentially, if not actually, disreputable source of competition. In this case it is the growth of shoe 'heel bars' which also offer key-cutting services. These have undergone massive expansion in the past 20 years yet give only minimal training and obviously, in practice, require no authorising instructions to enable them to cut security keys. There are a number of true and apocryphal stories in the business about security keys for safes that have been cut at 'heel bars' and have subsequently jammed in the safe lock – certainly, a perverse contribution to crime prevention. Other common tricks and sources of complaint and concern include the retention of spare keys by 'cowboy outfits' who offer to fit household locks, incidentally failing to give advice about window locks and who, whilst fitting the locks, can be safely 'casing' the premises. Many major representatives of the locksmith industry have therefore been in favour of at least some form of licensing and regulation.

The National Supervisory Council for Intruder Alarms has over 100 member companies, the figure fluctuating with the growth of the industry and the offsetting of increases following amalgamations. The NSCIA was established by the BSIA, with a brief to oversee adherence to British Standards for alarm systems. Being an *installer* of alarms is the sole criterion for eligibility for membership, although acceptance follows some degree of scrutiny of the *bona fides* of the applicant company. Acceptance to the Council's Roll allows companies to display the seal of approval of the NSCIA and carries some recognition from the insurance companies (the ABI is represented on the Council) and the police and supposedly also the general public, although this seems far less certain (see Chapter 4, p. 65). None the less, the NSCIA seems confident of its credibility and is generally unenthusiastic about the idea of licensing and regulation, although it has obviously considered the issue (see below). But in any case, the NSCIA is probably best considered in terms of its relationship to the BSIA, for in matters of broad policy concerning private security, where this would affect the NSCIA, then it would probably follow the BSIA's lead.

In the past, the Intruder Alarm Installers Association has been a visible if small, independent rival of the NSCIA and has attracted criticism from the BSIA/NSCIA Directorate. It is comprised of small independent installers nationally, claiming to work to similar high standards to the NSCIA, such as installing to British Standards and operating an internal system of inspection and discipline. Its attitude to licensing seems equivocal but, however much sympathy it might elicit as the underdog in a competition with the larger companies and the BSIA/NSCIA, it is clear that it has no real powers of discipline over its membership other than expulsion from what is in any case a small organisation. It lacks the credibility and contacts of the NSCIA and certainly cannot be taken to contribute anything to the arguments against licensing. On the other hand, the very fact of its existence, and the new SIMSSA, demonstrates the ineffectiveness and non-representative nature of the NSCIA. Only a system of licensing and regulation could clarify the muddied waters of the alarm industry.

The Association of British Investigators has tended to adopt a liberal public relations approach in presenting its identity, has decried the non-professional standards of some private investigators and has seen the benefit of such a strategy in indicators of acceptance such as the use of its membership list by the Law Society. An impressive sounding code of ethics and conduct urges its members 'to at all times conduct our investigations within the bounds of legality, morality and professional ethics . . . [and] to guard against inadvertent disclosures of private information', and so on. Needless to say, there is no mechanism for more effectively encouraging adherence to these highflown principles.

Further questions might surround other aids to the promotion of a professional image. For example, the Younger Committee (1972) heard evidence concerning private investigators which raised the possibility of misrepresentation if officially approved identity cards were issued, perhaps bearing a photograph and possibly being mistaken for possessing some police authority. As Draper (1978: 163) points out however, 'this problem is already with us. Members of the Association [of British Investigators] . . . are given identity cards to prove the membership of the holder and, although they are not very similar to police warrant cards, to the uninitiated they might be mistaken as such.' Such halfway house attempts to create respectability are not really very satisfactory on any criteria.

To some extent this is recognised by the Association which has gone on record as being in favour of some form of licensing system. In an undated report (c. 1978) the ABI notes that its 'efforts were acknowledged by the . . . Younger . . . Committee on Privacy . . . in July 1972: "We also note the desire of the Association of British Investigators – apparently the only large organisation of private detectives in this country to have a licensing system." ' The Association's document, submitted to the Royal Commission on Legal Services (1979) concluded its two pages with the following claim and request:

> With the exception of those investigators who are members of the Association of British Investigators, [others] are not bound by any code of conduct or ethics and it is therefore the wish of this Association that in the public interest, the Royal Commission on Legal Services support the various moves being made to control or license the private investigator.

No control was, or is, forthcoming, but two recent developments may indicate the future shape of self-regulation for private investigators. First, the BSIA has made clear its opinion that the private investigator is not a part of the private security industry because 'the role of security is crime prevention whereas a private investigator is not involved until after the crime has been committed' ('Private', 1987: 61). Strictly speaking, this is not true with regard to a number of services that private investigators undertake; however, the position remains that the BSIA will not represent private investigators. This can only result in further confusion with the creation of a parallel system of self-regulation for private investigators. This may emerge following the initiative of the Institute of Professional Investigators which is apparently inviting all private investigators in the UK to register with a new voluntary body that it hopes to establish. According to one trade report, 'it is understood that this new regulatory body is being established with the blessing of the government and is an indication that the IPI have now given up all hope of getting any form of registration law on the statute books' (*Security Times*, 1987: 29). In an occupation which relates to a wide range of sensitive issues, such a move can represent only limited progress and should not be allowed to foreclose genuine debate about the need for statutory regulation.

The role of the Home Office

Since the earliest soundings about the possibility of licensing private security in the 1960s, the Home Office has remained unmoved by arguments in favour of the merits of the case. Rather, regardless of political party in power, it has generally rejected the need to address the issue and, when occasionally moved to a token information-gathering gesture, has opted for the minimal response possible. Even the 1979 Green Paper (Home Office, 1979) was a case of brief momentum gathered in a way designed subsequently to clog the wheels for years to come. With the publication of the report, leaving an open-ended but wholly uncoordinated period for consideration, response and consultation, the wheels ground to a halt again and inertia was restored. To all intents and purposes – apart from some recognition of significance inherent in the preparation of a Green Paper – the status quo was resumed and the support of the Home Office, and the new Conservative and previous governments for self-regulation was reaffirmed. The Home Office has over time argued that an established range of legislation already controls and regulates the status and power of private security personnel (and hence their organisations) just as it does all other ordinary citizens. To offer some brief examples:

It is generally agreed that *uniforms* give private security a sense of corporate identity. For good or ill, they help the private security personnel to stand out and furthermore – and more importantly – they give the appearance of authority (Randall, 1976: 140; Scott and McPherson, 1971: 272). It is, of course, also widely agreed that the wearing of uniforms deliberately designed to resemble those of the police in order to gain further authority, respect and perhaps lay claim to police powers is not acceptable. The fact that it happens – albeit with varying degrees of subtlety – can be neatly forgotten. For the Home Office, the matter is rendered unproblematic because Section 52 of the Police Act 1964 makes it an offence for 'any person who is not a police officer to wear an article of police uniform or any article having the appearance of such an article where it gives him an appearance so nearly resembling that of a member of a police force as to be calculated to deceive' (*Turner* v. *Shearer*, 1973; Bunyan, 1976: 253). But the issues of intent to deceive and whether or not a uniform looks like that of a police officer do not exhaust the matter. Security services, such as the now defunct Night Watch Yeomen of Tunbridge Wells, may adopt a uniform style like white jackets and crash helmets evidently different to that of the police. None the less, they operate as a uniformed body patrolling the streets, which calls into question the effective application of legislation passed after the banning of the Blackshirts in the 1930s concerning uniformed groups on the public highway (Public Order Act 1936).

Arms, and their use, present an odd case in the late 1980s because, although the public is more familiar today than ever with the idea of the police being potentially armed in certain circumstances (and the experience of the Northern Ireland conflict is by no means any longer the only reminder of that), it is often now forgotten that for periods in the 1950s and early 1960s a number of private security companies were issuing firearms to their pay-roll guard services. Undoubtedly, other private security services, then and now, had and have access to arms. But the important point in providing a backcloth of what is *possible* is that in a society which prides itself on its control of firearms, for quite a few years private security organisations were able to issue selected members of their staff with firearms in a legitimate fashion under the benign, half-closed eye of the Home Office. The Home Office subsequently discouraged requests for, or licensing of permits for, firearms for private security organisations. But the role of the police is of major significance here as well. They were, of course, strong critics of the issue to and possible use of firearms by private security. Wide-ranging criticism eventually led the BSIA to adopt a policy position which it evidently feels is sufficiently reassuring to defuse the issue. To others it might be felt to contain an ominous secondary implication:

'While the British policeman remains unarmed, the British security guard will remain unarmed' (Bunyan, 1976: 236).

Not surprisingly, ex-police officers now working in private security fear a serious spiralling of the use of firearms if private security companies are ever able to issue and use them on any scale. The most obvious example that might be given here is that bank and pay-roll raiders would be even more likely than they are now to carry and use arms if they knew or thought that the security guards were armed. With regard to the adequacy of current control, however, the Home Office (and others) feel that existing restrictions and new legislation on the sale and holding of firearms are adequate. Furthermore, it is held that private security companies (by which is meant the larger, respectable companies) need to maintain good relations with the Home Office and the police and this acts as a most severe informal as well as formal source of proscription against the issue and use of firearms. None the less, what is common practice behind security guarded doors remains largely unknown and it is uncertain how idle was at least a part of the boast of the Knightsbridge Safe Deposit Centre when it opened in 1983 that it would be the most secure in the world, protected not only by a multitude of security devices but also by armed security guards. The centre's loss of around £10 million in July 1987, after thieves bluffed their way into the vaults on the pretext of wishing to check on its security arrangements before making a deposit, might be reminiscent of claims made about the *Titanic*, but it also means that had the armed thieves really been challenged by guards who were themselves armed then lives might also have been lost. Whether the guards were armed or not, such claims if made (Cohen, 1987: 2) should be the subject of official scrutiny based on regulations embodied in law. Neither in the short term nor the long is society well served by a situation in which private security guards might be armed and use their weapons against others who are armed, or where they are unarmed but assumed to be.

Truncheons have also been issued to and used by private security guards in the past. The Home Office again argues that existing legislation is and has proved to be sufficient to control and curtail such practices. According to the Prevention of Crime Act 1953, section 1, the courts shall be the arbiters of whether a person has 'lawful authority or reasonable excuse' to carry an offensive weapon, such as a truncheon. But generally it is held that 'Any person who without lawful authority or reasonable excuse, the proof whereof lies on him, has with him in any public place any offensive weapon, shall be guilty of an offence.' Security guards have been prosecuted on the basis of this understanding, and in 1973 a Court of Appeal ruled that 'the carrying of a weapon should not be treated as a matter of routine or as part of the uniform.' Three guards working for White Star Security were convicted following this ruling, having been prosecuted for carrying truncheons which were held to constitute offensive weapons (Bunyan, 1976: 236). Nevertheless:

> it may be lawful for a security guard to carry handcuffs and a truncheon out of sight of the public, *whilst he is on duty on private land to which the public are not admitted.* However, if a security guard decides to draw his truncheon where there is no justification for doing so, say, merely to frighten a trespasser, such an act may constitute an assault. ('Eye', 1987: 19)

A security guard may use a truncheon in the prevention of crime as long as he only uses 'reasonable' force, according to one interpretation of the Criminal Law Act 1967 (section 3). However, this reading, the implications of other provisions of the 1967 Act and the force of precedents set in a variety of past court cases need clarification. Members of the industry would themselves welcome such a move from the Home Office because, as one trade journal report recently observed, 'members of private security forces could be committing offences daily!' ('Eye', 1987: 19).

However, while truncheons no longer seem to be routinely issued by security companies, it is the lack of formal, official response to the issuing and potential use of truncheons, firearms and MACE canisters that was and remains disturbing. Private security guards are *not* the 'general public', who after all do not as a rule guard pay-rolls, safe-deposits, night clubs or computer facilities; rather, they are a very specific case. Even if the preferable option of specific legislation pertaining to the powers, authority, uniform and accoutrements of private security is viewed as too complex, potentially cumbersome and anyway unnecessary by the Home Office, there is no excuse for not maintaining a publicly accessible, *specific* watching brief overseeing the activities of and developments in the private security sector.

The standard response of the Home Office to such a case is that private security companies and personnel have no 'special privileges'. However, as legal commentators have often retorted, common law and the provisions of six Acts of Parliament provide for an individual's right to protect his or her property. This power can be made the responsibility of another party, such as a private security organisation, whose employees enjoy and can use the citizen's power of arrest and the right to use sufficient force as is necessary to prevent a crime being committed (Garner, 1978: 126; *Sunday Telegraph Magazine*, 8 December 1973). Under the Criminal Law Act 1967:

> Any person may arrest with reasonable cause any person suspected to be in the act of committing an arrestable offence (2. (2)). A person may use such force as is reasonable in the circumstances in the prevention of crime or in effecting or assisting in the lawful arrest of offenders or suspected offenders.

The provisions and wording of the 1967 Act have been in force for so long now and have formed a part of whatever little basic training security staff receive (where there *is* coverage of the relevant legislation) that it is unlikely that the new Police and Criminal Evidence Act 1984 will be familiar to many for some years to come. It is at present untested whether the provisions of the Act will materially change or affect practices of private security personnel in significant ways. It would appear that the Codes of Practice in the Act relating to the duty of 'investigating offences' do not apply to civilian security staff as they are not 'charged with the duty of investigating offences' (section 67 (9)). Section 24, however, may be relevant in so far as it redefines 'among other things, that any person may arrest without warrant anyone who is in the act of committing an arrestable offence or anyone whom he has reasonable grounds for suspecting to be committing such an offence' (*Police Review*, 1986: 479). This may seem a relatively unexceptionable and historically familiar civil power. However, proper compliance with the requirement of the Code of Practice on the Detention, Treatment and Questioning of Persons by Police Officers (*which also extends to 'civilian investigators'; Police Review*, 1986: 479) to administer a caution on arrest would be immeasurably aided by legislative requirement of adequate training for anyone employed in a security capacity that brings them into contact with the public in such circumstances as an arrest might be made.

This is not a question of 'special privileges': the point is that private security is a *special case*. Private security personnel do not act like ordinary citizens, indeed their commercial *raison d'être* is that they should not. I shall conclude this section by noting that it seems to have suited both the Home Office and the BSIA to attempt to maintain a generally low profile despite the importance of the relevant issues.

The Home Office Green Paper on *The Private Security Industry* issued in February 1979 acknowledged that: 'There is no modern society in which a government can provide total protection against crime' (p. 10, para. 30). '(It is inconceivable that the police should be expected to meet *all* demands for protective services as part of their public duties and to do so at the expense of taxpayer and ratepayer.)' (p. 11, para. 31). Four months earlier, Sir Robert Mark (then Commissioner of the Metropolitan Police) had generated an apparent wave of shock through the media when he had said the same thing: *The Daily Telegraph* headline announced 'Police force can no longer cope with thefts' (Davis, 1980: 21). Hardly a murmur greeted the Home Office echo of Sir Robert's statement, yet this represented a statement of official policy thinking whereas Sir Robert was well known as an outspoken individualist when it came to views on contemporary policing. This point is perhaps the very reason why Sir Robert's comment did make the news, but it does not explain why a report purporting to be a contribution to further debate and much-needed thinking on this subject somehow effectively *dampened* any such debate.

Perhaps part of the answer to this is that, like many bureaucratic documents designed to cover openly whilst simultaneously stifling a subject and its debate, the Green Paper was simply very bland. Furthermore, the private security sector – or at least its 'establishment' end – has ultimately been quite effective in blurring what measures it itself supports: some form of self-regulation merges with promises of consumer protection and 'independent' inspectorates which merge with occasional vague expressions of willingness to 'support' licensing. However, support for self-regulation of abuses within the private security sector merely reflects an inclination to minimise the conflicts and revelations which would be inherent in the real enforcement of regulation. The operation of this pseudo 'ombudsman' or consumer-protection agency type of 'informal institution' is well described by Abel (1982: 287) as based upon: 'scapegoating the exceptional enterprise that is totally irresponsible, thereby diverting attention from routine business practices and ensuring that regulation and publicity will have only a very limited general deterrent effect.' At the same time, it is clear, and no surprise of course, that where significant voices *are* raised in the private security sector in favour of some limited form of licensing (as opposed, it should be noted, to serious regulation and limitation) it is because they are generally those of the figureheads and public relations departments of those larger companies which might well be very happy to take up any slices of the market left by any legislation which pushed smaller companies unable to 'make the grade' out of business. This cynical truism is well understood throughout the industry.

Carson's work (1970, 1979) on the history of factory legislation illustrates a similar situation where large companies have over time been apparently happy to cooperate with the Factory Inspectorate. Quite simply, such companies can afford to come up to scratch whereas smaller companies often cannot. Ironically, the Factory Inspectorate in this respect can strengthen the monopolistic power of the larger companies as small competition is pushed out of business by the stringency of conditions that it cannot meet. The potential for abuse of regulations – and for hiding such abuse – increases as the dominant companies grow in size, respectability and power. The prospect of a similar development within a self-regulating private security sector or one minimally controlled by legislation is an issue to be seriously concerned about.

Note

1   The following section draws on publicly available BSIA reports up to BSIA (1987) and news in the trade press; on an extended interview with Mr John Wheeler, MP, Director General of the BSIA, 20 April 1978; and on interviews conducted between 1978 and 1987 with Mr Bruce George, MP, relating to his campaign to introduce licensing for private security.

8 Towards Effective Licensing, Regulation and Accountability

Other models and jurisdictions

With regard to the provision of public safeguards concerning private security, it is surely the case that Britain is seriously out of step with many of its European neighbours, with provisions in the United States and with developments in countries with dissimilar legal systems, such as Israel, and those with closely similar systems, such as Canada, Australia and New Zealand. Of course, not all of these nations have comprehensive, omnibus legislation covering every aspect of the private security sector, as I have outlined its range of activities. None the less, some exertion (and importantly symbolic effort) of control over some areas of private security activity has been made. At the same time lessons have been learned.

Before offering a short review of the principal criticisms and reservations about existing models of licensing and regulation, I will first outline the major provisions of relevant international legislation. In doing so I shall follow the format of Draper's excellent discussion of this area (1978: ch. 8), initially outlining legislation relating to private investigators and then going on to consider control measures relevant to other forms of private security.[1]

It is generally assumed that licensing and regulation are most strongly developed and well defined in the USA where 35 of the 50 federal states currently operate some sort of relevant system. However, as Draper (1978: 136-7) observes, it is the legislation adopted by New Zealand which probably offers a more adequate example of attempts to control both private investigators and security. Furthermore, developed in a similar society and legal system, it is a model which it has often been suggested might be followed in the UK. This system requires anyone working in the detection field to be approved as a 'responsible employee' and to have obtained a certificate to this effect from the regulatory body. The employee may then work for any licensed private investigator agency.

Applicants must apply to the police who can object to the granting of a licence or certificate of approval. Others can also register objections to the licensing process. In such cases there is recourse to a tribunal hearing where objectors and the applicant can present their cases. Applicants must be able to prove some degree of apprenticeship experience in the work, although a licence is required to practice independently. The process is guided by rules relating to age, prior convictions involving dishonesty and the previous revoking of a licence (Draper, 1978: 136–7). Obviously, the New Zealand model would need to be adapted in a manner which respected and was in tune with UK legislation (for example, with regard to the provisions of the Rehabilitation of Offenders Act 1974) and it would probably be the feeling of many that the police may not be the most appropriate body to process such applications: a position potentially open to abuse where other police interests may influence the fairness of the procedure. But it is fallacious to argue, as many have, that a licensing system could not be worked out or that it would be alien to the principles of our legal system. It is hardly the case that the legislative processes or legal traditions of New Zealand are dissimilar to those of the UK, and the recent passage of legislation relating to private security companies in Northern Ireland (see below) is a further challenge to such arguments.

There is not the space here to go into the positive features or the shortcomings of this system, though the requirement of a period of basic experience is usually praised (although without monitoring of this aspect this could be a double-edged feature) and once again, characteristic of the field internationally, there is little emphasis on training development and the gaining of qualifications.

Far less attention has been paid to the activities and control of private detectives in Europe and, when compared to the situation in the USA where they are more common and active in wider fields, this is relatively unsurprising. The Scandinavian countries regulate their private security industry which has been a long-established feature of their provision for property protection and crime prevention. However, neither there nor in France, Belgium, Holland or the UK is specific licensing legislation directed at private investigators. Germany's Central Association of Investigating and Detective Agencies operates a self-regulating code of ethics and private security organisations must be licensed by the *Länder* (Home Office, 1979: 29); Spain requires investigators to pass a proficiency test but, as Draper (1978: 137) points out, the most elaborate system for licensing private investigators in Europe seems to be that which operates in Italy.

This system forbids the carrying out of a whole range of investigative services without the granting of a licence issued by a Prefect. The Prefect must be satisfied that the applicant is of Italian citizenship, can be appropriately bonded and has not been convicted of a criminal offence. Police have access to inspect an agency's records and have the authority to enlist the services of private investigators for their own operations. This latter power is one that would almost certainly be unwelcome to most interested parties in the UK: the police, civil liberties groups and the industry itself. It must be clear that licensing should not be sought as a mechanism legislatively to empower or deputise a secondary police force. Licensing must be viewed in terms of what it licenses particular people to do in the course of the duties assigned to them, and who those qualified people are. It must also explicitly state what they *cannot* do. Licensing should be a process of *regulation*, in so far as it is clear about who can undertake certain roles and that it limits and is proscriptive in its description of what licensed persons can do, whilst prescriptive about requirements they must fulfil. Legislation directly controlling the activities of private investigators in Europe is, then, generally undeveloped except in Italy, and in the UK in any specific sense it is non-existent.

When we turn to look at international examples of licensing and control covering private security companies, a now familiar picture emerges. Concomitant with their massive expansion and increasing significance as part of the division of policing labour, private security organisations are now the subject of some form of regulatory legislation in most European nations as well as the USA, Canada, Australia and New Zealand. In Italy, the same system of licensing that operates for private investigators also covers private security employees. Further, it is sufficiently well developed not only to lay down standards but also to make extra provisions for different types of guards, including those who are 'sworn' and carry firearms. Where less elaborate systems exist elsewhere in Europe they none the less represent statutory requirements to be fulfilled by prospective employees seeking to be placed in positions of trust and which require responsible levels of sensitivity and discretion. At its most basic, the favoured method for some form of vetting is generally the requirement that the applicant can show he or she has no previous criminal convictions. Providing evidence of this is either the responsibility of the applicant seeking employment or else, as with the New Zealand system, the prospective employer may be expected to take on responsibility for complying with certification requirements. While the latter system is held to have some advantages of bureaucratic certainty and efficiency, it can also be criticised as involving too great an invasion of privacy.

Draper (1978: 143) argues this point, following Philip-Sorenson, Chairman of Group 4, who believes that the Scandinavian system of making it the responsibility of the employee to provide his or her own certificate by applying at a local police station is the most acceptable method of vetting. According to Philip-Sorenson, 'If the applicant does not return to the security company to which he has applied, then no one is any the wiser. He may have failed to get a certificate or he may, on the other hand, have found another job' (Draper, 1978: 143). This is true and the approach is one way of attempting to ensure respect for individual rights regarding the transfer of personal information. In this respect it is a system which certainly merits consideration as a vetting option that satisfies some civil liberties concerns, although, again, reservations about the police being the most appropriate agency to process applications must be raised. It might also be observed that suggesting that this arrangement involves less of an invasion of privacy by security companies is a dubious indication of concern for civil liberties, especially as the regulations of many major security companies suggest that employees will be expected to face further vetting procedures in the future. To what extent this actually occurs is, of course, open to question, but evidently the issues raised by the debate over vetting of personnel are by no means clear cut.

The 'personal application' system appears to be the means by which licences are issued in most countries with some regulatory legislation. As I have pointed out, its implementation in the UK would need to take account of the Rehabilitation of Offenders Act 1974 but this would not be a problem in the case of those more serious offences not covered by the Act and which constitute grounds for rejection of an application. Such a system is still less than adequate, but it does represent at least a tentative step in the right direction.

Slightly more developed systems operate in some states in the USA and provinces of Canada, but the most advanced at present would seem to be that developed in Sweden. Here the licensing system emphasises adequate training through government-approved programmes as well as the usual vetting requirement. A basic minimum of 214 hours, backed up by yearly refresher courses is a prerequisite for qualification. Specialist work, such as handling guard dogs, merits further training (Draper, 1978: 144). Additionally, the amount of overtime that can be worked is also limited. For an industry which is often reliant upon and exploits overtime working, this is a significant and positive provision. Thus, in reviewing other models of regulation in other jurisdictions there are lessons to be learned from mistakes and half-hearted responses, but there are also exemplary practices in existence which have been proved to be workable and which can be followed. The expanded legislation and licensing system now operating in Sweden is, however, still relatively new. To gain a different perspective on what is workable, it is useful to turn to the experience of licensing in the United States and Canada.

In their major Rand Corporation study conducted and published in the early 1970s for the US Department of Justice, Kakalik and

Wildhorn presented a clear picture of the inadequacy of then existing licensing. Following a survey which looked at procedures in 31 states, three counties and 46 cities, they made the following observations:

> First, the regulatory agencies' effectiveness is limited because they typically do not have extensive data on the security industry's problems. With the exception of reviewing license applications, the typical regulatory agency has very limited and, in some cases, no contact with the industry. Second, the agencies' effectiveness is limited because they very rarely invoke the post-licensing powers they possess to correct problems in the industry. Suspensions, revocations and fines are rare . . . the agencies have such limited resources and such ineffective channels for learning of problems that many specific problems do not come to their attention. Hence, controls are very rarely exercised. Third, there are wide variations in the toughness with which regulations are enforced among regulatory agencies. Finally, nearly every regulatory agency responding to our survey recommended that some aspect of the regulation of the industry be made stronger than it presently is in their jurisdiction. (Kakalik and Wildhorn, 1972, vol. 1: 56–7).

Despite my earlier comments about the extent of licensing regulation abroad *in relation* to the British situation, cases of long-established regulatory systems like the USA are instructive. Although it is sometimes assumed that the USA, in particular, has wholly embraced licensing, it remains the case that serious commitment to regulation and control of the private security sector has not really been embraced with great enthusiasm anywhere. Ten years on from the Kakalik and Wildhorn Rand Report, a municipal judge writing in *The Police Chief* (Schepps, 1982: 26–7) was seriously concerned about the inadequacy of the regulatory system. Thus Schepps writes: 'Since only 62% of the states have regulatory agencies for security services, one-third of the nation must rely solely on local regulation. Widespread local regulation discourages uniformity and standardisation necessary for maximum effectiveness and control of security services.' More broadly and fundamentally:

> While citizens have, in theory, some ability to alter police behaviour (through the courts, local government, political clubs, etc.) their control over private police behaviour is almost non-existent. Thus, if the citizenry is to have any success in halting the threats to individual liberties and privacy, it must create new mechanisms of control over private agencies.

Progress, however, appears to be slow, even with the existing framework of state legislation to build upon. For example, in a 1984 *New York Times* (4 June) report, 'Growing security-guard industry under scrutiny', the New York Secretary of State, Gail S. Schaffer echoed familiar past criticisms: 'It is an industry that lends itself to abuses.' According to the *New York Times* report: 'The New York State Investigation Commission in its report said attempts to license guards and increase controls had been blocked by "the vigorous lobbying efforts of the security guard industry." '

I cannot here cover all the diverse provisions of existing systems of licensing, though these raise many interesting issues – not least the extent to which licensing restricts and limits powers and activities versus the extent to which it enhances existing prerogatives and confers new ones. There is also an accompanying debate, so far little developed in the UK, which is less about whether private security should be licensed and regulated and more about whether private security arrangements and provision should be *required* by law. As Hamilton (1974: 95) points out, such a system has been introduced in Israel where:

> amendments passed by the Knesset to the Licensing of Businesses Law, 1968 give power to the Minister of the Interior to designate businesses requiring a license in order to ensure the 'prevention of danger to the public peace and protection against robbery and housebreaking'. The Minister of Police is then empowered to make regulations for the prevention of 'danger to the public peace . . . including protection at the time of the transportation of money, diamonds, securities and other valuables, where licensed and certain other businesses are concerned'. These regulations are enforced by the police but usually amicably and appeal mechanisms are built in.

It is highly unlikely that this sort of model will develop in the UK or indeed in many of the other jurisdictions mentioned. However, it *is* likely that the requirements for security in certain businesses and homes imposed by the insurance industry will become increasingly stringent.

In general, though, formal control, regulation and licensing of the private security sector has exhibited three key features in its concerns. To paraphrase the excellent discussion of these issues offered by Shearing and Stenning (1981: 230–1 and passim), until very recently most regulatory schemes have tended to share several characteristic features. First, they have focused on the contract security side: upon contract guards and investigation activities. Secondly, they have reflected concerns about 'competition' between private security and the public police. This has been the case in the past and remains evident today. Where licensing systems exist, some evidence for this is afforded by the frequency with which it is the public police that are designated as the licensing and regulatory authority. At the same time, in many jurisdictions, it is a high priority concern to forbid, or at least control 'moonlighting' by sworn police officers in the private security sector in off-duty hours.

Thirdly, the breadth and lack of precision of regulations (rarely accompanied by a breadth of actual powers and resources to back them up) has given rise to a high degree of *discretion* in the implementation of regulatory authority. Necessary baselines for effective assessment for certification are notoriously loose. Criteria such as character and competency have been consistently recommended or required yardsticks, yet the bases on which they should be judged are equally consistently unclear. While this discretionary type of system has probably often worked to the advantage of private security companies, it has generally been even more inadequate in lacking provision for proper and fair appeals and complaints procedures for the public, employees or the companies themselves.

The point of this tour through other jurisdictions and models of licensing has been to indicate that, with the exception of new legislation applying only to Northern Ireland, the UK is virtually alone in having *no* formal, legislatively empowered system of control over even the most visible and largest-scale operators in the private security sector, let alone those small-scale 'cowboy' and up-market specialist agencies that should elicit more concern. In conclusion, however, it is only fair to admit that examination of the various existing schemes gives little scope for optimism about their real efficacy. As Shearing and Stenning (1981: 231) conclude: 'Despite the apparently expansive scope of these regulatory schemes, research into the adequacy and effectiveness of such schemes has not produced encouraging results.'

I have already referred to the findings of the Kakalik and Wildhorn (1972) Rand Report. Their conclusions have been broadly confirmed in the wide-ranging studies conducted over more than a decade by researchers at the Toronto Centre of Criminology (see in particular Stenning and Cornish, 1975: ch. 6). This research into the regulation of private security in Canada concluded that:

> Regulatory agencies were typically understaffed and under-budgeted, with the result that they could rarely perform more than the most minimum of licensing functions. Administration of such regulatory functions as inspections, competency tests, the hearing and disposition of public complaints, and setting of standards for advertising, uniforms, and equipment was typically minimal or non-existent. (Shearing and Stenning, 1981: 233)

In going on to consider some of the *pros* and *cons* of proposals for licensing and regulation of private security in the UK, it should be borne in mind throughout that one of the most central issues is whether to provide the *absolutely necessary* resources to make any licensing scheme work if this gains support *and is intended to work*. The metaphor of the 'toothless watchdog' is a particularly appropriate one to use in discussion of the private security business. Without the appropriate resources to do its job then any regulatory authority ever appointed might well appropriate the image for its crested letterhead.

The case for licensing and regulation of private security in the UK

Unlike the formal system of overview of the police (whatever its inadequacies), there is in the UK no prescribed means for ensuring the accountability of the private security sector. There is no constitutional calling to account, nor even a universal regulatory code governing the relationship between private security and public services, from which private security benefits in gross disproportion to its input into the relationship.

In 1978 the Outer Circle Policy Unit (OCPU) presented a report on private security to the Home Office during the period that it was preparing its 1979 Green Paper, *The Private Security Industry: A Discussion Paper*. One of the key issues which the OCPU report addressed and which the Green Paper minimised was that of accountability. Private security interests themselves, not surprisingly, consistently trivialise this issue. As the OCPU report observed,

> the claim by the Managing Director of Securicor that as a public company it is 'at all times most effectively answerable to the press' (*Times*, 10 June, 1978) simply demonstrates a failure to grasp the constitutional issues involved in the concept of accountability. Occasional scrutiny by the press does not at all resemble the conventional idea of accountability or that which [has been] called the 'explanatory and cooperative mode' of accountability which is written into the Police Act 1964. (OCPU, 1978: 10)

Formally, the occupational and social role of the police is based upon the mandate of the state to appoint an agency to ensure the enforcement of its laws. In contrast, *prima facie*, private security has only a commercial *raison d'être* (South, 1984) and it is reasonable to state that there is certainly no 'mandate' here which is primarily intended to be coincidental with the general public interest. Rather, it is private interest that prevails. As the OCPU report pointed out, 'indeed since the initial abolition of compounding an offence, even the most exiguous protection for the public is lacking' (OCPU, 1978: 11).

Of course, the question also arises of protecting the civil liberties of ordinary employees in private security work. At one level, there is an unusual coincidence of opinion on this issue between civil liberties groups, private security employers and representatives of employees such as the trade union, MATSA, and the independent association, IPSA. All these groups, albeit to different degrees and with different ends in view, have supported some system of licensing which exempted private security employees from the provisions of the Rehabilitation of Offenders Act 1974. The most relevant part of this Act is section 4 which lays down that:

a person who has become a rehabilitated person for the purposes of this Act in respect of a conviction shall be treated for all purposes in law as a person who has not committed or been charged with or prosecuted for or convicted of, or sentenced for the offence or offences which were the subject of that conviction. (section 4.1)

Where a question seeking information with respect to a person's previous convictions, offences, conduct or circumstances is put to him or to any other person otherwise than in proceedings before a judicial authority – (a) the question shall be treated as not relating to spent convictions or to any circumstances ancillary to spent convictions and the answer thereto may be framed accordingly. (subsection 2) (see also the discussion in Draper, 1978: 42)

The provisions of the Act do not extend to sentences of over 30 months and the length of 'rehabilitation' can be up to ten years. But what seems to keep this hurdle at the forefront of proposals about how to introduce licensing and regulation is not only that it makes it difficult to make a credible start on vetting prospective employees but also the fear that it is not necessarily 'major criminals' who may have received substantial prison sentences who will find employment in private security attractive, but rather petty, small-time, small crime offenders who may have a string of two-year sentences behind them.

The 'clean slate' intentions of the Act are highly important but there have always been a number of occupations exempted from the Act. It is on the basis of pragmatic recognition of this that bodies like the National Council for Civil Liberties, which has favoured a system of licensing for private detectives for some years (recommending this as part of its evidence to the Younger Committee), have also extended their support to the licensing and regulation of private security generally, including – with provisos – the exemption from the Rehabilitation of Offenders Act 1974. A letter of March 1978 to Bruce George, MP, supporting his proposed Private Member's Bill to regulate private security, briefly set out the NCCL's position at that time:

We do not believe that licensing would either confer an unwanted appearance of official approval on Private Detectives, nor would such a system involve an invasion of privacy. As you know, it is our view that only the licensing body should have access to criminal records in order to find out whether an applicant should be licensed or not. We would, of course, be against any system where an employer could have access to criminal records in order to check the credentials of an applicant for a job as a detective or security agent.

On balance, the NCCL's position would seem the most proper one for a regulatory system with credibility, integrity and sensitivity to follow.[2] It would, however, require far more resources than the kind of approach allowing the employee or employer to apply for some form of certification from the criminal records system. Such large resources are unlikely to be forthcoming in the foreseeable future. It remains to be seen how much of a real dilemma any possibility of licensing and regulation, which could not concede this proviso for fiscal reasons, might be.

There are, of course, other parties with an expressed interest in seeing the control (if not the complete abolition) of private security. Not insignificant here is the opinion of many rank-and-file police officers. While attitudes to the private security sector seem to mellow further up the promotion scale, the attitude of many junior police officers and of the Police Federation has frequently ranged from the suspicious to the hostile. In familiar terms and with similar arguments, various representative voices of rank-and-file officers have demanded controls over private security through the past three decades and remain vocal over the issue in the late 1980s. Perhaps an increasing number of the rank and file have grown slightly apathetic about the issue or else come to accept, and to *some* degree welcome, the ancillary service functions of the contract private security industry. But on the platform of Police Federation conferences, and in the pages of *Police* and *Police Review*, the issue remains a live one. Typical was the editorial column of *Police Review* for 17 June 1983 headlined 'Ban bogus police' and revivifying a whole series of arguments which turn upon the contention that private security is usurping roles which should be the responsibility of the police. The scene is set in terms of the necessity of maintaining public confidence in the police – a concern which it is difficult reasonably to argue against.

> There is no law in this country to stop a private company setting up its own police force. There should be – if for no other reason than to maintain public esteem for genuine police forces. There are other reasons besides, but it is manifestly against the public interest to permit anything that might erode public confidence in the police.

Without the burden of having to acknowledge reasons for the growth of private security (including aspects of the law relating to access to private property and to police powers and responsibilities), there follows a familiar invocation of section 52 of the Police Act 1964 concerning the wearing of police-style uniforms and of the Public Order Act 1936 regarding 'associations of persons' who may be organised, trained or equipped to 'usurp the functions of the police'. It is not that these points do not have validity, either in law or argument, as I have indicated earlier; rather, they are simply tired and, by themselves, put forward from the position of a relatively narrow interest group, will receive little attention and less action. This is so because it really is not difficult to discern that the persistent core of these arguments amounts to 'leave the police alone to get on with their jobs'. This is clear in just one example of the continued correspondence in this vein in the police journals:

> Instead of hampering the legitimate law enforcement agencies, organisations like the NCCL, police monitoring groups and others should turn their attention to these ridiculous private armies – indeed, tighter legislation should be brought in to control them. (Balcon, 1986)

Concern for civil liberties seems a little overshadowed by self-interest here. None the less, as part of a *broader* range of arguments and sources of pressure for licensing, regulation and control then the significance of this particular lobby is profound.

Where we could expect to find strong and clear opposition to any form of licensing and regulation is among the free-marketeers and established figures at the helms of organisations in favour of self-regulation. But even in the arguments of those who seem most certain about the benefits of non-regulation or the adequacy of self-regulation, there are evident failings or concessions. In several papers which have contained arguments against licensing private security, and indeed supported further privatisation of certain 'policing' functions, the economist, R.L. Carter (1974, 1976) has viewed the private security organisations as providing a good and efficient service at competitive prices – the key to the fallacy of this argument is the belief that efficiency and good service can follow from uncontrolled competition.

Carter correctly points out that licensing would increase the cost of private security, as would proposals to create qualification barriers to entry into the business or the kind of proposal made by Seldon (1977) and others to employ the police for certain security services for they have higher standards, better pay rates and better conditions of work (Carter, 1976: 35–7). Carter sees the current situation as beneficial for both security organisations and their customers:

> So long as entry to the market remains easy with low capital barriers there should be no fears of the restrictive practices characteristic of oligopoly situations. Competition between firms should keep both prices and profits low. Moreover customers can always exercise the ultimate sanction of employing their own security staff if dissatisfied with the prices charged or service provided. Therefore under existing conditions there need be no fear of the exploitation of firms by a cartel of security companies, nor can they afford to operate inefficiently. (Carter, 1976: 35)

However, with regard to these conditions promoting efficiency, surprisingly for an economist, Carter misses the point that in the most competitive areas of private security they are likely to lead to the opposite. Precisely because 'competition between firms . . . keeps both prices and profits low' (though the latter is questionable), undercutting the prices of rivals is necessary for survival and low pay and inadequate training are inevitable consequences, in turn tending to attract workers to the occupation who are, by the professed standards of the private security companies, unsuitable. In short, the competitive marketing of the mass, non-specialised private security services actually means that firms (to paraphrase Carter) *cannot* afford to operate *efficiently*. What the arguments of writers like Carter expose is not the efficacy of the free market, but rather the need for intervention in it in the form of minimum wages and standards legislation.

Of the bodies in favour of self-regulation, the National Supervisory Council for Intruder Alarms has (*relatively* speaking) perhaps been the most successful (although see pp. 64–5 above). However, in musing upon the possibility of it attaining broader powers through legislation, its former Director, Admiral D. Callaghan, was quite prepared to acknowledge its ineffectiveness in dealing with serious cases of abuse of standards and practice. As Callaghan put it in a paper to the 1975 Edinburgh Conference on 'Major Property Crime': 'we are very much open to criticism for our impotence in the face of outrageous advantage being taken of a customer powerless to obtain redress without resorting to the Courts.' Once this admission is made, the next step can only be recognition of the need for some form of legislatively backed powers of control:

> it could hardly be questioned whether a legislated supervisory body would have the necessary powers, either under its own control or by virtue of its official access to the various consumer-protection departments of the Government, and we must therefore conclude that an independent body (e.g. the NSCIA) is at a disadvantage in this respect compared with a legislated body when acting as a consumer protector. (Callaghan, 1976: 147)

Obviously, if legal powers were to be bestowed on anyone, the self-regulation bodies would prefer that *they* were the recipients of such authority. But at least recognition of the advantages of legislated powers of control over private security starts the debate at a more appropriate point than the non-intervention, 'leave it to the market' stance. To quote the title of Callaghan's paper, it recognises that fundamentally the issue is that of the 'accountability of security in practice'.

The Green Paper 1979

In 1979, the then Labour government published a Green Paper, *The Private Security Industry: A Discussion Paper*. The introduction stated that:

(1) The Government are publishing this discussion paper because they recognise that there is public concern about the recent growth of the private security industry in this country . . .

(2) Arguments in favour of control are often based on the principle that the preservation of law and order is essentially a matter for the police and that if certain functions in this area are assumed by private organisations then at least these organisations should operate under strict government control . . .

(3) The present paper is designed to contribute to this debate by providing background information about the private security industry and discussing some of the issues raised by the question of control. (Home Office, 1979: 1)

Such a debate, however, has hardly flourished in the UK. It has instead kept relatively safely within its existing parochial boundaries. If the Discussion Paper was a sincere initiative then it should have had sincere support and sponsorship subsequently and genuinely encouraged debate involving all interested parties. Too often issues of legislative policy and criminological significance are debated by those whom the Home Office feels 'know best' but who in reality may in fact be those who know least about the day-to-day realities of, for example, policing, prisons, drug use or in this case the private security sector.

Indeed, one of the major problems of the adequacy of the Green Paper – as with much of the debate about private security – is that it has no conception of the significance of the *breadth* of the activities that private security organisations, agents and related bodies deal in. The parameters of its discussion are safely set out in a restricted view of 'the private security industry'. This very low-key approach did not surprise, but none the less disappointed, interested observers and especially those (including the present author) who had been involved in the compilation of information and evidence for submission to the Home Office with the precise intention of attempting to widen the working definition of private security that Home Office researchers had been briefed with.

It is certainly something of an indication of the dampening as opposed to enlivening effect that the Discussion Paper had on debate that the most cogent response came from observers in Canada. In a paper entitled 'Private security and private justice' published in the *British Journal of Law and Society*, Stenning and Shearing (1980a) provide a critique of the Green Paper in the kind of detail that cannot be offered here. It is important, however, to take up some of the key points that they raise, both in agreement and disagreement.

Stenning and Shearing (1980a: 262) promptly identify the nature of the Discussion Paper as a 'tentative governmental response to some quite specific pressures for the introduction of some form of regulatory legislation'. Echoing the feelings of UK observers, they go on to observe that 'in such circumstances, there is often as much, if not more, comment to be made on what the Paper did not talk about (and why it did not talk about it), as on what the Paper did talk about.' This is certainly true, and with regard to one of the key issues that Stenning and Shearing raise, there is a certain irony in some omissions.

As mentioned already, earlier official sources, ministerial statements and Home Office reassurances have at various times rejected the need for specific legislation pertaining to private security on the grounds that the existing body of laws is quite adequate to curtail abuses and illegalities. Up to a certain point, principally concerning one's definition of adequate, this argument has some limited force, although the adequacy of the law courts as one arena of accountability has also been shown to be wanting in a number of cases (for example, *Photo Productions Ltd* v. *Securicor, All England Law Reports*, 1980: 556).[3] Further, and of considerable significance with regard to the argument that legislation concerning private security is impracticable, in 1987 the government recognised that the existing body of laws was *not* necessarily adequate. It can be argued, as no doubt the government would, that this recognition pertains to very specific conditions: recognition of evidence that in Northern Ireland paramilitary groups have been using private security companies as fronts for some of their activities. However, such an argument is as myopic and locked into parochialism as past arguments against any form of regulation. The result of government concern is proof that licensing legislation *can* be enacted; however, it is regrettable, to say the least, that the circumstances which prompted such action have led to the 'host' legislation being the Northern Ireland (Emergency Provisions) Act 1987 (c. 35) (see below p. 146). This subsumes important issues about the regulation of private security within a highly emotive context and wholly inappropriate piece of legislation. It also lets pass an important opportunity to reappraise the matter generally, consider a licensing and regulation system applicable to the whole of the UK, and determine where the strengths and weaknesses of the existing body of law actually lie in relation to private security. This should, perhaps, be no great surprise. It merely reflects a consistent disinclination to consider seriously either the negative or the positive potential of existing law to contribute effectively to the regulation of private security. This reluctance to examine, in any depth, the proposition favoured by the Home Office that existing legislation is adequate for the control and accountability of private security, effectively closes off one further avenue of debate that the 1979 Green Paper was supposedly designed to open. Indeed, the 1979 Paper makes relatively little use of this argument, which seems a strange omission. This directing, and effective narrowing, of the debate was also noted by Stenning and Shearing in their response to the Green Paper:

> in emphasizing that the law makes no distinction between ordinary citizens and private security persons, the Discussion Paper seems to ignore the importance of the general law as a vehicle for more effective control over the private security industry. In this way the Paper prepares the way for its exclusive focus on various forms of regulation in discussing the alternative forms of control available. (1980a: 262)

As Stenning and Shearing suspect, the Paper was not designed to be an exercise genuinely considering the entire possible range of issues arising from the growth, activities and need – or not – for control of the private security sector. Its posture was defensive and purely responsive. It was not, whatever its claims to the contrary, intended to stimulate debate. It was intended to reply to certain pressures and proposals and, in reasonable tones and terms, defuse them.

What must be grasped is that genuinely adequate regulation, control and accountability of the private security sector will not follow from the pursuit of 'either/or' options. Standing, general laws should always, in any case, be employed to protect civil liberties, curb the abuse of power and privilege and prosecute in cases of criminal violation. As Stenning and Shearing go on to recognise:

> If private security personnel are in reality no different from ordinary citizens, a law which treats them alike seems most appropriate. But if in reality they are not, and the law still treats them as if they are, it becomes inappropriate . . . *We strongly suspect that in reality the personnel of modern private security organisations are growing increasingly less like 'ordinary' citizens.* (1980a: 263, emphasis added)

This latter point is pivotal to the argument for the necessity of specific regulatory legislation pertaining to the range of activities within the private security sector. The very development of this sector has been founded upon the need of various interested parties to create agencies and mechanisms of protection, detection, policing and social control which are quite different from the public police controlled by specific laws or the general public controlled by general laws.

Today the private security sector works effectively at various levels within the new division of policing labour as part of an acknowledged commercial compromise on the part of government (South, 1984). To some extent, this 'new' division of policing labour merely replays that 'new' division which took place in the nineteenth century when the 'new' public police began to displace some of the long-established local, private arrangements for security, protection and the maintenance of order (South, 1987a). The tremendous significance of this development must not be underestimated; nor should the medium and long-term social repercussions, adjustments in the criminal justice system and other effects. But there is a need and there is scope for a constructive legislative response now in order to provide public safeguards in relation to private security.

Conclusion

Given current and future trends, limited licensing and regulation can, in the long-term view, only be an inadequate stop-gap measure. It would none the less be a step in the right direction, even if only as a concession of recognition of the present and future significance of the private security sector. The current 'blind eye' of history and the Home Office is grist to the mill of suspicion and the musings of conspiracy theory. And their attraction is not confined to civil libertarians and the like. As the editorial comment of *Security and Protection* magazine put it in responding to the Home Office Green Paper, the document as a whole is 'pretty uninspiring'; it 'ignores in the main the extensive arguments for and against regulation/registration'; it 'suggests the need for public debate but provides nothing for the "public" to debate'; and generally, 'seems . . . an extended argument as to why the Home Office should not involve itself' (March 1979).

Nearly a decade on, the Home Office persists in trying to ignore an issue that won't go away. Even when forced to respond legislatively to abuses which have been known about for some years – as in the case of the use of private security companies by paramilitary groups in Northern Ireland – the opportunity to develop a regulatory system for the whole of the UK was rejected and the piecemeal approach of confining registration requirements to the Province alone adopted instead. Indeed, the Home Office seems to be wilfully and obstinately blinkered in the view it takes of private security. This view is narrow and either naive or negligent. Some support for the former interpretation may be found in the following Parliamentary exchange:

> 48. *Mr Holt* asked the Secretary of State for the Home Department if he will facilitate the use of the services of private security companies to assist police in the maintenance of law and order.
>
> *Mr Douglas Hogg*: Private security companies have an important role to play – for example, in protecting private property – but their role is not to patrol streets or other areas of public resort. The maintenance of law or order must remain the task of a properly trained and equipped police force with the support of the public as members, for example, of the special constabulary or of neighbourhood watch schemes. (*Hansard*, 1986: 650)

It would seem inconceivable that the Home Office does not know that, of course, private security companies quite routinely undertake the patrolling of a wide range of 'areas of public resort'. The Minister's knowledge of the rather more disturbing services which the private security sector offers may well be limited, though that in itself is disquieting, but perhaps that has been rectified by the wide media attention paid to the hiring of a private security firm by the Panamanian government to assist in evicting diplomatic staff from its embassy in London in March 1988. This resulted in the police visiting the offices of a south London security firm and holding seven men. The government expressed its concern, but what further action may be taken is unclear (*Newsview*, BBC2, 12 March 1988). Certainly, if the Home Office believes that there should be clear limits to the role of private security companies and, in addition, the information on which it bases its consideration of this issue is inadequate, then there is a strong case for re-examining the debates over licensing, regulation and accountability. This may not be what Mr Holt had in mind when he asked his Parliamentary Question, itself a cause for concern if some Members of Parliament are now proposing that the Home Office should facilitate the use of private security companies as surrogate police. But the exchange has significance in drawing attention to the fact that the division of policing labour in society *is* changing and has its supporters, no matter how reluctant the Home Office is to acknowledge this. Such a position is simply unrealistic, especially when in just one year (1987) the Home Office, on the one hand, extended the use of private security companies in the detention of immigrants, essentially an experiment in the privatisation of a detention facility, at a time when it was known that the government was considering privatising some prisons; while, on the other hand, it enacted the first major piece of legislation concerning the regulation of private security in one part of the UK.

This latter development is actually less of a dynamic initiative than a further illustration of Home Office inertia. It has been known for many years that paramilitary groups in Northern Ireland have been involved in a wide variety of illegal fund-raising activities involving 'drinking clubs, gaming machines, drugs, robbery, extortion and even protection rackets run by phoney security firms' (Ryder, 1987: 5). Part 3 of the Northern Ireland (Emergency Provisions) Act 1987 (c. 35) brought into force on 1 August 1987 and 1 January 1988 provisions which make it an offence to offer, provide or advertise security guard services without a certificate, or to pay money for such services to a person who does not possess a certificate. In the view of many who have been otherwise critical of the government's attitude to the introduction of licensing, this measure is seen as praiseworthy in its relatively comprehensive coverage. However, it is also recognised that the government has in no way fundamentally changed its attitude on the licensing and regulation issue. The Act is not seen by government as a precedent in this respect, rather it is a 'special case'. The fact that such legislation should have been enacted long ago is not acknowledged. Its limitations in only covering security guarding services are self-evident when, as I have illustrated, so many other private security services are equally deserving of regulation. The confinement of the application of the certification requirements only to Northern Ireland is simply short-sighted – it should not be presumed that similar corruption and extortion is unknown in London, Glasgow, Liverpool or any other major city in mainland Britain. A major opportunity genuinely to take the initiative on the regulation and accountability of the private security sector has been missed. As Bruce George, MP, put it in commenting upon the persistence of this faint-hearted approach, 'regrettably, it is going to require a catastrophe to compel the Home Office to do what it ought to be doing' (personal interview, 23 November 1987).

The relatively comprehensive nature of the certification procedures now applying in Northern Ireland – at least with regard to contract guard companies – shows that such legislation *can* be drafted and implemented. There are in any case several models for the establishment of regulatory mechanisms in other areas. For example, control can be directed through a government department, such as the Home Office or the Department of Trade and Industry (George, 1984: 50). One example would be the Office of Fair Trading (OFT), charged with enforcing statutory requirements and otherwise encouraging good practices in the self-regulation of commerce. There are advantages and disadvantages to this kind of proposal. On the positive side, such an existing mechanism as the OFT provides clear indicators on what may be successful and what may be unsuccessful approaches and criteria to adopt in establishing licensing procedures. Departmental control would already be served by an existing infrastructure that a new body with responsibility for regulation would have to build up slowly. From some quarters, this route may seem attractive in avoiding the creation of yet another quango; it may be more cost-effective than creating a new body; and civil servants might be held to be appropriate administrators of a regulatory scheme, being seen as neutral and independent of the private security industry. On the other hand, such independence would inevitably mean inexperience in dealing with the problems of the industry, this being aggravated by the frequent movement of senior personnel within the civil service. The inertia of the Home Office in relation to the regulation of private security would not be an encouraging precedent when considering how the efficiency of such a system might be hampered by bureaucratic delays or the susceptibility of regulation by a government department to influence by the government of the day (George, 1984: 50–1).

Public licensing by an independent body offers flexibility and independence. With a permanent administrative staff and Inspectorate with legal powers to enable it to fulfil its appropriate investigative, inspection and enforcement roles (as in the case, for example, of the Gaming Board for Great Britain), such a body would seem to be the most appropriate model to follow. The principal objection to this proposal, put forward by advocates of self-regulation, is its cost. At a time when the limitation of public spending is a high priority for the government, this objection obviously carries some weight. However, as Bruce George, MP, has argued:

> The first thing to be said is that whatever cost is incurred *is necessary*. The costs will in any case not be formidable and the costs of registration and licensing will be borne by the applicants, which could go a long way to meeting the costs of the [administering body]. The additional costs to the industry, both from licensing and from the requirements for training and so forth, will of course be passed on to the security consumer. Those who want security in addition to that provided by the police must be prepared to pay for it, and the improved efficiency and protection from a regulated industry should compensate for any additional cost while ensuring that improvements in efficiency do not encroach upon the civil liberties and legal rights of citizens. (George, 1984: 53)

The civil liberties and legal rights of *employees* in the private security sector are also, of course, of paramount importance, and the establishment of a neutral and independent Registration Body or Council would be the most effective means of ensuring that they were not compromised. Such a body could take on a role not envisaged in recent Private Member's Bills put forward by Bruce George, MP, and, most recently, by Don Dixon, MP (The Private Security Bill 1987), in acting as a clearing house for certification, with access to *relevant* data from the Criminal Records Office, thereby bypassing the direct involvement of the police in the application procedure.

The essential features of a practicable regulatory system which truly regulates are that it should: set minimum standards and conditions of employment and service, as well as providing for appropriate training; be backed by legal powers to regulate and enforce these requirements and to provide for a certification procedure sufficiently adequate to minimise the possibility of persons deemed inappropriate (by virtue of previous convictions relating to, for example, fraud or violent offences) becoming either employers or employees in private security companies; create a publicly accountable body itself responsible for the public accountability of the private security sector and empowered to establish a tribunal for the hearing of complaints and appeals and the taking of appropriate action. In developing its role, the regulatory body should obviously examine and seek to build upon the lessons to be learned from the experiences of other jurisdictions. It must have adequate financial and personnel resources to maintain a credible and effective Inspectorate with efficient administrative support. The expense of such a regulatory body should – and could – be met by licensing fees, imposed fines and central government funding.

Legislatively empowered regulation and procedures for ensuring accountability are necessary because it must be recognised that the private security sector cannot be simplistically viewed as no different from the private citizen in the eyes of the law. The diversity of, demand for and growth potential of the (frequently disturbing), services offered by the private security sector make it a special case requiring a special response.

Notes

1 Draper's starting point here follows from her particular interests as a lawyer (and hence the detailed exposition found in ch. 8 of her book). From an interest in legislative control alone, initial consideration of private investigators and issues of intrusion of privacy is quite necessary and logical, for this is where most legal interest has been directed. Having outlined the *broader* dimensions of the private security sector earlier then this same starting point can suffice here also. It must, however, raise one or two questions. One obvious and key question that Draper asks is *why* so much interest has been focused on private investigators. She suggests that, for the UK at least, anxiety over security companies 'is of a more sporadic nature, manifesting itself at intervals whenever a particularly worrying story hits the headlines' whilst, on the other hand, 'the activities of private detectives have come more regularly under review in Parliament and elsewhere, usually in the context of the controversial question of the invasion of privacy' (Draper, 1978: 146). What seems a more interesting and fundamental question is why, in the UK – and even in those countries which have developed some legislative control – activities engaged in by private security sector agencies do not generate *more* concern and on a more consistent basis. Certainly, the influence of the media in its selection of stories has something to do with it. Clearly also there is a more obvious link in the public eye, and to a large extent in practice, between the private investigator and issues like the invasion of privacy. However, there are other dimensions of the private security phenomenon which must be explored in order to be able to raise the appropriate questions and then attempt to answer them. I have addressed some of these broader issues elsewhere (South, 1984).

2 From correspondence with the NCCL in 1987 it is unclear to what extent this remains their formal position; however, neither it nor support for the proposals put forward by Bruce George, MP, appear to have been retracted.

3 It is fair to note, however, that the exclusion clauses written into the contracts of some, if not all, private security firms protecting them from liability against damage caused by their guards have been declared void in the past by the Court of Appeal. However this has only led to the more sophisticated redrafting of contracts (Wheatcroft, 1978: 2).
    I am grateful to Robert Reiner for his comments on this issue.

9 Conclusion: Limits, Possibilities and Cautious Proposals

A new division of policing labour

The post-war expansion of the private security sector has revolutionary implications for the nature of modern social control and the policing of society. For the foreseeable future, such a significant increase in resort to private arrangements for ensuring security has fundamentally changed society's division of policing labour.

The substantial role played by the private security sector in this new division of policing labour is one which is now well developed. Contrary to the proposition put forward by some commentators critical of this state of affairs (principally members of the police service), it is now highly unlikely that even the most generous increases in public police resources and establishment levels would lead to any considerable decrease in demand for and use of private security services. Quite apart from the advantages that commercial customers find in having security services that are directly answerable to them as paying clients and in the flexibility of a private justice system, both government and many senior police officers value certain services performed by private security. Forms of private security pre-date the nineteenth-century organisation of public policing (South, 1987a) and have expanded in post-war years alongside, rather than at the expense of, considerable growth in the scope, size and sophistication of the public police. Indeed, as the police have changed their force goals and operational priorities in response to changing circumstances, concentrating more selectively on certain crimes and public order responsibilities, so symbiotically has private security capitalised on this situation, offering services on a commercial basis where it perceives needs unmet by the public service. A more complex division of policing labour and service provision in society, simply reflects – at one level – a more complex society.[1]

The significance of the new division of policing labour would be difficult to describe or appreciate purely in terms of statistical indicators. How many people are engaged in forms of policing and security work matters less than what they are doing. The changes that are happening are most importantly of a qualitative nature. They reflect the priorities of the New Feudalism of the modern corporate community in which, in addition to the importance of the legal institutions that legitimate the security of private property, common-sense notions of the sanctity of private property are also emphasised to provide 'a moral basis' for corporate security authority (Selznick, 1969; Shearing et al., 1985c: 372). The police seek to enhance their effectiveness, and increase the sophistication, intensity and capability of their pro-active and reactive routine work and special operations in the public sphere. The private security sector follows a similar path, responding to and stimulating demand from the market in the private sphere, which increasingly includes areas of private property to which large numbers of the public have access whether as consumers, residents or employees. That private security should today be policing large areas of 'public' space without this situation being defined as a challenge to conventional notions about the responsibilities of the public police reflects the fact that such a development has followed from economic and social changes rather than political and legal ones (Shearing et al., 1985c: 371). Of course, this does mean that different economic circumstances will significantly influence the specific functions that private security will fulfil in different locations. But the dominant trend is clear, whether private security is working in the corporate towers of Toronto, the car plants of Detroit or the shopping centres and new housing estates of Milton Keynes.

Private security brings with it a conservatively orientated, privately employed and directed form of commercial justice (South, 1983, 1984). Such a system 'understands' the needs of commercial clients and deals with transgressions in an appropriate manner, avoiding the constraints of the formal legal processing of offences and the bad public relations that can follow from a court case where public sympathy may be elicited for the offender rather than the corporate victim (Shearing et al., 1985c: 377).[2] Private justice systems typically evoke a paternalistic image of the company and the workplace as a small community, but one which expects adherence to certain rules and understandings. Hence, it is legitimate for the company to exert its authority and to make arrangements for the workplace community to be policed and regulated with the aim of ensuring that employees comply with company expectations. This may involve surveillance, investigative, adjudicatory and penalising procedures, but also, as Cohen nicely observes, the staging of Durkheimian ceremonies of social control which resonate with broader trends seeking to stimulate 'community' involvement and responsibility:

> Citizens of today's suburbia or inner-city slum cannot through an effort of will recreate the conditions of an eighteenth century rural parish. Closed circuit television, two-way radios, vigilante patrols, private security

companies and police decoys hardly simulate life in a pre-industrial village. This is not for want of trying. In some large stores, private security police are posing as employees. They conspicuously steal and are then conspicuously 'discovered' by the management and ceremonially disciplined, thus deterring the real employees. (1985: 69)

Private security and private justice are market responses not simply to the crime and other loss-prevention needs of their customers, but also to deep-rooted needs to feel secure: to feel that lives and property which are personally valued are protected, and that offenders can be identified and redress obtained. Security is then, in one important respect, a commodity, to be bought and sold in the market place (Spitzer, 1987: 43). But as Spitzer (1987: 46) emphasises, the value of such a commodity reflects not only material criteria but also an inner human dimension of personal fear and feelings. Taking account of the 'mist-enveloped regions of fear and desire' we must 'place emotion at the centre of the analysis' argues Spitzer (1987: 46). Thus, in examining the process of how security has been turned into a commodity, Spitzer exhorts us to ask (for example) 'why and how . . . security has been separated from its true social context in human association and turned into something that seems to be beyond our control?' (Spitzer, 1987: 49). Spitzer's analysis is a complex one which suggests that security *as* a commodity 'is constituted primarily through a process of symbolic production – through the transformation of images and expectations as much as, if not more than, alterations of the material world' (Spitzer, 1987: 51). The symbolic nature of security, of what the desire for it represents and of the means, human and mechanistic, by which we attempt to achieve it are undeniable (South, 1987b). But as Spitzer recognises, such 'symbolic production' has material consequences, and indeed arises within a material social context. In many respects the authority and practice of private security *is* simply symbolic, but none the less the material world, as embodied in the institution of private property rights, is still the foundation on which the legitimacy of private security rests. Such rights and the dubious extension of their province to cover people and information are held to justify a wide range of activities. The nature of such unchallenged legitimacy and justification deserves further scrutiny and, as I have argued in the previous chapter, appropriate legislative response.

Private security is not in business to serve the general public good; it is in business to serve the needs of its paying clients. It clearly does make a contribution to, for example, crime prevention in some respects, although how much this is offset by a displacement effect, which means those less able to pay for additional security become more heavily victimised, is unknown but probably significant. So public acceptance of private security, in terms of who it serves, its image and the activities that it engages in, remains puzzling. In one sense, private security is probably accepted simply because it is *there*. And it is *there*, increasingly, in all the publicly accessible private places to which people need everyday access: banks, hospitals, shopping centres, office complexes and so on.[3] Not only may many people be pleased that private security is being employed to keep the non-respectable out of these respectable locations, but also there is general common accord about the property owner's right to make arrangements to protect that property. Of course, some ambivalence about this can emerge from uncertainties about what constitutes 'private' property, whilst the public image of private security itself is ambiguous and unclear. The very term 'private security' carries many 'different nuances of meaning' for members of the general public (Shearing et al., 1985b: 227).

Private security does not fit with the common culturally accepted image of the 'protector' or readily offer a neat label or stereotype (Reiss, 1987: 33). The low regard with which private security is viewed does not evoke high confidence in it or a perception of it as the guardian of the public interest but of 'someone else's interests' (Reiss, 1987: 33). If such perceptions are fairly universal, then this does not bode well for public acceptance of the further extension of the role of private security within society's division of policing labour. As I have indicated, such extension is taking place and has strong advocates. The Adam Smith Institute, for example, has argued that, however the efficiency of the public police is measured,

> there is still a strong case for extending the private sector involvement that has already started to undertake several aspects of the police function. Not only do the private services take pressure off the publicly provided police force, but they can be used as a yardstick for comparison, for providing ancillary functions cheaply, and ensuring that new methods are explored. (1984: 23)

But it is short-sighted to raise the question of the efficiency of the public police without at the same time expressing concern about the low standards of training and performance in contract security, especially if one is proposing that private security should undertake yet more work currently performed by the police. As Williams et al. (1984: 46) have observed, 'neither the security industry nor its clients are under any obligation to evaluate the effects of private security arrangements on the problems of crime prevention and order of the wider community.' In the absence of any basis of evaluation, it is difficult to see how private security can be used as a yardstick by which to judge the efficiency of the public police or what reasonable basis there is for holding them up as a role model to encourage greater efficiency or innovation on the part of the police. In reality, such propositions as those put forward by the Adam Smith Institute and others are merely embellishments to a bottom-line ideological belief that low-cost services provided in a highly competitive market are still efficient and hence cost-effective. This is disputable (Borna, 1986: 330; LeGrand and Robinson, 1984; Millward, 1982; Walker, 1984).

Efficiency and the encouragement of a broader contribution to society's needs for crime-prevention services (and the discouragement of antisocial activities) on the part of private security could follow from a system of regulation and accountability which enhanced standards. I shall not reiterate here the other arguments for such a system. However, there are some obvious points about the limitations of what might be done that should be noted, whilst some possibilities should be raised for inclusion on the policy agenda. Of course, limits and possibilities should also always inform each other and if, on the one hand, we should take seriously the 'limits of the possible' then, on the other, in the case of this particular subject, we must also consider the *desirability* of the possible. With this in mind, my concluding comments must be cautionary, although at the same time they harbour some ambition to move *beyond* a concern with *private* security *per se* and towards considering how crime prevention, insurance and victim-support services could be more universally provided to contribute to a greater ensuring of *social* security.

Private security, unequal protection

From the late 1970s, and through the 1980s, there has been a growing acceptance by police and public of the respectable and visible operations of the private security sector. Police disapproval of the less reputable private security companies understandably persists and public opprobrium is occasionally aroused when media revelations point to particular abuses, shortcomings or practices that challenge the comfortable notion that 'things like that can't happen here'. Meanwhile, the private security sector expands rapidly, benignly encouraged by government and increasingly indispensable both to its more parochial and multinational, public and private employers. The contribution of private security to crime prevention is welcomed as a public good, and its role in systems of management, surveillance, protection and control is embraced as a contributor to private profit.

Safeguards to protect the individual against abuses, intrusion into his or her private life and so on do exist. For example, the Rehabilitation of Offenders Act 1974, the legislation now applying to private security companies in Northern Ireland and that concerning data protection, credit references and the like, the new telephone tapping regulations (the Interception of Communications Act 1985), civil and criminal law regarding powers of 'stop and search', inter-rogation and detention and a variety of other provisions in law (and custom) should all counter the extension of private security activities beyond their supposedly right and proper limits.

In practice, such piecemeal safeguards are themselves the real subject of limitation. It is the necessity of establishing an effective system of accountability and regulation to safeguard civil liberties and curtail certain specialist (and not so specialist) activities that is my primary concern.

It must be recognised immediately, however, that it is clearly problematic to be in a situation where the choice is between uncontrolled inadequacy and controlled efficiency, especially if part of the problem is the *threat* to civil liberties posed by very efficient private security services. On the one hand, the majority of non-specialised services that are playing (and will increasingly play) a significant role in the provision of services which affect the public as private citizens, employees, taxpayers, consumers and so on must demand attention. Given their prevalence, they must make the grade of acceptable public service standards and, correspondingly, be made accessible to an effective mechanism of public scrutiny. At the same time, precisely because certain parts of the private security sector are already highly competent and efficient in the specialist services that they offer, but are *not* subject to public scrutiny, the case for regulation and accountability is strong here also.

Obviously, serious doubts can (and in a constructive frame of mind *should*) be entertained about the role of private security as a 'public service' and about the adequacy of systems of public scrutiny, regulation and accountability. Such doubts hinge on realistic per-ceptions of the situation but can also embrace what, at present, seem rather optimistic prescriptions for really effective change. For example, Flavel in what is otherwise a most astute and realistic paper, can ultimately offer little that can be done *now*:

> If organised private security is seen as an exercise in selective policing, biased in favour of wealth and power, then for example developing a superficial system of public accountability, or improving police-security relations will make no difference. Radical change would seem to be necessary in the ownership and control of property, in the meanings attached to the term security, and in the aims and motivations of security organisations, before the systematic application of property security could be seen as a broadly based social service. (1973: 15)

One can but agree, but such 'radical change' is unlikely to happen in the immediately foreseeable future and in the meantime the power and impact of private security as a 'biased' and 'selective' system of 'policing' increases.

In similar vein, the important work of Shearing and Stenning ultimately eschews practical policy in favour of a somewhat utopian recommendation that the nature of changing forms of property be reconceived. As Weiss notes,

> in the face of the threat to individual liberties that private security poses, Shearing and Stenning suggest as a remedy *not* the attempt to regulate the private security industry, but to declare 'mass private property' as 'new property', hence subject to the 'elaborate protections of publicly-owned public space.' Just how such a revolution is to be achieved is left to the reader's imagination, but even if such a transformation were to occur, it would be a dubious achievement. (1984: 18)

Even with a re-conceptualisation of property and legal and other forms of 'protection' surrounding it, such a proposal offers little in the way of tangible action for dealing with the private security sector and its growth, power and activities. Unless within this vision it has simply disappeared from society, which seems an unlikely consequence, such a proposal produces no effective system of accountability or guarantee of civil liberties. Changes in the nature of property form and distribution would undoubtedly have profound implications for private security, as for the entire social, economic and political structure of society. But in the absence of likelihood of such change we have to bear in mind the immediacy of influences that private security currently has on aspects of social inequality, policy matters and everyday visions of the way that society is ordered and policed. As Flavel (1973: 15) puts it: 'a secondary system of policing which provides unequal protection to different groups in society is in itself socially divisive but it also has a direct influence on the operational priorities of the public police and perhaps affects people's attitudes to policing in general.' Realism and practicability dictate that while we might look to change in the future there are matters to recognise as priorities for more immediate intervention. The private security sector is not going to 'go away'. It is expanding rapidly and massively. As it does so it seeks to make itself and its services more indispensable, proselytising about its contribution to crime prevention, public safety and security in what it can point to as an ever more dangerous and unstable world.

In his Annual Report of HM Chief Inspector of Constabulary for 1977, Sir James Haughton, referred to the original objective of crime *prevention* of the Metropolitan Police Force when first established and noted a re-awakening of interest in preventative aspects of policing among some forces in England and Wales. Haughton's Report was confident that prevention would receive 'increasing attention throughout the police service', yet in the same year Sir Robert Mark was drawing public attention to the difficulties that the police were facing in being able to provide anything more than 'fire brigade' policing. In an interview with the magazine *Security Gazette* in July 1977, Sir Robert commented on the role to be played in crime prevention by private security and on the 'limited educative role of specialised crime prevention activities'. One implication of this state of affairs, according to the editorial in the same issue of *Security Gazette* (1977: 215) was that, 'the result of applying preventive measures to particular types of risk is to divert crime to other targets and to encourage the development of new forms of criminal activity.' This is, of course, a widely held view, and to tackle the problem there have been various suggestions concerning wider cooperation and coordination between the police and other agencies operating with crime prevention or related functions. A 1984 interdepartmental document (Home Office et al., 1984) was only one of a stream of proposals from various sources urging the need for cooperation and coordination. In its 1977 editorial, *Security Gazette* suggested that crime prevention should become less a separate police departmental function and more one of the everyday duties of the police in 'active cooperation' with other contributing agencies which 'would undoubtedly include a reliable, competent and fully accountable security industry, which through licensing or other means would be acceptable to the police as a partner.'

Subsequently, James Anderton (1978) Chief Constable of the Manchester force, suggested the establishment of a 'Central Crime Prevention Agency' to coordinate and disseminate information to the affiliated network of agencies. In Anderton's view there is no reason why the police service should not assist in this manner those security companies which wish to improve the range and standard of their services. If Sir Robert Mark's pessimistic portrayal of the ability of the police service to stretch to protect property from burglary and similar crimes has only half the validity that it seems to have had, then these proposals, from both sides of the policing fence – private and public – may well still be important pointers to real trends in the development of the private security sector. Indeed, the comments of Sir Kenneth Newman, the recently retired Commissioner, quoted in Chapter 1 (p. 14) indicate that there is continuing momentum in this direction.

Besides the trends in inter-agency proposals, other initiatives and possibilities are encouraged, sharing at least one principal consideration – that of reducing *cost*. The USA is often over-played as an indicator of 'the shape of things to come' in the UK, but in the current economic climate there is no shortage of reliable parallels, and approaches to dealing with crime problems may seek to emulate some US developments. In the most recent major US study of private security, 384 law enforcement administrators were surveyed and 'indicated a willingness to discuss [some] transfer of responsibilities to private security'

(Cunningham and Taylor, 1984: 4): 'They cited a number of police tasks "potentially more cost-effectively performed by private security" – among them public building security, parking enforcement and court security.'

The offloading of crime prevention and detection services from the public to the service sector is limited and cautious even in the USA, although privately run prisons are a new growth phenomenon (Weiss, personal communications, 1984, 1985: *New York Times*, 25 February 1985, see above p. 109). However, even in the UK, the increased availability of private security services has commended itself strongly to advocates of the general privatisation of public services as a means to reduce direct taxation.[4]

Whilst such advocates tend to be unclear about the extent of public expenditure cuts which are workable and about the remaining adequacy of public provision of services for the less well off, there is one element of the argument which should be highlighted here. Seldon (1977: 106), for example, presents the argument that 'You pays your taxes, but you gets no choice'. In relation to crime prevention services, he argues that:

> generally police patrols seem in principle to be a typical public good from which all in the patrol area benefit, from which they cannot be excluded, and for which they cannot be charged. But patrols benefit homes or buildings not according to their size (roughly reflected in their rates) but according to the value of the property (and life) protected. These values are reflected more accurately by insurance cover. (1977: 108)

According to Seldon's proposition, then, 'police charges could therefore be made to reflect the varying value of patrol services to individuals or firms in the area according to the lives or property at risk.' However, such proposals to privatise public services, especially in key areas of state responsibility such as health and criminal justice (Adam Smith Institute, 1984) inevitably reproduce and compound existing and familiar inequalities and contradictions (South, 1988). But such proposals do not come only from 'market-orientated' economic commentators. Proposals similar to Seldon's – to charge for policing services, whether with public and private police in commercial competition or having integrated them – have also come from and been discussed by senior representatives of the police force.

Philip Knights, former Chief Constable of the West Midlands police, in a paper to a Joint Conference of the Association of Chiefs of Police, Association of Metropolitan Authorities and Association of County Councils, noted that:

> the police committee of the AMA in 1976, when considering the role and development of local authority police forces and private security felt that it would be desirable for all types of policing to come under one large

umbrella, and interest was expressed in establishing a multi-tier police force comprising, for example, police officers as we generally understand the term, existing 'private' police forces, private security forces and traffic wardens, together with, perhaps, persons to patrol high-rise flats, covered shopping centres and the like. It was felt that the total cost of running the full, proposed organisation would be the same as now and charges could still be made to firms and individuals for the services of the 'security' section of the force. (1979: 7)

Knights suggests that:

such a move would no doubt have its supporters, but it does of course raise the whole politically sensitive question of 'municipal trading' and whether it is right that in the matter of police protection the more affluent citizen should be able to purchase a better service from his local Police Authority than that which the authority might be able to make available to the less affluent. (1979: 7)

Here Knights echoes (knowingly or not) the deliberations of the United Nations Committee on Crime Prevention and Control, quoted in a circular to the fifth United Nations Congress on Crime Prevention (Stead, 1975: 381). The Committee observed that:

the development of private law enforcement very often introduced an inequality of protection, since the richer groups in the society could afford additional security services while the poorer sections were left to manage with whatever services the state could provide. In a modern, complicated society, private services might be required, but they should be carefully supervised by the official police and standards should be established by Governments for their recruitment and performance. Too much private security, favouring some groups against others, could foster insecurity on a large scale.

Government, private security and public benefits

'Self-policing' and 'community protection' are the kind of slogans that have emerged out of long-overdue debates about how to provide accountable systems of crime prevention for local communities, particularly the traditionally disadvantaged. The future development of these debates must be considered elsewhere, but they resonate with policy-orientated observations which have been around slightly longer.

In the late 1970s and early 1980s a wave of research – most evidently in the USA – was directed at the 'link between crime and the built environment' (Murray et al., 1980; South, 1987b). Such studies occasionally offered familiar conclusions ('not enough is yet known about this area' etc.), but none the less suggested eminently reasonable and desirable minor policy goals, such as the installation of better locks as cheap and cost-effective and the reduction in the number of families per floor or per building. In the UK, the Department of the Environment saw the need for the rehabilitation of housing estates, including provision of some resources for elementary security fixtures, as embodied in its Priority Estates Programme. But as Kirsch points out:

> resident caretakers, adequate Direct Labour Organisations to cope with speedy repairs, and more council officers based directly on estates and in neighbourhoods are precisely those services which have been hit by the Tory government squeeze on rates and the rate support grant. As for safer designs of new estates, with public housebuilding ground to a halt by Tory policy there is a grim irony in this suggestion. (1983: 2)

Contradictions and dangers abound in trying to provide security in an insecure world. Hence we need to ensure that the community action and concern about crime that has found a new voice does not get into the dangerous position of talking to itself. It must engage with local government and national levels of policy planning and implementation. Correspondingly, government must (and we must work towards ensuring that it does) listen to the small voice from below. The issue of private security, and more broadly issues around crime prevention and privatisation of various public services, must be viewed, and hence promote realistic responses, within a social, economic and political context which contains powerful cross-currents. If on this basis the following suggestions seem ambitious it is only because there is nothing wrong in having grand goals as long as we have the sense to accommodate and work on small-scale incremental gains.

Just broadening the policy focus in one direction would suggest that the insurance industry might provide us with some idea for alternative systems of offering forms of financial and social security as well as security from crime. This is not to deny the need for increased provision of physical security that communities may feel and genuinely experience. However, in providing for the protection of life, limb and property it is reasonably common and reasonably advisable not only to seek a good lock but also a reasonable insurance policy, although even such basic measures are beyond the means of many. Yet more desirable would be a universally accessible scheme which provided for both physical security *and* insurance. According to Pease: 'the position of the insurance company is clearly critical [in the field of crime prevention], since it is the only agency in a position to offer the householder who wishes to be insured, financial incentives for crime prevention measures, in the form of reduced premiums' (1979: 32). Pease goes on to project some imaginary 'futures' for the contribution of insurance to crime prevention. I would like briefly to take up one of these 'futures', one in which the provision of a particular kind of insurance is a nationalised enterprise. As Pease outlines this particular model:

> in this future the insurance companies are nationalised. Many insurance surveyors join the police as specialised crime prevention officers and the crime prevention units take over the responsibility of surveying properties for theft insurance purposes. Theft insurance on properties becomes compulsory along the lines of third party motoring insurance and crime prevention officers have annual right of access to all properties for the purpose of survey. Actuarial rate of the calculation of premiums is available but social factors are incorporated into the calculation of premiums. In this way, insurance is no longer a fully commercial enterprise. For example, those living in inner cities are subject to high rates of crime but only low premiums are exacted, although premiums do vary with precautions taken by the individual property holder. Certain classes of citizen, for example old age pensioners, are allowed free crime prevention devices to bring them to the lowest premium rates. Lack of competition between companies means that high-risk individuals cannot use their insurance brokers in such a way as to allow them to minimise the required levels of crime prevention measure. (1979: 33)

In my conception of this 'future', the insurance industry is nationalised as a wholly or majority-owned, state-directed enterprise. I say 'directed' because for the purposes of any transition for such a complex system of financial institutions, from being a literally capital-intensive and orientated body to one reorganised as a system of social security and insurance, then retention of existing expertise and administrative processes would clearly be needed. A system, not unequatable to a fairer tax structure, could bring a categorised range of property forms under the provisions of legislation requiring subscription to a system of National Property Insurance, with subsidy or free subscription in cases of the unemployed, those with low incomes, the elderly and so on. A similar arrangement could provide for life and health insurance, taking the kind of benefits expected from private schemes into the arena of provision given by state schemes. In what would presumably still be a mixed economy, financing of the schemes could come not only from the state but also from the kind of investment that private insurance engages in currently. As a medium-term development, this is not a far-fetched proposition. As Bottoms observes, schemes set up to provide criminal injuries compensation in various Western countries have:

> run into substantial criticism, especially on the ground that if the state is to make grants to the victims of misfortune, there is no reason to single out the crime victim; rather, it is argued, the movement should be (as in New Zealand it has been) towards a more general scheme of state insurance and compensation for personal injuries. (1983: 171)

Such a shift could be profitably accommodated in a *socially* profitable and useful way within a system of Nationalised Insurance. Regulated private security, private insurance plans and selective and discretionary criminal injuries compensation could provide the basis for a nationalised and universally applicable system of provision of this whole range of services.

The cautionary point here lies in the suggestion that Smart finds in Foucault's later work that society has seen: 'a relative decrease in the significance of techniques of discipline, and a concomitant increase in the importance of mechanisms of insurance and security; [this] represents the insertion of a "principle of cohesion" in the very fabric of society, the constitution of a particular kind of solidarity' (Smart, 1983: 80). The argument for optimism lies in agreeing that social cohesion has its desirability: that what has to be changed and developed is the accountability of the institutions that shape that cohesion. Another and different 'kind of solidarity' can be worked towards, constructing and constructed by a different 'social fabric'. Significant, realistic and just social change can take place through some reorganisation of existing social and economic institutions.

Conclusion: Beyond *1984*

George Orwell apparently arrived at his choice of year for the depiction of his totally surveilled and security-conscious society of *1984* by simply reversing the last two numerals of the year in which he was writing. Hence, the significance of 1984 as a motif for totalitarian society was less strict prophecy than simple ironic gesture on the part of a prescient writer. The preceding chapters in this book depend less on foresight than on simply describing what has already happened, is happening and what might be proposed by way of response. But, writing several years after a different 1984 from the one that Orwell envisaged, it is still well worth considering the words of Philip Selznick, written at the same time as Orwell was outlining his 'Big Brother' society:

> Do we need or want agencies of control so efficient . . . that every actual offence has an equal chance of being known and processed? . . . I am concerned that we do not respond too eagerly and too well to the apparent need for effective mechanisms of social control. In the administration of justice, if anywhere, we need to guard human values and forestall the creation of mindless machines for handling cases according to set routines. Here vigilance consists in careful study of actual operations so that we may know what will be lost or gained. (Selznick, 1948: 84)[5]

As I hope to have demonstrated, in the modern spectrum of formal/commercial/private/informal dimensions of social control and justice, the actual operations of the private security sector have a significance demanding very serious vigilance.

A call for the accountability of such agencies is obviously a call for the establishment of machinery to administer such provision in a democratic fashion. A goal might be accountability guaranteed by public right of inspection, for example of training, information collection, operational activities and so on. It would, however, be to simply reproduce the 1984 nightmare to follow Bentham's solution to the old question of 'who guards the guards' by pursuing the ideal of 'omnipresent inspection, of everyone, by everyone' (Ignatieff, 1978: 78). Beyond 1984, it is precisely this kind of future that democratic accountability can and must guard against.

Notes

1 Such complexity includes not only the growth of the phenomena of mass private property to which the public has routine access (such as shopping complexes) but also the extension of personal private space compared to previous centuries. Concomitant with this has come the demand for more protection from the invasion of such space (Reiss, 1987). This complexity extends, too, to varying possibilities about how the future division of policing labour will develop. While one plausible scenario is that we will see increasing differentiation, there is also evidence to suggest that roles and the foci of work will increasingly converge. Reiss (1987: 42) for example, suggests that: 'Employers of private police . . . may be shifting from their major focus of protecting corporate property against loss to protecting their employees and clients. The public police, correlatively, may need to shift from major reliance on reactive policing in response to citizen complaints of intrusions to proactive compliance policing. Both appear to be shifting toward compliance policing.'

2 For more extensive discussion and analysis of the operation of private justice systems in the workplace, see the pioneering work of Stuart Henry (Henry, 1983, 1987a, b, c; see also Scraton and South, 1981, 1984).

3 In recent years local authorities have hired private security companies to patrol their housing estates, and such 'experiments' have received the wholehearted approval of the police (see *Evening Standard*, 19 June 1985: 13). Proposals to use private security to guard government offices where confidential papers are kept has drawn criticism (*Evening Standard*, 3 June 1985: 9); tenants concerned about drug dealing and prostitution in blocks of council flats called for action and the response has been the hiring of private security (*Evening Standard*, 11 November 1986: 15), whilst hospital staff concerned over attacks on nurses are now provided with security escorts (*East London Advertiser*, 5 September 1986: 1; *The Daily Telegraph*, 13 August 1986). Media commentators observe that as the fear of crime rises, so too does demand for security technology, guards and even arms (*The Sunday Telegraph Magazine*, 26 April 1987: 22). The regulation of car-parking on the public highway is being privatised and companies with low standards and disturbing attitudes enthusiastically seek the higher returns that come from the zealous pursuit of clamping with the 'Denver Boot' (*London Daily News*, 29 June 1987: 20–1; *Time Out*, 11 February 1987: 10). Recently, a further stimulus to the growth of private (non-police) security patrols

has come with the use of Manpower Services Commission funding by local authorities. Such Community Programme security schemes have received mixed reactions but will mean a higher profile for non-police security patrols in the localities which set them up (see *Guardian*, 4 January 1986: 3; *Police Review*, 17 July 1987: 1428).

4 As this book goes to press the government has issued a Green Paper, *Punishment, Custody and the Community* (Home Office, 1988), which indicates that it is considering the part that private security organisations could play in proposals for various forms of house arrest for offenders. One suggestion is that the probation service could contract out some of its work to outside organisations and that private security could, for example, be responsible for monitoring curfews imposed on offenders.

5 This quotation is edited in so far as Selznick refers to 'impartial' agencies of control which, as I have illustrated, is precisely *not* the point of private security.

References

Abel, R. (1982) 'The contradictions of informal justice', in R. Abel (ed.), *The Politics of Informal Justice*. New York: Academic Press.

Adam Smith Institute (1984) *The 'Omega File': Justice Policy*. London: Adam Smith Institute.

Adams, J. (1986) *The Financing of Terror*. London: New English Library.

All England Law Reports (1980) *Photo Productions Ltd* v. *Securicor Transport Ltd, All England Law Reports*, 1980, volume 1. London: Butterworth. pp. 556–7.

Allen, M. (1925) *The Pioneer Policewoman*. London: Chatto and Windus.

Anderton, J. (1978) 'Crime and the community', unpublished address to IFSSEC Conference. London, 25 April.

Arendt, H. (1958). *The Human Condition*. Chicago: University of Chicago Press.

Bailey, M. and Leigh, D. (1987) 'Bugging plot detective in Foreign Office link', *Observer*, 22 February.

Balcon, J. (1986) 'Far from secure in their powers', *Police Review* (Letters), 17 October: 2109.

Becker, T. (1974) 'The place of private police in society: an area of research for the social sciences', *Social Problems*, 21 (3): 438–53.

Beet, T. (1906) 'Methods of American private detective agencies', *Appleton's Magazine*, October.

Bell, G. (no date) *Bell's Security Handbook – Managers and Security*. London: Bell and Sons.

Borna, S. (1986) 'Free enterprise goes to prison', *British Journal of Criminology*, 26 (4): 321–34.

Bottoms, A. (1983) 'Neglected features of contemporary penal systems', in D. Garland and P. Young (eds), *The Power to Punish*. London: Heinemann.

Bowden, T. (1978) *Beyond the Limits of the Law*. Harmondsworth: Penguin.

Bridges, C. (1978) 'Risk management and the security officer', *Security and Protection*, June: 46, 48.

British Security Industry Association (1987) *The British Security Industry Association*. London: BSIA.

Brogden, M. (1981) 'All police is cunning bastards' in R. Fine, A. Hunt, B. Moorhouse and D. McBarnet (eds), *Law, State and Society*. Beckenham: Croom Helm.

Bunyan, T. (1976) *The History and Practice of the Political Police in Britain*. London: Quartet.

Burden, P. (1980) *The Burglary Business and You*. London: Macmillan.

Cain, M. (1985) 'Beyond informal justice', *Contemporary Crises*, 9: 335–73.

Calder, A. (1969) *The People's War*. London: Panther.

Callaghan, D. (1976) 'Accountability of security in practice', in P. Young (ed.), *Major Property Crime in the United Kingdom: Some Aspects of Law Enforcement*. Edinburgh: School of Criminology, University of Edinburgh.

Campbell, D. (1978a) 'Personal surveillance devices', *New Scientist*, 23 November: 600–2.

Campbell, D. (1978b) 'The pedigree dogs of war', *Time Out*, 21 July: 7–11.

Campbell, D. (1987) 'Government may use new prison ship', *London Daily News*, 10 July.

Carson, W. (1970) 'White collar crime and the enforcement of factory legislation', *British Journal of Criminology*, 10 (4): 383–98.

Carson, W. (1979) 'The conventionalisation of early factory crime', *International Journal of the Sociology of Law*, 7 (1): 37–60.

Carson, W. (1982) *The Other Cost of Britain's Oil*. Oxford: Martin Robertson.

Carson, W. and Young, P. (1976) 'Sociological aspects of major property crime', in P. Young (ed.), *Major Property Crime in the United Kingdom: Some Aspects of Law Enforcement*. Edinburgh: School of Criminology, University of Edinburgh.

Carter, R. (1974) *Theft in the Market: an Economic Analysis of Costs and Incentives in Improving Prevention by Government and Private Police and Reducing Loss by Insurance*. London: Institute of Economic Affairs.

Carter, R. (1976) 'Economic aspects of major property crime', in P. Young (ed.), *Major Property Crime in the United Kingdom: Some Aspects of Law Enforcement*. Edinburgh: School of Criminology, University of Edinburgh.

Clayton, T. (1967) *The Protectors*. London: Oldbourne.

Cohen, N. (1987) ' "Safest vault in the world" raided', *The Independent*, 14 July: 2.

Cohen, S. (ed.) (1971) *Images of Deviance*. Harmondsworth: Penguin.

Cohen, S. (1979) 'The punitive city', *Contemporary Crises*, 3 (4): 339–63.

Cohen, S. (1983) 'Social control talk: telling stories about correctional change', in D. Garland and P. Young (eds), *The Power to Punish*. London: Heinemann.

Cohen, S. (1985) *Visions of Social Control*. Cambridge: Polity Press.

Critchley, T. (1978) *A History of Police in England and Wales, 1900–1966*. London: Constable.

Cunningham, W. and Taylor, T. (1984) 'The growing role of private security', *National Institute of Justice, Research in Brief*, October. Washington: US Department of Justice.

Daily Mail (1986) 'Crime curb package', 23 June.

Daily Mirror (1982) 'Crooks get into uniform', 10 August: 6.

Davies, N. (1987) 'Ministers face new quiz on links with security company', *London Daily News*, 5 March.

Davies, N. and Edwards, C. (1987) 'Secret army', *London Daily News*, 6 March: 18, 31.

Davis, A. (1980) 'Cooperation', *Security Gazette*, January: 21–4.

Ditton, J. (1977) *Part-time Crime: an Ethnography of Fiddling and Pilferage*. London: Macmillan.

Dobson, C. (1987) 'Running the risk with Sir Kenneth', *Evening Standard*, 16 June: 31.

Dorn, N. and South, N. (1987) 'Some issues in the development of drug markets and law enforcement: notes for a criminological perspective', paper to European Community Workshop on Drugs: Side Effects of Control Policies, Luxemburg, 22–23 October.

Draper, H. (1978) *Private Police*. Harmondsworth: Penguin.

Dring, D. (1972) 'The growth of alarm systems', in P. Wiles and F. McClintock (eds), *The Security Industry in the United Kingdom*. Cambridge: Institute of Criminology, University of Cambridge.

Edwards, P. and Scullion, H. (1982) 'Deviancy theory and industrial praxis: a study of discipline and social control in an industrial setting', *Sociology*, 16 (3): 322–40.

Evans, P. (1980) 'Nuclear attack – there's a job for private security', *Security Gazette*, June: 33–4.

Evening Standard (1986) 'Changes in law "make life easier for shoplifters" ', 6 February.

'Eye' (1987) 'Handcuffs and truncheons for security guards', *Security Times*, September: 19.

Fine, B., Kinsey, R., Lea, J., Picciotto, S. and Young, J. (eds) (1979) *Capitalism and the Rule of Law: from Deviancy Theory to Marxism*. London: Hutchinson.

Fish, D. (1962) *Airline Detective*. London: Collins.

Fitzgerald, M., McLennan, G. and Pawson, J. (eds) (1981) *Crime and Society: Readings in History and Theory*. London: Routledge and Kegan Paul.

Flavel, W. (1973) 'Research into security organisations', unpublished paper, Second Bristol Seminar on the Sociology of the Police, April.

Fosdick, R. (1969) *European Police Systems*. New York: Patterson Smith.

Foucault, M. (1977) *Discipline and Punish*. London: Allen Lane.

Freedman, D. and Stenning, P. (1977) *Private Security, Police and the Law in Canada*. Toronto: Centre of Criminology, University of Toronto.

Frieden, K. (1986) 'Public needs and private wants', *Social Policy*, Fall: 19–30.

Friedenberg, E. (1975) *The Disposal of Liberty and Other Industrial Wastes*. New York: Doubleday.

Garland, D. and Young P., (eds) (1983) *The Power to Punish*. London: Heinemann.

Garner, A. (1978) 'The guardians: a study of the commercialised police in Britain'. BA thesis, Manchester Polytechnic, Manchester.

Gatrell, V. (1980) 'The decline of theft and violence in Victorian and Edwardian England', in V. Gatrell, B. Lenman and G. Parker (eds), *Crime and Law: the Social History of Crime in Western Europe since 1500*. London: Europa.

George, B. (1984) 'The case for public control', in D. Williams, B. George and E. MacLennan (eds), *Guarding against Low Pay*. Low Pay Pamphlet 29. London: Low Pay Unit.

Gleizal, J. (1981) 'Police, law and security in France: questions of method and political strategy', *International Journal of the Sociology of Law*, 9: 361–82.

Golding, P. and Murdock, G. (1983) 'Privatising pleasure', *Marxism Today*, 27 (10), October: 32–6.

Gower, L. (1984) *Review of Investor Protection*. Cmnd 9125. London: HMSO.

Gregory, J. (1986) 'Sex, class and crime: towards a non-sexist criminology', in R. Matthews and J. Young (eds), *Confronting Crime*. London: Sage.

Guardian (1987) 'Staff warn on private prisons', 22 May.

Guarino-Ghezzi, S. (1983) 'A private network of social control: insurance investigation units', *Social Problems*, 30 (5): 521–31.

Gurr, T. (1977) *Rogues, Rebels and Reformers: a Political History of Urban Crime and Conflict*. London: Sage.

Hall, S. and McLennan, G. (1982) 'Custom and law: law and crime as historical processes', in *Issues in Crime and Society*, Milton Keynes: Open University Press.

Hamilton, P. (1967) *Espionage and Subversion in an Industrial Society*. London: Hutchinson.

Hamilton, P. (1968) 'Security is an attitude', in N. Currer-Briggs (ed.), *Security: Attitudes and Techniques for Management*. London: Hutchinson.

Hamilton, P. (1972) *Computer Security*. London: Associated Business Programmes.

Hamilton, P. (1974) 'Legislating for security', *Security Gazette*, March: 94–5.

Hamilton, P. and Norman, A. (eds) (1975) *Handbook of Security*. London: Kluwer/Harrap.

Hanna, M. (1987) 'Jail security scare over lying workers', *The Observer*, 14 June.

Hansard (1986) 'Private security companies' (Written Answers), 18 December: 650.

Hansard (1987) 'Police computers' (Written Answers), 26 February: 342.

Hasler, G. (1978) 'Risk management consultancy – the need for the independent expert', *Security and Protection*, June: 44–5.

Helm, S. (1987) 'Sales pitch for his lordship', *The Independent*, 12 September: 4.

Henry, S. (1978) *The Hidden Economy*. Oxford: Martin Robertson.

Henry, S. (1983) *Private Justice: Towards Integrated Theorising in the Sociology of Law*. London: Routledge and Kegan Paul.

Henry, S. (1987a) 'Disciplinary pluralism: four models of private justice in the workplace', *Sociological Review*, 35 (2): 279–319.

Henry, S. (1987b) 'Private justice and the policing of labour: the dialectics of industrial discipline', in C. Shearing and P. Stenning (eds), *Private Policing*. Beverly Hills: Sage.

Henry, S. (1987c) 'The construction and deconstruction of social control: thoughts on the discursive production of state law and private justice', in J. Lowman, R. Menzies and T. Palys (eds), *Transcarceration: Essays in the Sociology of Social Control*. Aldershot: Gower.

Hilliard, B. (1985) 'Interception poser: will police prosecute MI5?', *Police Review*, 22 March: 57.

Hindess, B. (1973) *The Use of Official Statistics in Sociology*. London: Macmillan.

Home Office (1973a) *The Disappearing Profits: Pilferage from Smaller Shops: a Home Office and Police Guide*. London: HMSO.

Home Office (1973b) *Shoplifting and Thefts by Shop Staff*. London: HMSO.

Home Office (1979) *The Private Security Industry: a Discussion Paper*. London: HMSO.

Home Office (1986) Standing Conference on Crime Prevention: Reports of the Working Group on Commercial Robbery. London: Home Office.

Home Office (1988) *Punishment, Custody and the Community*, London: HMSO.

Home Office, Departments of Education and Science, Environment, Health and Social Security and Welsh Office (1984) *Circular on Crime Prevention 8/84*. London: Home Office.

Hougan, J. (1979) *Spooks – the Haunting of America: the Private Use of Secret Agents*. New York: Bantam.

House of Commons Home Affairs Committee (1987a) *Contract Provision of Prisons*. London: HMSO.

House of Commons Home Affairs Committee (1987b) *Report on the State and Use of Prisons*, 2 vols. London: HMSO.

Hussein, A. (1978) 'Extended review of *Discipline and Punish* by Michel Foucault', *Sociological Review*, November: 932.

Hyder, K. (1987) 'Privatisation of jails next?', *Labour Weekly*, 15 May: 8.

Ignatieff, M. (1978) *A Just Measure of Pain*. London: Macmillan.

Independent, The (1986) 'Security offers key to reduced insurance costs', 22 November.

Institute for Employment Research (1983) *1983 Economic Review*. Coventry: University of Warwick.

Jeffries, F. (ed.) (1974) *Private Policing and Security in Canada: a Workshop*. Toronto: Centre of Criminology, University of Toronto.

Jones, M. (ed.) (1974) *Privacy*. London: David and Charles.

Jordan and Sons (Surveys) Limited (1983) *British Security Companies*. London: Jordan and Sons.

Kakalik, J. and Wildhorn, S. (1972) *Private Police in the United States: Findings and Recommendations*, vol. 1. Rand Corporation Study for US Department of Justice, Washington DC: Government Printing Office (five volumes).

Vol. 2: *The Private Police Industry: its Nature and Extent*.

Vol. 3: *Current Regulation of Private Police: Regulatory Agency Experience and Views*.

Vol. 4: *The Law and Private Police.*

Vol. 5: *Special-Purpose Public Police.* Washington DC: National Institute of Law Enforcement and Criminal Justice, LEAA of the US Department of Justice; US Government Printing Office (1972). (Originally published 1971, Santa Monica, California: Rand Corporation.)

Kerr, M. (1979a) 'Confrontation or cooperation', *Police Review*, 26 January.

Kerr, M. (1979b) 'Who should control the security industry?' *Police Review*, 2 February.

Kidd, S. (1986) 'Advance and be recognised', *Security Times*, January: 11–4.

King, S. (1983) 'Not guilty', *Girl About Town Magazine*, 11 October.

Kirsch, B. (1983) 'Crime prevention', *Marxism Today*, 2 October: 2.

Klare, M. (1975) 'Rent-a-cop: the private security industry in the US', in Centre for Research on Criminal Justice (ed.), *The Iron Fist and the Velvet Glove: an Analysis of the US Police.* Berkeley, California: Centre for Research on Criminal Justice.

Knapp Commission (1972) Report by the Commission to investigate allegations of police corruption in New York City, Whitman Knapp, Chairman, 3 August 1972. Extracted in Chambliss, W. (ed.) (1975) *Criminal Law in Action.* Santa Barbara: Hamilton.

Knights, P. (1979) 'Policing – public or private?', text of talk to ACPO/AMA/ACC Joint Summer Conference, Harrogate (shortened version published 1979, *Police*, 11 (2): 12, 14).

Kulis, J. (1983) 'Profit in the private pre-sentence report', *Federal Probation*, 14, December.

Labour Research (1987) 'Getting to know what's right and wrong', October: 7–11.

Labour Weekly (1986) 'Escort service "insults Britain"', 7 November: 7.

LeGrand, J. and Robinson, R. (eds) (1984) *Privatisation and the Welfare State.* London: Allen and Unwin.

Lipson, M. (1975) *On Guard: the Business of Private Security.* New York: Quadrangle/ New York Times Book Company.

Lowman, J. (1982) 'Crime, criminal justice policy and the urban environment', in D. Herbert and R. Johnston (eds), *Geography and the Urban Environment*, 5, New York: Wiley. pp. 307–41.

Lowman, J., Menzies, R. and Palys, T. (eds) (1987) *Transcarceration: Essays in the Sociology of Social Control.* Aldershot: Gower.

Luzon, J. (1978) 'Corporate headquarters private security', *Police Chief*, 6 (45): 39–42.

McIntosh, M. (1971) 'Changes in the organisation of thieving', in S. Cohen (ed.), *Images of Deviance.* Harmondsworth: Penguin.

McIntosh, M. (1975) *The Organisation of Crime.* London: Macmillan.

Mack, J. (1975) *The Crime Industry.* Hants: Farnborough Press.

Madgwick, D. and Smythe, T. (1974) *The Invasion of Privacy.* London: Pitman.

Mars, G. (1974) 'Dock pilferage', in P. Rock and M. McIntosh (eds), *Deviance and Social Control.* London: Tavistock.

Mars, G. (1982) *Cheats at Work: an Anthropology of Workplace Crime.* London: Allen and Unwin.

Marwick, A. (1977) *Women at War.* London: Fontana.

Marx, G. (1987) 'The interweaving of public and private police in undercover work', in C. Shearing and P. Stenning (eds), *Private Policing.* Beverly Hills: Sage. pp. 172–93.

MATSA (1983) *Report on the Security Industry.* Esher: Managerial, Administrative, Technical and Supervisory Association.

MATSA (1986) *Security Industry: 1986 Wages and Conditions Survey.* Esher: Managerial, Administrative, Technical and Supervisory Association.

Matthews, E. (1972) 'Automatic burglar alarms – a police viewpoint', in P. Wiles and F. McClintock (eds), *The Security Industry in the United Kingdom*. Cambridge: Institute of Criminology, University of Cambridge.

May, D. (1978) 'Juvenile shoplifters and the organisation of store security: a case study in the social construction of delinquency', *International Journal of Criminology and Penology*, 6: 137–60.

Meek, V. (1967) *Private Enquiries: a Handbook for Detectives*. New York: Wiley; London: Duckworth.

Metropolitan Police (1985) 'Commissioner opens international security exhibition', Press Release, Metropolitan Police Press Bureau, 15 April.

Mills, C. Wright (1959) *The Sociological Imagination*. New York: Oxford University Press.

Millward, R. (1982) 'The comparative performance of public and private ownership', in E. Roll (ed.), *The Mixed Economy*. London: Macmillan.

Momboisse, R. (1968) *Industrial Security for Strikes, Riots and Disasters*. Illinois: Charles Thomas.

Murphy, D. (1986) *Customers and Thieves: an Ethnography of Shoplifting*. Aldershot: Gower.

Murphy, D. and Iles, S. (1983) 'Dealing with shoplifters', *Home Office Research Bulletin*, 15: 25–9.

Murray, C., Motoyama, T., Rouse, W. and Rubenstein, H. (1980) *The Link between Crime and the Built Environment: the Current State of Knowledge,* (vol. 1). Washington: American Institutes for Research.

Nelson, D. (1987) 'The boat people', *New Society*, 3 July: 7–8.

New York Times (1984) 'Growing security-guard industry under scrutiny', 4 June.

New York Times (1985) 'Studies planned over trend toward privately run jails', 25 February.

Newsweek (1986) 'Private eyes' new look', 15 September: 39–40.

Now Magazine (1979) 'Private armies on the march', 16 November.

Observer, The (1983) 'Anger at Securicor guard on migrants', 27 March: 3.

O'Toole, G. (1978) *The Private Sector: Private Spies, Rent-a-Cops and the Police Industrial Complex*. New York: W.W. Norton and Company.

Outer Circle Policy Unit (1978) *The Private Security Industry* (unpublished report, July). London: Outer Circle Policy Unit.

Owings, C. (1925) *Women Police: a Study of the Development of the Women Police Movement*. London: Hitchcock.

Parks, E. (1970) 'From constabulary to police society: implications for social control', *Catalyst*, 5, summer: 76–97.

Pead, D. (1985) 'Alarm bells over subliminal security system', *Police Review*, 27 September: 1947.

Pease, K. (1979) 'Some futures in crime prevention', *Home Office Research Bulletin*, 7, November: 31–5.

Penrose, B. (1987) 'Police chief is set to join private security firm', *The Sunday Times*, 14 June.

Philip-Sorenson, J. (1972) 'Employment and training in manned security services', in P. Wiles and F. McClintock (eds), *The Security Industry in the United Kingdom*. Cambridge: Institute of Criminology, University of Cambridge.

Phillips, Baroness (1982) 'APTS looks to the future', *Crime Prevention News*, 4. London: Home Office.

Pitkin, H. (1981) 'Justice: on relating private and public', *Political Theory*, 9 (3): 327–52.

Plummer, K. (1979) 'Misunderstanding labelling perspectives', in D. Downes and P. Rock (eds), *Deviant Interpretations: Problems in Criminological Theory*. Oxford: Martin Robertson.

Police Review (1983) 'Ban bogus police'. Editorial, 17 June.

Police Review (1986) 'PACE and security officers', 28 February: 479.

Police Review (1987) 'More police needed if prisons go private', 15 May: 968.

Police Review (1988) 'Eight accused of PNC misuse', 29 January: 212.

Policing London (1987) 'Prison ship runs aground', December, 5 (30): 30.

'Private' (1987) 'Private investigators – the industry's lepers?', *Security Times*, September: 61.

Radzinowicz, L. (1948–68) *A History of English Criminal Law and its Administration from 1750*, vols 1–4 (vol. 1: 1948; vol. 2: 1956a; vol. 3: 1956b; vol. 4: 1968). London: Stevens and Son.

Randall, W. (1979) 'Activities, policies and trends in the security industry', in P. Young (ed.), *Major Property Crime in the United Kingdom: Some Aspects of Law Enforcement*. Edinburgh: School of Criminology, University of Edinburgh.

Randall, W. and Hamilton, P. (1972) 'The security industry of the United Kingdom', in P. Wiles and F. McClintock (eds), *The Security Industry in the United Kingdom*. Cambridge: Institute of Criminology, University of Cambridge.

Reiss, A. (1987) 'The legitimacy of intrusion into private space', in C. Shearing and P. Stenning (eds), *Private Policing*. Beverly Hills: Sage.

Reppetto, T. (1976) 'Crime prevention and the displacement phenomenon', *Crime and Delinquency*, 22 April: 166–77.

Robinson, K. (1977) 'Are you being observed?' *Punch*, 7 September: 377–8.

Rock, P. (1983) 'Law, order and power in late seventeenth and early eighteenth century England', in S. Cohen and A. Scull (eds), *Social Control and the State*. Oxford: Martin Robertson. pp. 191–222.

Rojek, D. (1979) 'Private justice systems and crime reporting', *Criminology*, 17 (1), May: 100–11.

Rowbotham, S. (1973) *Hidden From History*. London: Pluto Press.

Royal Commission on the Police (1962) *Final Report*. Cmnd 1728. London: HMSO.

Royal Commission on Legal Services (1979) *Report*. Cmnd 7648. London: HMSO.

Rusbridger, A. (1987a) 'Men from SAS traded with Contras at highest level', *London Daily News*, 12 May.

Rusbridger, A. (1987b) 'London link exposed in Irangate hearings', *London Daily News*, 6 May: 12.

Ryder, C. (1987) 'Blitz on terrorist rackets', *The Sunday Times*, 15 February: 5.

Schepps, D. (1982) 'Why private police standards must be raised', *The Police Chief*, February: 26–7.

Scott, T. and McPherson, M. (1971) 'The development of the private sector of the criminal justice system', *Law and Society Review*, 6 (2), November: 267–88.

Scraton, P. (1982) *Policing Society; Policing Crime*. Issues in Crime and Society Course, Block 2, Part 6. Milton Keynes: Open University Press.

Scraton, P. and South, N. (1981) *Capitalist Discipline, Private Justice and the Hidden Economy*. Occasional Papers in Deviance and Social Policy, no. 2. Enfield: Middlesex Polytechnic.

Scraton, P. and South, N. (1983) 'In the shadow of the welfare police', *Bulletin on Social Policy*, 13, spring: 45–53.

Scraton, P. and South, N. (1984) 'The ideological construction of the hidden economy: private justice and work-related crime', *Contemporary Crises*, 8: 1–18.

Searchlight (1985) 'The column and the convoy', July, 121: 3–4.

Searchlight (1986) 'Murder conspiracy against *Searchlight*', April: 2–3.

Searchlight (1987) 'Front "military commander" hiring mercenaries', July, 145: 3–4.

Security Gazette (1977) 'Crime prevention planning', Editorial, July: 215.

Security and Protection Magazine (1979) 'Editorial Comment', March.

Security Times (1986a) 'News from APTS', January: 14.

Security Times (1986b) 'The mole', January: 8.

Security Times (1987) 'Registration again', September: 29.

Seldon, A. (1977) *Charge*. London: Temple Smith.

Selznick, P. (1948) 'Foundations of the theory of organization', *American Sociological Review*, 13.

Selznick, P. (1969) *Law, Society and Industrial Justice*. New York: Russell Sage Foundation.

Sennett, R. (1977) *The Fall of Public Man*. New York: Knopf.

Shank, R. (1986) 'Privacy: history, legal, social and ethical aspects', *Library Trends*, Summer: 7–18.

Shearing, C. (1981) 'Subterranean processes in the maintenance of power: an examination of the mechanisms coordinating police action', *Canadian Review of Sociology and Anthropology*, 18 (3): 283–98.

Shearing, C., Farnell, M. and Stenning, P. (1980) *Contract Security in Ontario*. Toronto: Centre of Criminology, University of Toronto.

Shearing, C. and Stenning, P. (1981) 'Modern private security: its growth and implications', in M. Tonry and N. Morris (eds), *Crime and Justice: an Annual Review of Research*, vol. 3. Chicago: University of Chicago Press.

Shearing, C. and Stenning, P. (1983) 'Private security: implications for social control', *Social Problems*, 30 (5): 493–505.

Shearing, C. and Stenning, P. (1984) 'From the Panopticon to Disney World: the development of discipline', in A. Doob and E. Greenspan (eds), *Perspectives in Criminal Law: Essays in Honour of John Ll.J. Edwards*. Aurora: Canada Law Books. pp. 335–49.

Shearing, C. and Stenning, P. (eds) (1987) *Private Policing*. Beverly Hills: Sage.

Shearing, C., Stenning, P. and Addario, S. (1985a) 'Police perceptions of private security', *Canadian Police College Journal*, 9 (2): 127–53.

Shearing, C., Stenning, P. and Addario, S. (1985b) 'Public perceptions of private security', *Canadian Police College Journal*, 9 (3): 225–53.

Shearing, C., Stenning, P. and Addario, S. (1985c) 'Corporate perceptions of private security', *Canadian Police College Journal*, 9 (4): 367–90.

Smart, A. and Hodgson, P. (1979) 'Security problems on an oil platform', *International Security Review*, April.

Smart, B. (1983) 'On discipline and social regulation: a review of Foucault's genealogical analysis', in D. Garland and P. Young (eds), *The Power to Punish*. London: Heinemann.

Smith, P. (1975) 'BSIA should be judged by realistic standards', *Security Gazette*, November: 382–3.

Smith, P. (1979) 'Who watches the watchdogs?' *Police*, 11 (11): 29–30.

South, N. (1982) 'The informal economy and local labour markets', in J. Laite (ed.), *Bibliographies on Local Labour Markets and the Informal Economies*. London: Social Science Research Council.

South, N. (1983) 'The corruption of commercial justice: the case of the private security sector', in M. Clarke (ed.), *Corruption: Causes, Consequences and Control*. London: Frances Pinter.

South, N. (1984) 'Private security, the division of policing labour and the commercial compromise of the state', in S. Spitzer and A. Scull (eds), *Research in Law, Deviance and Social Control*, vol. 6. Greenwich, Conn.: JAI Press.

South, N. (1985) 'Private security and social control: the private security sector in the United Kingdom, its commercial functions and public accountability'. PhD Thesis, Middlesex Polytechnic, Enfield.

South, N. (1987a) 'Law, profit and "private persons"': private and public policing in English history', in C. Shearing and P. Stenning (eds), *Private Policing*. Beverly Hills: Sage. pp. 72–109.

South, N. (1987b) 'The security and surveillance of the environment' pp. 139–52, in J. Lowman, R. Menzies and T. Palys (eds), *Transcarceration: Essays in the Sociology of Social Control*. Aldershot: Gower.

South, N. (1988) 'Reconstructing policing: differentiation and contradiction in post-war private and public policing', in R. Matthews (ed.), *Reconstructing Crime, Law and Justice*. London: Sage.

Spitzer, S. (1975) 'Towards a Marxian theory of deviance', *Social Problems*, 22: 638–51.

Spitzer, S. (1979) 'The rationalisation of crime control in capitalist society', *Contemporary Crises*, 3: 187–206.

Spitzer, S. (1987) 'Security and control in capitalist societies: the fetishism of security and the secret thereof', in J. Lowman, R. Menzies and T. Palys (eds), *Transcarceration: Essays in the Sociology of Social Control*. Aldershot: Gower.

Spitzer, S. and Scull, A. (1977a) 'Social control in historical perspective: from private to public responses to crime', in D. Greenberg (ed.), *Corrections and Punishment*. Beverly Hills: Sage.

Spitzer, S. and Scull, A. (1977b) 'Privatisation and capitalist development: the case of the private police', *Social Problems*, 25 (1): 18–29.

Starr, P. (1987) 'The limits of privatisation', in S. Hanke (ed.), *Prospects for Privatisation*. New York: Proceedings of the American Academy of Political Science, 36 (3).

Stead, P. (1975) 'Regulation of the security industry as an international problem', *Security Gazette*, November: 381–3.

Stenning, P. and Cornish, M. (1975) *The Legal Regulation and Control of Private Policing in Canada*. Toronto: Centre of Criminology, University of Toronto.

Stenning, P. and Shearing, C. (1980a) 'Private security and private justice', *British Journal of Law and Society*, Spring.

Stenning, P. and Shearing, C. (1980b) 'The quiet revolution: the nature, development and general legal implications of private security in Canada', *Criminal Law Quarterly*, 22 (20): 220–48.

Stevens, J. (1987) 'Brain drain that robs the police of top talent', *Evening Standard*, 6 January: 15.

Sunday Times, The (1980) 'Army men enlist the "pirate tappers" ', 10 February: 1.

Sullivan, P. and Warren, P. (1987) 'Out of control', *Computer Talk*, 16 February: 1.

Task Force on Private Security (1976) *Private Security: Report of the Task Force on Private Security*, Washington, DC: National Advisory Committee on Criminal Justice Standards and Goals, US Department of Justice.

Taylor, I. and Walton, P. (1971) 'Industrial sabotage: motives and meanings', in S. Cohen (ed.), *Images of Deviance*. Harmondsworth: Penguin.

Taylor, I., Walton, P. and Young, J. (1973) *The New Criminology*. London: Routledge and Kegan Paul.

Taylor, I., Walton, P. and Young, J. (eds) (1975) *Critical Criminology*. London: Routledge and Kegan Paul.

Thompson, A. (1970) *Big Brother in Britain Today*. London: Michael Joseph.

Walker, A. (1984) 'The political economy of privatisation', in J. LeGrand and R. Robinson (eds), *Privatisation and the Welfare State*. London: Allen and Unwin.

Weiss, R. (1978) 'The emergence and transformation of private detective industrial policing in the United States, 1850–1940', *Crime and Social Justice*, spring/summer: 35–48.

Weiss, R. (1981) 'The private detective agency in the development of policing forms in the rural and frontier US', *Insurgent Sociologist*, 10 (4)/ 11 (1): 75–91.

Weiss, R. (1984) 'The growing privatisation of security: neo-feudalism or changing parameters of the state?', revised version of unpublished paper, Conference on the Decentralisation of Social Control, Simon Fraser University, Burnaby, April.

Weiss, R. (1987) 'The reappearance of the "ideal factory": the entrepreneur and social control in the contemporary prison', in J. Lowman, R. Menzies and T. Palys (eds), *Transcarceration: Essays in the Sociology of Social Control*. Aldershot: Gower.

Weiss, R. (1988) 'The community and prevention', in E. Johnson (ed.), *Handbook on Crime and Delinquency Prevention*. Westport, Conn.: Greenwood Press.

West, G. (1986) 'The second economy in Nicaragua is the second front: Washington's efforts to destabilise any succeeding American revolution', unpublished paper.

West, G. (1987) 'Vigilancia revolucionaria: a Nicaraguan resolution to public and private policing', in C. Shearing and P. Stenning (eds), *Private Policing*. Beverly Hills: Sage.

Wheatcroft, P. (1978) 'Ridin' shotgun on Securicor', *The Sunday Times*, 13 August: 2.

Wiles, P. and McClintock, F. (eds) (1972) *The Security Industry in the United Kingdom*. Cambridge: Institute of Criminology, University of Cambridge.

Williams, D., George, B. and MacLennan, E. (1984) *Guarding against Low Pay*. Low Pay Pamphlet 29. London: Low Pay Unit.

Williams, R. (1976) *Keywords*. London: Fontana.

Worsley, J. (1983) 'And they have the nerve to call it crime prevention', *Police*, 12–14.

Wright, K. (1972) *Cost-effective Security*. London: McGraw-Hill.

Young, J. (1981) 'Thinking seriously about crime: some models of criminology', in M. Fitzgerald, G. McLennan and J. Pawson (eds), *Crime and Society: Readings in History and Theory*. London: Routledge and Kegan Paul.

Young, P. (ed.) (1976) *Major Property Crime in the United Kingdom: Some Aspects of Law Enforcement*. Edinburgh: School of Criminology, University of Edinburgh.

Younger Committee (1972) *Report of the Younger Committee on Privacy*. Cmnd 5012. London: HMSO.

Index